D1189682

Sherwood Anderson: The Writer at His Craft

(Circa 1926)

Sherwood Anderson:
The Writer at His Craft

Edited by
Jack Salzman, David D. Anderson
and Kichinosuke Ohashi

PAUL P. APPEL, *Publisher*
Mamaroneck, New York

Copyright © 1979 by Paul P. Appel

Library of Congress Card Catalog Number 78-68648

International Standard Book Number: 0-911858-37-7

Distributed in the United Kingdom, Europe and Commonwealth by George Prior Associated Publishers Ltd., 37-41 Bedford Row, London, W.C.1, England.

PHOTO CREDITS: Frontispiece by Eugene Hutchinson; photograph facing Page 274 by Dave Greer. Both photographs reproduced by courtesy of The Anderson Collection, Newberry Library, 60 West Walton Street, Chicago, Illinois 60610.

Printed in the United States of America

The Contents

v

Preface

Sherwood Anderson's literary reputation rests firmly on *Winesburg, Ohio* and his great short stories, as indeed it should, and critical recognition is coming belatedly to his novels and journalism as the re-assessment of his literary career continues. From its low point in 1951, when Irving Howe relegated Anderson to a minor role in American literary history, critical assessment has increased that role until now, supported by the statements of Saul Bellow, Nobel Laureate, he is recognized as both a central figure in the making of modern American literature and a first-rate literary artist.

The dimensions of that new assessment were made clear in three recent volumes, *Sherwood Anderson: Dimensions of His Literary Art,* edited by David D. Anderson, *Sherwood Anderson: Centennial Studies,* edited by Hilbert H. Campbell and Charles E. Modlin, and *Twentieth Century Literature*'s special Anderson issue, guest-edited by Jack Salzman, as well as by the substantial centenary observances at Michigan State University, Clyde, Ohio, and Marion, Virginia, in September, 1976. More of Anderson's works are currently in print than at any time during his life, and they are standard works in university literature courses.

This collection of Anderson's works, all of them previously uncollected, represent an added dimension of Anderson's work: his substantial and varied contributions to periodicals. Although he had himself collected many of his periodical essays, articles, and stories, there are many he did not, particularly from a period hitherto neglected by those who denigrate his place in literary history. That period is the decade of the nineteen thirties, a period of great productivity and profound social consciousness for Anderson.

The works in this volume are not, however, restricted to that decade, but in themselves they provide a cross-section of Anderson's entire literary career. In them are the embryo writer unsure of his art but certain of his aspirations; the conscious literary artist, the social critic, the man who has examined life from the perspective of a long creative career and found it fundamentally good.

This collection is particularly important and convenient because it includes material largely ignored in many earlier appraisals of Anderson's work, and the works included shed a good deal of light on the later unpublished material in the Newberry Library, just as that material is relevant to these works. In future assessments this dimension—largely that of his last years and his journalistic contributions—must play a larger role than any critic has given it thus far. In closing the gap between previously published but uncollected works, this collection makes convenient the search for the complete portrayal of Sherwood Anderson that is yet to come.

                                                                    1978

Introductions and Forewords

THEODORE DREISER'S

Free *and Other Stories*

THEODORE Dreiser is a man who, with the passage of time, is bound to loom larger and larger in the awakening æsthetic consciousness of America. Among all of our prose writers he is one of the few men of whom it may be said that he has always been an honest workman, always impersonal, never a trickster. Read this book of Dreiser's, *Free and Other Stories,* and then compare it with a book of short stories, say by Bret Harte or O. Henry. The tradition of trick writing began early among us in America and has flowered here like some strange fungus growth. Every one knows there are no plot short stories in life itself and yet the tradition of American short story writing has been built almost entirely upon the plot idea. Human nature, the strange little whims, tragedies and comedies of life itself, have everywhere been sacrificed to the need of plot and one reads the ordinary plot story of the magazines with a kind of growing wonder. "Is there no comedy, no tragedy, no irony in life itself? If it is there why do not our writers find it out and set it forth? Why these everlasting falsehoods, this ever-present bag of tricks?"

One is sometimes convinced, in thinking of the matter, that, among most of our prose writers, there is left no feeling at all for life, and the prose writer, at least the tale teller, who has no feeling for life is no artist. There is the man or woman who walks beside me in the street, works beside me in the office, sits beside me in the theatre. What has happened in the lives of all these

3

people? Why do our writers so determinedly spend all their time inventing people who never had any existence—puppets—these impossible cowboys, detectives, society adventurers? Are most of our successful short story writers too lazy to find out something about life itself, the occasional flashes of wonder and strangeness in life? It is apparent they are. Either they are too lazy or they are afraid of life, tremble before it.

But Theodore Dreiser is not afraid. He does not tremble. Often I have thought of him as the bravest man who has lived in America in our times. Perhaps I exaggerate. He is a man of my own craft and always he has been a heroic figure in my own eyes. He is honest. Never in any line he has ever written will you find him resorting to the trick to get himself out of a hard situation. The beauty and the ironic terror of life is like a wall before him but he faces the wall. He does not mutter cheap little lies in the darkness and to me there is something honorable and fine in the fact that in him there is no lack of courage in facing his materials, that he needs resort to tricks of style to cover.

Dreiser is a middle-westerner, large of frame, rather shy, brusque in manner and in his person singularly free from the common small vanities of the artist class. I often wonder if he knows how much he is loved and respected for what he has done by hundreds of unknown writers everywhere, fellows just trying to get ground under their feet. If there is a modern movement in American prose writing, a movement toward greater courage and fidelity to life in writing, then Theodore Dreiser is the pioneer and the hero of the movement. Of that I think there can be no question. I think it is true now that no American prose writer need hesitate before the task of putting his hands upon his materials. Puritanism, as a choking, smothering force, is dead or dying. We are rapidly approaching the old French standard wherein the only immorality for the artist is in bad art and I think that Theodore Dreiser, the man, has done more than any living American to bring this about. All honor to him. The whole air of America is sweeter to breathe because he had lived and worked here. He has laid a foundation upon which any sort of structure may be built. It will stand the strain. His work has been honestly and finely done. The man has laid so many old ghosts, pounded his way through such a wall of stupid prejudices and fears that today any man coming into the craft of writing comes with a new inheritance of freedom.

In the middle-western country in which Dreiser grew to manhood there could have been no awareness of the artist's obligations. How his own feet found the path they have followed so consistently I do not know. One gets so little from his own writings, from those little flashes by which every artist reveals himself in his work, that helps toward an understanding of his fine courage. Grey smoky hurried towns, Terre Haute, Indiana, Chicago, St. Louis, and the other places wherein he worked and lived, a life of hard work for small pay in dreary places. Twain had at least the rough and tumble heartiness of western life, the romance of the old Mississippi river days, and as for the eastern men who came before Dreiser, the Hawthornes, Emersons (and one is compelled to include the Howellses) they grew out of a European culture, were the children of a European culture, a fact that no doubt advantaged them while it has been of so little help to the Americans who are seeking masters to aid them in finding a life and a basis for a culture of their own.

Our earlier New England writers knew Europe and Europe knew them and accepted them as distant cousins anyway, but in Terre Haute, Indiana, in Dreiser's day there, when his own life was forming—if any of his fellow countrymen of that day and place ever crossed the sea I dare say they went to the Holy Land and came back with a bottle of Jordan Water. The only knowledge they had of the work and the aims of European artists was got from reading that most vulgar of all our Mark Twain's books, *The Innocents Abroad*. The idea of an artist, with all of the strange tangle of dreams and hopes in his brain being also a workman, owing something to his craft and to the materials of his craft, would have been as strange to the Terre Haute or the St. Louis of twenty-five years ago as a camel sitting and smoking a pipe on the court-house steps.

And it was out of such a grey blankness (from the artist's point of view, at least) that the man Dreiser came and he came alone, making his own path. What a figure he has made of himself, always pounding at the wall of stupidity before him, throwing aside always the cheap triumph to be got by trickery, always giving himself fully and honestly to the life about him, trying to understand it, never lying to himself or to others. One thinks of such a life and is appalled.

There is that story we have all heard of the young Dostoevsky, when he had written his first book *Poor Folks*. He gave the manuscript to a writer friend who took it home and read it and in the middle of the night drove to the home of a publisher, filled with excitement. The two men sat up together and read the manuscript aloud and then, although it was four in the morning drove through the wintry streets to the young writer's lodgings. There was joy, excitement, happy fellow craftsmen, even tears of joy. A new and great writer had come into Russian life. What glad recognition. It was like a wedding or a birth. Men were happy together and you may imagine how the young craftsman felt.

That happened in Russia and in America Dreiser wrote his *Sister Carrie* and it was published and later buried out of sight in the cellar of a publishing house, for some ten years I believe, and might have been there yet but for the fighting impulses of our critics, our Hacketts, Menckens and Dells. Some woman, a relative perhaps of some member of the publishing firm, had decided the book was immoral and today one reads with wonder, seeking in vain for the immorality and only made glad by its sympathetic understanding of life.

Theodore Dreiser, whose book *Free and Other Stories* is now included in the famous Modern Library series, has lived out most of his life as a comparatively poor man. He might have grown rich had he but joined the ranks of the clever tricksters or had he devoted his energies to turning out romantic sentimentalities. What amusing and clever men we have had in his time, what funny fellows, what masters of all the tricks of writing.

Where are they? What have they given us?

And what has Dreiser given us? A fine growing and glowing tradition, has he not, a new sense of the value of our own lives, a new interest in the life about us, in offices, streets and houses.

Theodore Dreiser's nature is the true artist's nature, so little understood among us. He is no reformer. In his work, as in the man himself, there is something bold, with all the health of true boldness, and at the same time something very finely humble. He stands before life, looking at it, trying to understand it that he may catch its significance and its drama. He is not always crying,

"Look at me! See what I am doing!" He is the workman, full of self-respect, and—most strange and wonderful of all for an American writer—full of respect for his materials, for the lives of those who come close to him, for that world of people who have come into life under his pen.

As for my trying to make in any detailed way an estimate of the value of the man's work, that is beyond me. The man has done, is doing, his job, he has fought his way through darkness into the light and in making a pathway for himself he has made a pathway for us all. Because he had lived and worked so honestly and finely America is a better place for all workmen. As for his work, there it stands—sturdy, strong, true and fine and most of all free from all the many cheap tricks of our craft.

And as for the man himself, there he also stands. One knows Dreiser will never stoop to tricky, second rate work; cannot, being Dreiser, ever so stoop. He is, however, not given to advertising himself. He stays in the background and lets the work speak for the man. It is the kind of fine, honest work that is coming to mean more and more every year to a growing army of sincere American craftsmen.

STEPHEN CRANE'S

Midnight Sketches and Other Impressions

AN explosion in a city street. People in the street, thousands of them. They are mechanics, housewives going to market, young men trying to get on in business, newspaper men, street-car conductors, drivers of trucks, corner policemen, old men who sell newspapers, dirty-faced boys selling newspapers, women going to meet their lovers, country people in the city for the day, travellers passing through the city.

You can imagine such an explosion. Let us say nobody has been hurt.

Stephen Crane never hurt any one. He was an explosion all right.

The strange thing to think about is such an explosion happening and no one paying any attention. You might have imagined every one was dead—that only ghosts of people were walking in the street.

I am thinking about Stephen Crane coming along—as a writer. Writing in America must have been pretty dead then. There are signs enough of the same kind of death now.

People think they can write about people with their fingers. In Stephen Crane's day America was pretty full of individualists. Look at the pictures left of early Americans. An individualist hasn't much time to think of others. He is hot on freedom, liberty—that sort of thing. Of course he means himself, his own liberty, his own freedom.

9

There isn't any such thing, but people persist in thinking there is. America was built up on that sort of ideas.

Pretty bad place for such men as Mark Twain, Frank Norris, Stephen Crane, Walt Whitman, Herman Melville.

You can't be an individualist and write as Stephen Crane sometimes did. You can't do it with your fingers or your arms.

You have to feel people, things. I can imagine Stephen Crane going along a street in a city and hearing a truckdriver swear at a street-car conductor. That is when the explosion occurred. Something inside a man suddenly expanding, taking in everything—self forgotten.

The real writer writes with every nerve in his body—all his nerves aroused. Clever men can write any time. They know a little bag of tricks and can just reel it off. Stevie learned to do that. I'm bound to say I think he wrote some pretty bad stories. I suppose the magazine editors of his time and the other and more successful writers told him how to do it and he listened.

I remember that I was a boy when he began to write. I had left a country town and was working in an advertising agency. One day a man named Marco Morrow, who worked as a copy writer in the same agency, came in from lunch with a book in his hand. His eyes were shining. It was a Steve Crane book, one of the early ones. I cannot remember whether it was "Maggie," THE RED BADGE OF COURAGE, or what it was. I remember our excitement. Marco made for me, hauled me away from my desk. We cut out for the day. This was in Chicago. I fancy we spent the afternoon in the back room of some little saloon, drinking beer and Steve Crane.

Suppose they opened the saloons now—after this prohibition business. Cozy warm places to go on winter afternoons. Men about, telling stories, bragging, lying, laughing.

There was literary prohibition in Steve Crane's day all right. He defied them and at least partly got away with it. He sold real whisky, beer, wine, for a while anyway. What I mean is that he was a writer really writing when it wasn't being done. That is the wonder of the man. It is time he was getting a hearing. If the man wrote some bad, easy, tricky stuff, what of it?

A country gets real writers by having them. Writers who are trying to do decent work in America now do not know what they owe to Walt Whitman, Herman Melville, Steve Crane. Future writers here will—some of them—hate to admit how much they owe to such present-day men as, say, Theodore Dreiser. Men of talent are not always generous.

It does not matter. What I am trying to say is that the culture of a country—a new country—builds up slowly. There is a house being built. It takes time and the labour of real craftsmen. Stephen Crane was a craftsman. The stones he put in the wall are still there.

Another thing I want to speak about. You will see I am not—in writing of Steve Crane—holding myself down to this present volume, MIDNIGHT SKETCHES. But you read it. Notice something.

Notice the colour of the prose. Something splashy—men, women, rainy nights. Colours in buildings, skies, men's faces, caught and put down.

Once long ago in Chicago I was talking with Carl Sandburg. We were walking in a city street and I was railing at American writers because their prose was so colourless. "Look at that," I said. We were walking over one of the bridges that cross the Chicago River. I pointed to the smoky skies, the buildings rearing up, the marvelous colour of the river down below the bridge.

"It's all splashy with colour, washed with colour, and none of them ever catch any of it. They make life too colourless, too eternally grey," I said.... "You lie," said Carl.

He referred me again to Steve Crane, sent me off to the Chicago Public Library to find a little book of Crane's early verse.

Pure colour, experiments, a man finding his way, feeling his way. What that man knew he never got said. Writers in America who do not know their Stephen Crane were missing a lot. Suppose he did a pretty little patent-leather finish on some of his later tales. Take him for what he was—his importance. Think of what was going on all around him then.

All the painters of that day painting in low tones—going in for facile brush work. The arts all grey. Grey cities, grey people.

A young man coming along, not too strong physically, touched with consumption, broke most of his life.

Standing up against the almost universal greyness of the art expression of his day. Putting in great splashes of colour—the

tales in this volume, "Maggie," THE RED BADGE OF
COURAGE—others too.

The thing to do is to have all his books on your shelves. Get
him in relation to his times, the drama of the man, of his life.

He did a lot. He was an explosion all right. It's about time
people began to hear the explosion.

EUGENE JOLAS'

Cinema

I MET Eugene Jolas in New Orleans last Winter. He was
working there on a newspaper. My son, who also worked on the
paper, came home one day all excited. "There is a real poet down
there, working on our paper," he said.

Later I found Eugene Jolas just the poet. He is unsure of
himself, quick and sensitive to the life about him. Most young
poets are impossible as companions. They are so dreadfully sure
no poets have ever lived before their time. Jolas is not like that.

He is Alsatian, with a mixture of German and French bloods,
married to an American woman.

As a lad he came over here to live and he has been coming back
over here since. At this moment I have on my desk a letter from
him. He is just sailing for Europe. The letter is full of regret that
he must go. "I'll be back," is the burden of it.

Jolas is a poet feeling his way. The energy of America, the fast
pace here, the growth and development of our industrial life,
New York, Pittsburg, Chicago, the Kentucky derby, the bootlegger, our sky scrapers, our great mills, the Ford.

All of these things excite and fascinate the man.

He wants to be thought of as an American himself. Well, his
heart is here.

He is one of the young poets intent on expressing the age in
which he lives and he believes America best expresses the
present age.

He is, I am very sure, one of the few important new singers—
here lifting up his voice to Americans.

PHILIP McKEE'S

Big Town

THERE it is, the American Big Town. There are the drifting crowds of people in the streets, people in the houses. This town isn't so big but that there will be the biggest crowds of people on a Saturday night. The best people won't be out that night. That is the night for workers and for the farmers who still come to this town. All day and every day a river of motors in the streets. Lights are flashing at street intersections and there are well-dressed girls driving sporty-looking roadsters. You will see beautiful women in the Big Town. The Middle West can produce them. There will be strongly-made free-walking women with heads held high. You'll turn to have another look.

There are young men growing up, sons of prominent men. They also drive sporty cars. You will see some of them standing before drug stores, memories of small-town life.

You drift in and out of the towns, look about, go from the little places to the Big Town. There is a brave show of keeping something up. It may well be that the time will come when this period in the history of America will be looked back upon as a peculiarly heroic period. "There was poetry written even then," men will say. They will read books and learn that lovers lived and loved, that a few men thought clearly, walked occasionally in fields, saw the young corn coming up, saw new leaves coming on trees in the Spring, saw the Fall wood, felt rain and wind on flesh, made music, even made painting.

America is paying. There is a price to be paid. Go anywhere and you will see the debt being paid. We are paying for lack of courage, for lack of brains. Look at what we were given. Look what we have done with it.

Are we cowardly or only confused?

You look back upon the mess of the World War. No one tries much any more to make a thing of glory out of that. They keep still. Were the boys who went into it a mess? Hardly. They did a job they were asked, urged, begged to do, a dirty ugly killing job. They got nothing much out of it. Some of them found a few comrades they can remember with pleasure.

"I have given the best of myself here, the fire and fineness of my youth. I marched and fought through filth and dirt, hoping to come out into the light.

"You said I would. You said that.

"What I got was increased darkness.

"Now they are rigging the game to do it again. You watch. They'll do it again. They'll do it to my son."

Here is a book about a Big Town of the Middle West. There are thousands of miles of rich long cornfields in the Middle West. You drop down into the great valley out of the Appalachian Range and travel across the floor of the valley at speed for days and days. You pass over broad rivers, you pass white farmhouses set in clusters of trees, you see big towns and little towns. You go on at last into the great rolling stretches of wheat fields . . . the wind playing in the wheat, mountains seen in the distance. At last you come to the western rim of the valley, the Rockies.

God, what a country!

What a din going on in the valley now, what a racket, what a lot of meaningless noise. Everywhere in the floor of the valley the roadways are lined with advertising boards. There are thousands of cars flying up and down, people going nowhere specially. Voices are everywhere, flashing lights.

The talkies are everywhere . . . intensified vulgarity at Los Angeles, spreading itself out. It has learned how to cover a lot of territory. There is a roar overhead. "Look. We've got progress. Look. There goes an airplane."

They did think they were up to something, didn't they? They thought they were getting culture and progress with a bang...culture with a kick in it. Are they all just noisy, vulgar children? Books like this make you wonder.

As though the big gods and the little gods wouldn't come back and laugh. They are laughing now. "Do you think you can do what you have done to this valley and get away with it? Pshaw. Wake up."

When it comes to what was, when men had been in there but a short time...there were the Libs and Flos of the old "Line," the streets of prostitution in the bigger towns...there were the P. T. Barnums, Blaine, the plumed knight of Maine, Brigham Young. This book gives you another peep back. There was the age of the tobacco chewers, the spitting men...of Billy Sunday, his glory just gone from him...of Henry Ward Beecher back of him. Let's have no more of them.

It's a time for ripping open now. Go ahead. Come on, disillusion us. Let's have a look. Let's look at the inner workings of the Y.M.C.A., at the big churches, at industry, at prohibition, at the Anti-Saloon League. Let's look 'em all over.

Let's look at everything. Let's have a look. We need a little education. These are tough times. We are nearly all broke. That's good. Lots of us haven't any work, no money coming in. Let's try thinking. We might as well try.

Pretty soon there will be voices enough. I look for hot times in the Big Towns some of these nights. There is just a thin skin over everything now, over the savagery underneath. It may be savagery and there may be courage, suppressed hunger for something of nobility in lives, for growth of intelligence, down under there.

Money. Money. Money.

Suppose suddenly money began not to mean anything. That would make the gods laugh. Suppose the doctrine of John Marshall, Mark Hanna, Hamilton, Henry Cabot Lodge, the doctrine of government on which all this we have is built, suppose if began to show up for what it is.

Eyes popping open, eh? A new time of discussion, of men finding words again, trying to think their way through. We might as well try. They've got us all herded in now, pretty well hushed up. This is their time of victory, of triumph. Something may get touched off any time. Some book may start it. Who knows when it will come? It's coming.

Money. The Machine.

We are at the end of something. When men build perhaps they have to build blindly. Perhaps minds have to go temporarily dead. If men stopped to think, thinking of the shortness of lives, of the obvious uselessness of most effort, they would do nothing. The mind perhaps has to stop working. Men have to live by shibboleths. The hands go on making the beginning of a new, perhaps even a better world.

Then, after the work time, after the time of the men of action, after the blind time, men have to begin to try to see. Their hands have built a new house. They may have to open their eyes to find their way in. They may have to bathe themselves. The mind has to have its turn. That's something. It may be a groping for a new life.

Stop. Look. Listen.

We are going into a time of deeper discussion than men, in America, have ever known. We are going into a time like the pre-Civil War days. I'm no prophet. I don't know when it will come, what will touch it off. It's coming. I've faith in its coming. It is going to cut across everything, tangle everything. There will be questions asked, questions and more questions. There will be toys taken away from children. They'll cry.

It's coming.

The machine has made a new world for men. It has made new towns, new cities. Here's one. You wait. You will see presently what a tangled strange time there will be, in the great cities, in the little places, in the Big Towns.

WALT WHITMAN'S

Leaves of Grass

Come close to me warm little thing. It is night—
I am cold. When I was a boy in my village here in the
West, I always knew all the old men. How sweet
they were—quite Biblical too—makers of harness and
wagons and plows—soldiers and sailors and pioneers.
We got Walt and Abraham out of that lot.[1]

WHITMAN is in the bones of America as Ralph Waldo Emerson is in the American mentality, but what is wanted and needed here now is a return to the bones and blood of life—to Whitman. We Americans need again to have and to be conscious of land hunger, river hunger, sea and sky hunger. For one, two or three generations now the drift of our young American men and women has been away from the land and toward the towns. Industrialism must go on and the machine must be made subservient to man, but there must be also a rebirth of feeling for the fact of America. Now we work too much with our heads. When I was myself a young man and had got into the advertising business, as a writer of advertisements, I had an experience more common to young Americans than is generally believed. I kept getting into a blue funk. It seemed to me that I couldn't go on, day

---

[1] *Mid-American Chants.*

19

after day, using words to praise and sell some one's soap, tooth paste, or what-not. Other men about me were in the same case. We were often desperate. Why, as to that, we were making money enough, doing very well. We were in the current of our times, swimming with the current. We continually turned to Emerson and he bucked us up. How many days of stupid advertising writing have I myself got through on the strength of Emerson's "Self Reliance." Alas....!

This self-reliance, where is it, where does it take us?

There is something beyond this success we Americans have been so intent upon. Where is it? What is it?

It is in the land, waving cornfields of Illinois, Kentucky, Tennessee and Virginia hills, piny woods of Georgia, hot red lands of Georgia, Alabama, Mississippi, gigantic flow of the Mississippi River, forests that surround Wisconsin lakes, deserts, skies, men plowing....

Push hard against horse-collars, broad-breasted horses....

There are men of the farms going into the towns and bellyaching. "There is no money in farming any more," they say. Well, what of it? What has money being in a thing or not being in it got to do with anything?

Don't laugh. This isn't sentimentality. It's a matter of getting back national health. Once, I swear, we had men here.... Walt Whitman, lone Abe Lincoln, John Brown, others I could name, men with a sense of soil in them, men with guts, patience, stand-up men, men not intent upon success. If I, an American man, cannot learn to love one strip of countryside, turn of a flowing river, white farm house on a slope in an apple orchard, if I cannot love some one spot ... (if I am a strong man perhaps a dozen such spots) how can I love America...?

...or a woman or a brother man?

Whitman is the singer of the strong lustful ones of the men who could love a woman or a field or the sky above prairies, forest or seas. He walked far and wide, bare-throated, brown-armed, and singing ... not up in the mind only but with his whole body. He was thought too crude, too lustful. They turned away from him. As a boy and young man I myself went into respectable middle-class homes and found there volumes of Whitman's "Leaves of Grass" with the so-called ugly lustful passages cut out with scissors.

How shameful! How can there be real delicacy without strength? I proclaim Whitman the most delicate and tender of all American singers. Here is this volume of his songs, the American artist Charles Cullen having made alive glowing pictures for it, pictures full of pregnant strangeness. I hail it. Read again "When Lilacs Last in the Dooryard Bloomed."..."Out of the Cradle Endlessly Rocking." Read the rocking long and short American verses. Who was it who said only the negroes had brought real song into America? Hail, all hail, negro workmen, river hands, plantation hands, makers of songs, but hail also, always Whitman, white American, lustful one....

Singer of the great land, the broad land...singer of growing cities, horses plowing, men sowing seed, soft waves breaking on sea shores, forest singer, town and dusty country road singer.

The great sweet land that Walt Whitman sang so lustily is still here. People now forget what America is...why forget how huge, varied, strong and flowing it is? We gather too much and stay too long in holes in cities. We forget land-love, river and sky-love. To these we must return before we begin again to get brother to brother love of which Whitman sang and dreamed.

Whitman is in the bones and blood of America. He is the real American singer. What is wanted among us now is a return to Whitman, to his songs, his dreams, his consciousness of the possibilities of the land that was his land and is our land.

GEORGE SKLAR AND
ALBERT MALTZ

Peace on Earth

THE theatre, like every other form of human expression in the arts, has to keep trying and trying—always apparently to lift itself by its bootstraps. It can be done. There is an old lesson to be learned over and over.

Do it.

Do it.

Do it.

Half the ills of our present society are due to eternal talk of doing when nothing is done. How many conferences have I myself attended. God help me, I have been a speaker at some of them. We come out of such a conference. "Where are you going, Tom?"

"I have to hurry home to dinner."

"I have to go get a haircut."

Anyway, in this play, "Peace on Earth," at the old Civic Repertory Theatre, something is done.

Conferences. Talks. Lift up the theatres. Bring in new life; new meaning. The ills of labor—of our Negro population—committee of writers against lynching—men and women in a warm room, drinking cocktails or tea—"Isn't it terrible?"

"Let's sign something. Bring it here. Let me sign it."

The telephone jangling.

"Do you protest?"

"Do you protest?"

23

"Sure. Here are a million signed protests. Take them. Run and scatter them in the streets. Someone is being brutally killed over here, over there an injustice is being done. Protest. Protest."

What I like about the Theatre Union and their play "Peace on Earth" is that it is something real done, and I think well done. The play itself is vital and alive. It is full of the curious dramatic realism of everyday American life right now. There is the pathetic hungryness of the kindly intentioned man—author, college professor, liberal—dramatically set over against the realism of men shot, broken heads—the thing so likely to happen when men and women stand up against the combined little fears of a frightened society. Whiff of cold mornings by factory gates— half-crazed young girl radicals screaming with shrill voices at stolid-faced citizens on street corners—smell of sweaty overalls—horror of prisons where men are locked up and sometimes hanged for dreams. Do you like it? The Theatre Union has proven that it is good drama.

All of this caught up and fixed into dramatic form so that you and I going into the old Civic Repertory can see and feel as we might have seen and felt had we been present last week sitting in a court room at Decatur, Ala., as we might feel and see were we present and participating some rainy morning when a strike breaks in a gloomy factory street or at a mine shaft.

So there it is again—the good thing. . . . (It may go haywire in a month. What difference would that make?) . . . . the thing again pushing up from below—new vitality again achieved. I think that the Theatre Union has succeeded with this play. It means something. After months of work, begging money to get a start— men and women working night and day, as they always will work when they feel some forward thrusting thing being done.

Prices are cut to depression pockets. I shall not try to tell the story of the play. Go and see it. It will give you one evening's glimpse of the drama now going on, down below, in our American life.

Tributes and Appraisals

CARL SANDBURG

HE comes into a room where there is company heavily and slowly, staring about. His eyes are small and blue-faded. Everyone knows a personage has arrived but there is no swagger to him.

He is not a physically strong man although he looks like the stuff out of which champion middleweights are made—a fighter who has given up fighting, gone out upon another road, out of condition for fighting. His eyes are not strong and he reads little. He is an eternal sitter-up o' nights drinking quantities of black coffee.

In conversation concerning the two subjects that absorb him—labor and poetry—he is unsure of himself, makes startling statements hesitatingly and covers his uncertainty with a blustering manner. There is no intellectual smartness and oddly enough no intolerance.

A distinguished Frenchman came to my house and wanted much to meet Sandburg so I had him up for an evening. They sat and stared at each other—both helpless. Sandburg took from his pocket a paper covered with figures and began to tell the Frenchman of the number of tons of coal mined in the state of Illinois each year, the number of miles from Chicago to Dallas, Texas, how many railroads come into Chicago, what Mr. Gary said at the time of the steel strike.

27

Silence settled down upon the two men. One might have cut the silence into little squares and rolled it into balls.

I led Sandburg to the piano and he began to sing, thumping steadily on two or three chords.

His voice is mellow and rich and he has the gift of song. He sang nigger songs, a song of the boll-weevil, one about Jesse James, another about a tough girl of the city streets whose lover had proved unfaithful.

Sandburg singing, naively, beautifully, was something the Frenchman understood and loved. Later he told me that the evening was one of his really fine experiences in America. On that evening we were all so absorbed that while Sandburg sang a robber crawled in at a window and going into his sleeping room robbed the Frenchman of his clothes, his money, and his luggage—thus giving him, in addition to his evening with Sandburg, a strikingly true picture of what life in Chicago is like. I've a notion that he went home to France inclined toward the suspicion that Sandburg and I were in league with the robber.

There is a growing tendency, as his fame goes up in the world, to speak of Carl Sandburg as a He man, an eater of raw meat, a hairy one. In Chicago newspaper local rooms he is spoken of as John Guts. I do not think of him so although I've a suspicion that he sometimes writes under the influence of this particular dramatization of his personality.

Buried deep within the He man, the hairy, meat eating Sandburg there is another Sandburg, a sensitive, naive, hesitating Carl Sandburg, a Sandburg that hears the voice of the wind over the roofs of houses at night, a Sandburg that wanders often alone through grim city streets on winter nights, a Sandburg that knows and understands the voiceless cry in the heart of the farm girl of the plains when she comes to the kitchen door and sees for the first time the beauty of our prairie country.

The poetry of John Guts doesn't excite me much. Hairy, raw meat eating He men are not exceptional in Chicago and the middle west.

As for the other Sandburg, the naive, hesitant, sensitive Sandburg—among all the poets of America he is my poet.

ALBERT MAURER

NOTHING could be more delightful for me to think about than an exhibition of the work of Mr. Alfred Maurer. These paintings are such living things, plucked out of the life of modern cities. The young girls are like desert flowers, flashing into quick beauty just caught; the old women, like gaunt, barren old hills. I own but two of his canvases. Would that I owned two dozen.

It is several years ago now that a friend, Mr. Arthur Dove, took me into Maurer's neat little workshop and I came away owning one of his street girls. What a charming companion she has been. I have carted her about with me ever since. On mornings when I have awakened unable to quite face what I thought the discouragements of my own life, I have looked up at her hanging on my wall and a smile has at once begun playing over my inner self. She sends me out into the streets again believing in the inextinguishable charm and reality of life.

Life twisted, beaten down, perverted often enough, life as it is—in young girls in the back streets of cities, in tired old women—life everywhere having its wonder moments, this poet has caught.

Always the strange half mystic wonder of reality.

Long have I been convinced that Mr. Maurer is one of the really great modern painters. It is evidence of the persistence of life in us all that the subtlety and understanding of this painter is beginning to be recognized. Would that I owned two dozen.

NATHANIEL WRIGHT STEPHENSON

Lincoln

ONE of the really beautiful stories in the world is the Abraham Lincoln story. I am told that the poet Sandburg is this year to publish a Lincoln book, but as I sit writing I have not seen his book.

Recently, however, I read a Lincoln—by Nathaniel Wright Stephenson—that seems to me destined to live. It is a beautiful book, beautifully conceived, felt and written.

And what a story is the Lincoln story, the Lincoln myth, if you will! The poor boy of the forests with the long, grotesque body, the slovenly no-account father, the hard-working, crude tobacco-chewing, hog-raising, swearing, fighting people, the mud, the dirt, the vulgarity, always the vulgarity.

The boy escaping by the sheer force of his inner sweetness and patience. War, politics, graft. The man seeking through war, through crowds of scheming men and emerging at last to establish, through the force of his own personality, the greatest American story, a story that has been written many times, that will be written many times.

Let me a little explain my own attitude toward this Lincoln written by Mr. Stephenson, a man of the colleges, an erudite, cultured man. My approach to the book was amusing—at least to me. I am myself a writing man and the writing man—after he becomes a writing man—is rarely a consistent reader. His interest is in people, in life rather than in books and often very

31

dull books are the only ones he reads. Well-written books have to be approached cautiously. There are, for example, certain very beautiful writers I am unable to read at all. Their reaction to life is so much finer and clearer than my own that they fill me with gloom. After all, if I am to go on expressing myself through the written word, I have to find my own way of saying things, of feeling and seeing things. These superlatively apt and skillful fellows get me off my track. I find myself later using their words, feeling through them, getting my own reactions to life all coloured and changed, making something oddly unreal and untrue to myself.

Their books, then, for the most part, I have on the shelves of my library. My wife reads them, and often in the evening we speak of them. Surely I have read them once—I speak so knowingly. Situations are discussed. "Do you remember the scene—the two men in the boat on the dark river—the lights dimly seen in the distance. There was a young girl running in a path through the forest toward the river's edge. Surely that was Balzac at his best."

My wife is aware that I am cheating. She is onto my curves and when I invent scenes, attributing them to Dostoievsky, Hardy, Flaubert, she smiles and lets the matter pass, but when there are guests in for the evening they are often confused.

"But in what story of Balzac's did that scene occur?"

"Do you not remember? It was in a tale of his called 'Night Again.' Surely you remember."

After all I am a writer. Am I to let people know how little I read? Reading and writing are after all linked in people's minds.

But let's be honest for a moment. After all what do writers read?

Writers like myself read little except when they are in one of the dreary blank periods, between outbursts of writing, when they are very young, and when they are ill.

I am myself seldom ill, but every now and then I am knocked over by a period of what my friends have learned to call one of my psychic sicknesses. The sickness lasts sometimes for months, often for weeks and occasionally, when I am lucky, a day or two will see me clear and all right again.

The periods, that is to say the times between, have to be got through however, and it is at such times most of my own reading is done. Life has become for the time dull and meaningless, my bones ache, and I look at my fellows with jaundiced eyes, so I escape into books.

Mostly I read histories, biographies of statesmen, of presidents, of generals. Such books are written usually by college professors—who get better jobs, I am told, after writing and publishing a book—by secretaries to the great, by wives and daughters of the great. Mr. Joseph Tumulty writes the Life of President Wilson, a general's wife writes a long book to prove that her husband was not responsible for the loss of the battle of Shiloh during the American Civil War, a successful business man writes a long book to tell how he learned to save pennies. The late World War has already produced a flood of deliciously dull books that will in the future, I am sure, most admirably serve my purpose and cure me of many an illness.

The books will get into the second-hand book stores. I will buy them, two for a quarter, and store them away.

Presently I shall have one of my psychic illnesses and shall spend the time, until I am well again, and do not want to read, in consuming facts. Having found life, as seen through the eyes of these writing men, inconceivably more dull than my own life can ever be, I shall become well again.

All of this fanfare, only to speak of a man who has betrayed me. I am being constantly betrayed these days. Something dreadful is happening. Historians, college professors, all such fellows, men who should read Mr. Henry Mencken and remain in the place he has provided for them, that is to say properly dull and commonplace, are writing, many of them, so much better than most of our novelists. It is dreadful. A man like myself hardly knows where to turn.

Recently, during one of my illnesses—of the kind just described—I picked up the story of Abraham Lincoln by Nathaniel Wright Stephenson—a perfectly proper college professor I had been told, expecting of course to be lulled into my normal healthy state of self-complacency by its dullness. Had I not read most of the Lincoln books? Did I not know what to expect?

Throwing myself on a couch I began to read. Pshaw! The

deuce! What a betrayal! The book was beautifully written, beautifully imagined. All my life I had been dreaming of writing, sometime, just a certain kind of Lincoln book and here was a man who had made the task impossible to me.

Mr. Stephenson had realized with the quick, sensitive feeling of the artist toward his materials that the true life story of such a man as Lincoln cannot be got at by the old, dull method of piling up facts. Having before him a wonderful story, he told it with warmth and gusto. He had gone at his job as an artist goes at it, by feeling with Lincoln, living in him and with him, putting his fingers with marvellous intuitive certainty on the very heart and soul of the drama in the life of the greatest and finest American figure.

And what had resulted was a book—a very, very fine book.

The Lincoln of Nathaniel Stephenson will, I am sure, live. The Lincoln story—the Lincoln myth, if you will—will surely live, for many hundreds of years and as long as it lives this book should live with it. It has stirred me more deeply than any American book I have read for years.

Surely it will stir many other Americans who, like myself, will be rejoiced to find the whole Lincoln story given a new turn toward greater subtlety and understanding.

However, I had been betrayed. The book was written by an educated man, and is there not another American myth that says very clearly that educated, cultured men cannot write, that they are dull? In adding so beautifully to the American Lincoln myth, Mr. Stephenson is helping to destroy, rather ruthlessly, another and, to me, very precious myth.

The whole situation, you see, the new turn our historians are taking toward beautiful, imaginative prose, leaves a fellow like myself, who at certain times must have dull books and who has always so depended upon the college professors, with practically no place to turn. Mr. Stephenson's book made the period of psychic illness, during which I read it, one of the most prolonged I ever had to go through. He wrote so well he made me sick. No college professor, no cultured, educated man should be allowed to act that way. It isn't right. No historian has any right to be so charming in prose.

JEROME BLUM

HOW very satisfying and comforting it would be if any man could walk into the studio of a painter and, as he stood there before the painter's work, could know definitely what makes the man's work beautiful or not beautiful. It would be such a cinch, so satisfying, such an ego boost to the bystander. I am thinking of this because I have had an experience.

I went recently to see the new work, done within the last two years, by the American painter, Jerome Blum. I was in New York and hearing that this painter had recently returned to America, went to see him. I went into a room where there were some twenty, twenty-five, perhaps thirty canvases piled against a wall. It was late in the afternoon and I am a provincial. All day I had been seeing people and was tired. I was full of my own affairs. "Come on," I said, "let's see." Then it came...the fine, rare experience that no man has too often. There is a new poet or a new proseman who suddenly begins to write beautifully. What a tightening of the heart strings when you come upon such work. It's a little odd...half beautiful work often makes you half jealous or envious. Clever work always does that to me, but really beautiful work doesn't. You are simply and naturally glad that another man has succeded in getting into his work something you are always so stumblingly trying for.

I think Jerome Blum has done it. I think that this work of his, this gorgeous painting, done in the last two years, tells a fine

35

story. I don't know what the story is. Blum has always been a strong, bold painter. He has never been afraid of color, but in this new work there is something, I swear, that was never there before...something ripe, alive, glowing. Any one of these paintings placed against the wall in a room makes the whole room suddenly and miraculously alive. I stood before them tired and confused and suddenly I was not tired. I was simply glad and happy. I suddenly wanted everyone to see them. That is why I am writing this. I hope it may induce someone else to have the stirring, fine experience I have had.

An awakening, a coming back to life and sense of life through the work of another. I started to speak of these paintings by saying I did not know what it was that suddenly comes into another man's work that gives it such dignity and integrity, and I do not stake my judgment on what I am here saying about the new work of Blum. What I stake is my senses. I am glad enough to stake that.

ALFRED STEIGLITZ

City Plowman

THEY have all been trying to stand up on their feet. I have
been trying. I have seen others trying. It has been going on since I
was a child.

The cities try to stand on their feet. The buildings in the cities
try.

There is a great uncertainty, roots trying to go down into
American soil.

I remember when I was a young man and first went to Europe.
I saw much there. There were the cities, the cathedrals, old kings'
palaces, all of the things we wide-eyed Americans go eagerly to
see, to come home and talk about. Water from the river Jordan,
a swim in the Seine. Here the Disciples walked. There marched
Napoleon. There, at a desk in a room in that great building, sat
Bismarck.

These things to be seen and wondered over, but there was a
greater wonder. I saw it in the body, in the eyes ... it was in the
hair, in the clothes, of a French peasant, driving a dusty cart along
a French country road, under trees.

It was in a man in a field near an English village. He was
binding grain into sheaves. He arose from the ground and
stretched. I remember standing in a path near by and
watching ... feeling something I find it hard, even yet, to put
down.

It was English skies in the Englishman, French skies in the

Frenchman, sense of fields, horizons, of place in man. Man in a place he knows, feels related to. "Life has gone on a long time here. Our sins on our own heads.

"We are men standing here. We will not pretend to be something greater, more splendid than we are.

"I will accept myself in my own place and time, in this moment, under these skies. My feet walk on the soil of this field. I will not leave this field. I will stay here.

"There will come bad years and good years. I am a man who belongs in this country town, on this farm. I am a man of this city.

"The city streets are mine. I am walking in the streets of this city. Watch my feet go down.

"In the city my feet strike upon stone, cement, asphalt. What does it matter? Something within me, tiny sap roots in me, go down through stone, cement, asphalt, to the dark ground.

"I admire my place. I want it.

"What does it matter to me that life constantly changes? The old relationships, man to man, man to woman, woman to woman, go on. I need the tiny veins in me, reaching down, to bring sap of earth up...that I may live, love...be brother, be sister...be friend, be foe.

"I need my own land, my place, my city.

"Let them change it, remodel it. 'Go on, men. Build your great buildings, bring your machines.' We men and women remain. We ourselves will get it or lose it."

There is something that constantly gets lost, that is occasionally, in a man, in a woman, regained. I have seen proud men in America, a few of them, a few proud women.

What gives me pride, life pride, is ability to love, vitality to love.

If I am a painter, this canvas can be my home, my place, my field, my hill, my river...if a sculptor this piece of stone, if a writer these white sheets, here before me. I have dirtied too many white sheets myself, seen others dirty city streets, American streams, dirty farms, dirty towns.

Something spoiled things too much for us here in America.

I declare it isn't our own fault. That, I know, doesn't let us out, but still I declare it.

They asked too much of us...Goddam 'em...giving us this.
They didn't give it. It happened. No one is to blame. As you
live along you find that out. No one is to blame for anything.
Still. Still. Still.
It was too much. It was too splendid.

You have to think of men coming here, to this America...not
supermen.
Just men...and women...their old European sins thick on
them. Your grandfather and mine...to say nothing of
grandmothers...Jews, Germans, Irish, Swedes.
Roumanians, Poles, Italians.
New blood mixtures, new streams forming.

Here the deep rivers, the forests, the rich valleys.
Wealth coming. It had to come. All the things men wanted and
needed...or thought they wanted and needed...were here in
abundance. Is it any wonder we got out of touch? The wealth was
outside man, in forests, mines, rich earth, slowly built up by
nature through thousands of years. One of the great crimes
against the Holy Ghost...is the crime of soil destruction that has
gone on here. Thirty million acres of it in one state I know of, land
once rich thrown aside.
Cities built blindly, factories stuck in anywhere, railroads
stealing river fronts, blind building, building, building...never
for the inner man.
It takes so long, so long here to get a bit of ground under your
feet. "What is my relationship with all this?"
They tell themselves so many little lies. Where is the man who
will not lie to himself or others?
I used to feel man's ultimate lie so much, in myself and others
when I was a younger man, out in Chicago. I had come there from
the backwoods, was what Henry Mencken loves to call "a Yahoo."
I didn't care. I didn't feel much like apologizing to the city
Yahoos.
I remember that just before I came to the city for the first time
I went out along the Sandusky Pike to Uncle Jim Ballard's farm
near my home town in Ohio, for a last visit. Uncle Jim was not my
real uncle, and Aunt Mary was not my real aunt. I had adopted

them. I walked out, the seven miles, and stayed overnight.

It was in the spring. I remember that the dogwood was blooming. I had been out there a week before to leave my clothes. Aunt Mary was mending them for me, getting me ready for my city adventure. Uncle Jim had laughed at me. "I guess you think you have to do it. You have to go. All the young fellows think they have to go."

He chuckled, making me uncomfortable. "You want to turn out to be something big, eh?" he said. Why, whenever I think of my friend Alfred Stieglitz do I think also of Uncle Jim, of Uncle Jim in relation to his farm, his barn and house, his friends?

There was a field that went away from the barn to a distant wood and, on the next morning, during my visit there, Uncle Jim was plowing in the field. He was a little wiry old man, just such a figure as Stieglitz is now. He was hatless in the field. The spring wind was blowing through his thin gray hair as he followed his team along a plowed furrow.

Uncle Jim always had a good team. He came down along a furrow toward the barn, and I am quite sure that, even then, I felt something of the splendor in the breasts of the great work horses, in the clean furrow rolling up as the plow marched.

He turned the team at the furrow's end and stopped. He went into the barn. It may have been a call of nature. Anyway, I put my hand to the plow in his field. "I'll make a few rounds for him," I thought. I wasn't really a plowman. What I did to his field might have passed unnoticed by any other farmer along that road.

A slight twist to my furrows. I spoiled the clean lines across the face of his field and it hurt Uncle Jim as though I had made an ugly mark on the face of his wife.

I remember the hurt look in his eyes as he stood looking at the field. It was something to remember. He cared. It wasn't in Uncle Jim to throw the hurt back to me by cursing, but I had spoiled his day's work. A little perhaps I had spoiled all the work of the year for him there in that field.

And what has all of this to do with this other man, this Alfred Stieglitz? There was Uncle Jim's relationship to the fields he had already plowed for some fifty years when I first knew him, and Stieglitz's to the city where I found him. He also made a clean furrow. There was the man and his environment, something fitting, going together. They were both men unashamed. They belonged.

It must be something very hard to get, and that most of us, here in America, never do get. I myself have been a passionate traveler, a lover, but where has it brought me in the end? I am here, facing these white sheets, as Uncle Jim his field and Stieglitz his white sheets. It must be nonacceptance that has brought this mouth-weariness, eye-weariness to so many of us. There are voices crying, "Accept, accept."

Other voices—a few..."Put it down. Put it down."

Stieglitz is a voice. He is a putter-it-down.

Fear of not making good. Who ever heard of Uncle Jim? Who ever bothered about him? What did he care? The young full of the diease: "I must make a noise, get big."

"But I don't want to."

"But you must. You must."

I think there must have been too much big talk in America, long ago. "America, the new sweet land," etc., etc. All the earlier ones flocking here from old Europe, the old human shame on them.

"Land of opportunity."

"Land of opportunity."

"Make good now, make good."

"If you can't do it really, make a bluff. Turn out showy work. Get attention."

Uncle Jim, back there, on his Ohio farm, never got off any of that stuff they were so full of in town. "Boy, I know you are going to make good now." He would have asked, "What's the matter with you as you are now?" He wasn't ashamed of his own position, on his little farm, warm with it, alive with it...his little strip of woodland, little fields, barns and sheds. "It's in me, and I am in it."

Later Stieglitz, in a city street walking. The man in his workshop. He catching, with his photographer's plates, city lights, significance of tall skyscrapers, light on the face of stone, on skies. There is an old gelding, standing weary after the day's work—something to make your throat hurt looking. How are you going to tell the story back of such work?

A dead tree by a road near the little house in the country to which he has gone in the hot months for thirty, forty, fifty years. He in his environment as Uncle Jim in his. "Make it yours, then give.

"Give them a farm, wide Ohio horizons. Give them the city. Make it your city and then give it."

Uncle Jim, by the clearness and honesty of his relationship to a field, giving me, standing and watching, sense of all fields, stretching away in a flat country, skies above fields, towns in the distance, so that later, fields and towns could live also in me, my own fancy released, my own imagination playing over farms, going into farm houses, going into streets in towns. . . .

And so Stieglitz to me. He in the city releasing the men about him, turning the imaginations of other men loose in his city. I get him so, as I get Uncle Jim . . . his workroom and the city, the fields he plows, he giving me thus also the city, as Uncle Jim the fields.

Making the city live as reality.

His relations with others, men and women, artists, his photographs. . . .

Himself asserting, sometimes preaching. His preachings and his assertions haven't mattered half as much to me as his devotion. . . .

Just brother, I think, to the devotion of my uncle Jim. . . .

That bringing in something healthy . . . love of work, well and beautifully done . . . the work of others as well as his own work.

Nonsense, eh?

It is the thing for which America cried out. It is the thing the city needs. A few more New Yorkers like Alfred Stieglitz and the city would change.

Take him away and the city will again change. I never did dare go back to Uncle Jim's farm after he and Aunt Mary turned up their toes to the daisies.

CARL CARMER & LANGSTON HUGHES

Paying for Old Sins

CARL Carmer went to Alabama a bit too anxious to please. He is so sunny and good-natured about everything from grits and collard gréens to Scottsboro that it rather makes your bones ache. These Alabamans are so persistently and so confoundedly cute, even in their cruelties, the old aristocracy is so aristocratic and the niggers so niggery. Thank you kindly. Hand me the Bill Faulkner.

Sample, page ninety-three: "We had planned a few days' tour before the visit Mary Louise had planned was to begin. An hour or so after we had started we had seen the red-gold of the dust turn to white. Below that white surface black soil—the Black Belt from whose dark and fertile land rose pillared glories with names that are poems—Rosemont, Bluff Hall, Gainswood, Oakleigh, Farmdale, Snow Hill, Tulip Hill, Winsor, Chantilly, Athol, Longwood, Westwood, Waldwie."

Poems man? You do not make words poetic by asserting they are poetic. Where is your poetry?

The book promises well. There is poetry in the title and the foreword excites. And then, too, Farrar and Rinehart have made the book well. Physically it is beautiful and Mr. Cyrus LeRoy Baldridge has made some drawings that are charming, but for me the book doesn't come off. I have already seen that some critic has said that it was not made for home consumption and I think he is wrong. I think the Southerners will love it, particularly the professional Southerners of New York and Chicago. Mr.

Stribling you are quite safe. This man will never steal your Alabama from you.

Nerts, say I. All this fuss because some Alabama farmer invites you to supper. It always did annoy me, this business, some Yank going South. No one shoots him. A Negro woman brings a cup of coffee to his bed in the morning. He eats hot bread. The hotel rooms are dirty. Now he is off.... "Oh this gorgeous land, home of old romance," etc., etc. Not that it isn't all true enough, if you could get below Alabama life, down into it.... Indiana life for that matter... what makes people what they are, the real feel of the life around you, get down into you, become a part of you and come out of you.

I don't think Mr. Carmer does it. He skirts it now and then and when he becomes what he really is, a very competent gatherer-up of names of fiddlers' tunes, collector of folk tales told by others, etc., the book begins to have real value. He should have confined himself to that work. The man is not a story teller.

And, as I have said, this other business, this damned half apology before Southerners for being born a Northerner, this casualness about Southern cruelty. There is an innocent school teacher taken out to a tree and hanged because he had a relative who was a murderer. "Give me a cigarette. Let's go down to Mary Louise's house. These Alabamans are so cute, don't you think."

There is one favorite Southern tale I didn't find in the book. It is about the white farmer who came down to the cross-road general store. Several other white farmers lounging about. "Well," he says, "I killed me a nigger this morning." Silence. He yawns. "Boys," he says, "I bet you that nigger will go three hundred pounds." To make his book quite perfect, Mr. Carmer should have got that one in. It is so cute.

"The Ways of White Folks" is something to puzzle you. If Mr. Carmer goes one way, Mr. Langston Hughes goes another. You can't exactly blame him. Mr. Hughes is an infinitely better, more natural, story teller than Mr. Carmer. To my mind he gets the ball over the plate better, has a lot more on the ball but there is something missed. Mr. Carmer is a member of the Northern white race gone South, rather with jaws set, determined to please and be pleased, and Mr. Hughes might be taken as a member of the Southern colored race gone North, evidently not determined about anything but with a deep-seated resentment in him. It is in his blood, so deep-seated that he seems himself unconscious of it. The Negro people in these stories of his are so alive, warm, and real and the whites are all caricatures, life, love, laughter, old wisdom all to the Negroes and silly pretense, fakiness, pretty much all to the whites.

It seems to me a paying for old sins all around, reading these two books. We'll be paying for the World War for hundreds of years yet and if we ever get that out of us we may still be paying interest on slavery.

Mr. Hughes, my hat off to you in relation to your own race but not to mine.

It is difficult. The difficulties faced by Mr. Hughes, as a story teller, are infinitely greater than those faced by Mr. Carmer. Mr. Carmer has but to take the old attitude toward the American Negro. "They are amusing. They are so primitive." If you go modern and go so far as to recognize that Negro men can be manly and Negro women beautiful. It is difficult to do even that without at least appearing to be patronizing. You begin to sound like an Englishman talking about Americans or a Virginian talking about a Texan. Even when you don't mean it you sound like that.

The truth is, I suspect, that there is, back of all this, a thing very little understood by any of us. It is an individualistic world. I may join the Socialist or the Communist Party but that doesn't let me out of my own individual struggle with myself. It may be that I can myself establish something between myself and the American Negro man or woman that is sound. Can I hold it? I am sitting in a room with such a man or woman and we are talking. Others, of my own race, come in. How can I tell what is asleep in these others? Something between the Negro man and myself gets destroyed...it is the thing D. H. Lawrence was always speaking of as "the flow." My neighbor, the white man, coming in to me as I sit with my Negro friend, may have qualities I value highly but he may also stink with old prejudice. "What, you have a damn nigger in here?" In the mind of the Negro: "Damn the whites. You can't trust them." That, fed constantly by pretense of understanding where there is no understanding. Myself and Mr. Carmer paying constantly for the prejudices of a whole race. Mr. Hughes paying too. Don't think he doesn't pay.

But story telling is something else, or should be. It too seldom is. There are always too many story tellers using their talents to get even with life. There is a plane to be got on—the impersonal. Mr. Hughes gets on it perfectly with his Negro men and women. He has a fine talent. I do not see how anyone can blame him for his hatreds. I think Red-Headed Baby is a bum story. The figure of Oceola Jones in the story, The Blues I'm Playing, is the most finely drawn in the book. The book is a good book.

BURT EMMETT

I CAME out of The Little Church Around the Corner in New York, where I had been sitting with perhaps two or three hundred other men and women and listening while certain men, ministers of the gospel, had been saying certain words over the dead body of my friend. I am afraid I did not hear many of the words. I arose when the others did, I bowed my head as prayers were said; I was thinking, thinking. "He is dead, this friend, this man I have loved."

"Man who has been kind to me, who stood by me once when I was terribly puzzled, half desperate."

I began thinking of a certain summer Sunday morning in the deserted streets of the city when Burt Emmett came to me.

I had been rude to him. He had tried to help me. "Oh, to hell with you," I had said, but he was determined. I remember how he walked around with me, fought with me. There was always, to the very last, a kind of eternal boyishness. In the church I was thinking, "All of these others must have felt at some time the same thing in him." When he could no longer fight me down that day, we walked, I remember, for a long time through the deserted streets of the city in silence and then I looked up at him. There were tears in his eyes. The face was the face of a young boy deeply hurt. There was a pleading look in the eyes. "I can't fight with you. Come on. Let me be your friend," the eyes said, and I surrendered.

47

There should be a new funeral ceremony written for the modern man. We are all nowadays cast into such a new changing puzzling world. It is so hard to draw close to others. Some great, some powerful poet should write new words, filled with a new music, expressing a little a new hunger in man, the new hunger of man for man.

I was thinking of that on the day when they buried my friend Burt Emmett. We, his friends, were on that day all so solemn, so apart from each other. As I came out of the church I kept looking about at other men. They were nearly all strangers to me. "And this man, now dead, has at some time, in some moment of his life drawn close to each of these men and women as he drew close to me." I wanted it said, sung, shouted. "He was my friend, and mine, and mine. He had the gift. He is gone and there is a great hole left, there is this emptiness."

I cannot write of Burt Emmett, as young man... already friend-worshipper... as the young fellow who went from town to town as advance man for some group of players....

Then young newspaper man, advertising man, lover of fine printing, collector of rare first editions, collector of paintings by struggling young American painters. There are a hundred faces to the life of Burt Emmett I did not know much. I knew him, and I think that all of the others who knew him best must have thought of him always first of all for a certain gift. It was the gift of belief in others, a kind of profound eagerness, humbleness before the fact of friendship. It had a curious effect on us all. All of Burt Emmett's friends will bear me out in this. He dignified our lives by his friendship, by the curious gift he had of giving love and belief... a belief, freely given, that made any man fortunate enough to be Burt's friend also believe in himself.

He dignified the life of every man to whom he gave his friendship. What more can any man do?

LINDSAY and MASTERS

I T WAS the last two chapters of Edgar Lee Masters' beautiful and stirring biography of his friend and fellow American poet Vachel Lindsay that moved me most deeply. In the last chapter of the book Masters has his own say and I like that. He has been writing of his friend. He is moved and angry. I like this kind of healthy male indignation. It is good, like the healthy strong anger of that other American, Theodore Dreiser, fighting for some friend, fighting some stupid injustice done someone he loves....

Masters must have written this final chapter just after finishing that other chapter in which he put down Lindsay's finish. And what a death that, what an unrelieved, stark tragedy.

There is the Lindsay house in Springfield, Illinois, Lincoln's home town, town of the struggles of the great and forgotten Altgeld, town to which the beaten and defeated Grant went to make a new start, town in the midst of the fat rich Illinois country, land of corn, of corn like forest trees. There is a picture of the house opposite page 28 in the book. I think Edward Hopper should go to Springfield some day and make a painting of that house... house full of haunts it would be for the poet born into it. There are not many houses in the Middle Western corn country in which one family has lived so long. It was the house in which Lindsay was born. He died there. That was good.

House haunted, after death, by Lindsay's father, old Doc Lindsay, by the insistent, determined, religious mother... she

49

must have put the bee on Lindsay all right...by colorful grandfathers from both sides of the family...Lincoln adorers, Lincoln haters, Northerners and Southerners...these coming there in the years after the Civil War...neither side knowing exactly what they had fought for...in what war did the fighters ever know...angry, perhaps in their hearts knowing both sides had been defeated.

One wonders if Lincoln would have seen down through it if he had lived on for a time.

Lindsay living on in that house through childhood, through boyhood, and young manhood, through death, in that house, in that town. He must have been a boy or young man there when John W. Gates came down from Chicago to stand on the State House steps and pass out money to legislators who put through his Chicago street-car franchise. Gates a big and important man in the state; Lindsay and the men who were his father and grandfathers unimportant. Of what importance is an old doc, going about in his buggy, long after automobiles came in, delivering babies, taking care of the sick...I dare say, most of the time, forgetting to send his bill...of what importance the boy who was to become one of the three or four important American poets. Hopper, you'd better go down there and paint a picture of that house, or Charles Burchfield you go. Let's try to keep the banner up for Lindsay; Masters has done his stint.

Vachel Lindsay's end in that house. Let me just lift a few paragraphs from the pages of the book. It has the stark simplicity of great writing:

Ill and exhausted, with only $76 in his pocket as the profit of a grilling lecture experience, and with $4,000 in debts for living expenses for his wife and little children and for himself, there was no place for him to turn for solace. He was in the fatal trap, the door had sprung to and fastened itself, and there was nothing for him to do but to wait for the end. The wait was not long, it was but a week, but the torture of that week defies words.

He was up and down in bed, at times too weak to go about safely. He was having auditory hallucinations. He thought he heard voices on the porch plotting his death and the death of his wife, and blackmail. His wife could not assure him that he had been merely dreaming. After he took her word that it was all a dream he would recur to the wild belief that enemies were about the house seeking his death. He was taking bromides and Luminal, but sleep fled him.

At dinner [on the evening of his death] he fell into pitiful tears, saying that he was an old man, and that his life and work were finished. After dinner Mrs. Lindsay got him upstairs again, and then she descended to the living room to read. He had asked her to leave him, he wanted to be alone.

In about half an hour he came downstairs full of energy and fury about every real or imagined wrong that had ever been done him; he stormed with accusations against Mrs. Lindsay for the injury she had done him in her double role of tyrant-mother and scarlet woman who had taken his virginity. He wanted to get away from her and the children, and so announced himself. He wanted to go back to Hiram College, there to begin over the dreams of twenty-one, and to write more magical songs. His wife told him that she would not stand in his way, that she was only concerned for his care and support if he left her. Lindsay replied to this that He who watches over the sparrows would take thought for him. This frightful frenzy, these whirling words lasted for three hours; then he was exhausted, and in the wrath an angry ghost he stalked upstairs. Mrs. Lindsay after a time followed him, and found him pretending to read.

She closed her eyes, finally, though not in sleep. Then Lindsay arose and descended to the lower floor again. Mrs. Lindsay in anxiety for him followed him. She found him in the dining room putting up the family pictures, those of Mrs. Lindsay and the children, those he carried with him on his lecture tours. He looked calm and peaceful, now, and when she asked him if he were all right, he replied, "Yes, dear, I'm quite all right. I'll be up in a moment."

Mrs. Lindsay went back to bed, and fell into sleep. In about fifteen minutes she was awakened by sounds of something crashing downstairs. And then she heard footsteps heavy and fast, and then the sound of Lindsay coming upstairs on his hands and knees. Mrs. Lindsay rushed out to get him, fearing that he was making for the room where the children were asleep. By this time, Lindsay was running through the upstairs hall, with his hands up, looking white and scared. As Mrs. Lindsay screamed he fell. When he was put in bed he asked for water, saying, "I took Lysol." The doctor was quickly summoned, but when he arrived Lindsay had ceased to breathe. His last words were, "They tried to get me; I got them first." It was December 5, 1931, at one o'clock in the morning.

Can you wonder after that, after reading these few paragraphs from the book, that Masters, after writing them ... himself a poet, land-lover, Illinois-lover, America-lover, that he turned then, full of fine male anger, to the writing of another chapter, accusing America?

For allowing it, for allowing itself to forget earlier American dreams, to forget Jefferson, to forget what Lincoln must at least have thought he meant ... Illinois forgetting Altgeld ... the West and the Middle West going whoring after the East and the money of the East, after money, money, money ... the East whoring after the tired, wornout culture of Europe ... the old dignity of old beliefs gone....

The great broad sweet land that Lindsay did love, that he sang of, often with such glowing gusto ... with such clear sweetness often enough....

Trying, in his flaming days, always to lay the foundation for an American culture. What matter if he sometimes went religiously fantod? Johnny Appleseed, Boone, Jefferson, Altgeld, John L. Sullivan, Bryan in his good days before they got him into the money racket ... Lindsay trying to set up in America a nest of heroes, to do for American life what Greek heroes once did for Greek life.

The man Lindsay doing this most of his life, in a kind of religious ecstasy ... tramping ... strange enough figure, God knows ... through the streets of cities ... the long walk South, from New York to Florida ... North again, then later West, toward the Pacific ... Talking, talking, talking ... singing some-times ... shouting sometimes ... land-love, town-love, city-love....

Garages, livery stables ... I dare say factory doors where

workers pour out, drug stores, hardware stores, doors of
farmhouses...shoes often enough worn-out, clothes worn-
out..."I had an apple and a can of beans, bought at a store,
yesterday. I walked fourteen miles."

Then sudden fame, as it would come to such a man here...his
queerness, strangeness, helping a lot to bring it on. Bang! Bang!
Bang! Here comes General Booth on his way to heaven. If it were
to be a Lindsay heaven it would be a strange enough place. It, that
is to say fame, was no heaven for Lindsay. They do it to you if you
let them.

The usual story. They took him, I think, most of all, for a kind
of freak...this sugar-lame boy who couldn't grow into
something. It might be what manhood is, the thing we must grow
to. Call it sophistication. It's being on to the racket.

They petted him for a time, made much of him—I dare say
spoiled him a lot—and then forgot him. They found someone
else to entertain them, be freak for them. Wear-your-hair-long
boys. Parade for them.

Then for Lindsay, lecture touring for the women. That will
finish a man O. K.; it's almost as sure as going to Hollywood. The
Hollywood boys get more dough. His spirit strength ebbing
away, the realization coming of what he was doing to himself,
knowing his power to see going, to feel going, to love going. Then
the Lysol. It's a disinfectant, isn't it?

It's a story O. K., this one of Lindsay that Masters tackled and
has done so well. To me it is a story of a writer, by a writer, for
writers, but I may be wrong about that. It may be a story for all
young Americans.

And I dare say that if painters do go some day to Springfield, to
paint the house Lindsay lived and died in, they'll find it has
become a museum. We do very well by our poets here, when they
are dead.

EVAN SHIPMAN

Free for All

IT doesn't happen too often, the arrival of a book like this, by a young American writer—a book that makes an older American writer's heart jump with joy. Evan Shipman, in coming into writing, hasn't stayed in New York's Greenwich Village or about Union Square, taking up the current fad of romanticizing the proletariat. He cut out into the back country and found there something pretty swell and real going on, mostly among the unromanticized proletariat. In the midst of industrialized towns, the machine, the rivers of automobiles in the streets of the towns, he found man and the horse.

Not the running horses, mind you—that world of big gamblers and wealthy owners, with little wizened lads, half dwarfs, starved down to their ninety pounds, taking the danger and the real excitement

...not that such horses as Sun Briar, Man o' War and Omaha aren't beautiful enough

...the man end of that racket is not so good....

Shipman found something else—the trotters and pacers—the glory of that, still going on at state fairs in farming states, in county-seat towns, in the vast American hinterland. It is, in its own way, poetry out of a people.

Time was—it's not so long ago—when it was in every town, this poetry. There was a country doctor, merchant, saloon keeper, often a farmer and sometimes even a preacher, who simply had to have at least one or two good ones. We never did get a fair break from our writers on some of the sweeter sides of our American life. President Roosevelt's father owned Gloster, a good one.

Men and lads together on chairs and on upturned boxes before livery-stable doors or before country-town hotels at evening, breeding lines being discussed and fought over, great names mentioned, the master reinsmen, Murphy,.Budd Doble, Walter Cox, and the great master of them all, Pop Geers.—"And did you once see Shelley plain?"—They didn't speak of him as Pop. They called him Mr. Geers. He died at seventy-four, in the sulky, in the home stretch, those powerful old hands of his holding the reins over a good one.

The owner not walking about, so expensively tailored, on running-track clubhouse lawns—millionaires. Owners and trainers stayed with the trotting horses, worked with them, drove them in long bitterly fought heats, in danger always of being cut down, trampled, even killed.

Vicious men, gentle ones, firm ones. Boys running away from home to be stable boys, "swipes," to get a glimpse of the big world, be near a good one. All the boys dreaming of some day being a driver. They knowing in their hearts that it was a fine art—Shipman's Fred Dunbar, Leon Farmer, Will Broderick, Tommy the Dancer, Aroostook Slim.

The death of the old bum Pete on a night when rain fell over a lonely fair ground, the story of Stamina's last race, and that other story of the way Fred Dunbar brought on the colt Black Worthy. I could write pages about Shipman's book—read it, have yourself a warm real American evening. Excuse me. I put the book with the best of Hemingway or Faulkner and even with Chekhov and with the finest of Turgenev, his glorious "Annals of a Sportsman."

The book is illustrated with beautiful little drawings that really illustrate, by Robert Dickey.

V. F. CALVERTON

V. F. Calverton, known to those who knew him well as George—I never did know the meaning of the V. F.—was one of the men to whom I cannot be other than grateful, who, it seemed to me, understood what I myself was trying to do, at a certain time when I needed the encouragement he gave me.

I had long been trying to emphasize in my stories and novels the importance, and the drama, of ordinary life among ordinary people. Perhaps this was not a conscious effort. I felt myself very close to the people I was trying to write about, and in several pieces I wrote, George Calverton did seem to understand what I was driving at and I could not be other than grateful to him.

It seems to me that Calverton had one of the best of modern critical minds. He must have been frequently, perhaps always, confused as we all have been by all this modern use of big words, the determination to group people and think of them in the mass rather than as individuals. But if you did try at least to keep in mind that people are people, that all men and all women, regardless of this new passion to put people in pigeonholes and thus to understand where there is no understanding—if you had tried to avoid all this, Calverton, seemed to sense what you were at and to appreciate it.

I am sure Claverton had, deep down, real inner integrity. And what is more wanted now, the world being as it is? I hated the fact that he died. There is too much death in the world today.

Some day, perhaps, we will get out from under this modern cloud of death and into the clear again. Living will become again of supreme importance. I always felt, during the few times I was with him, a great eagerness for life in Calverton. That was what made me so regret his death.

Certainly what is more and more wanted now is men who have this eagerness for life.

Maury Maverick
in San Antonio

THERE is one man, mayor of an American city, who is having a grand time. It is Maury Maverick down in San Antonio, Texas. Maury has lost none of his magnificent swagger. He is full of laughter, is eternally busy. He is like a man attempting to lift an entire city on his shoulders—carry it forward into something new.

I suspect there are many people in San Antonio who have no great fondness for Maury. They managed to beat him for re-election to Congress but it may well turn out that they will end by being glad he is back there at home, in his own city, among his own people. There is something very Texan about Maury. There is a Texas sweep to the man. He is Texas in a way I imagine that other Texan—Jack Garner—never was, never could be. Out there, where they know their Cactus Jack personally, they speak of him always with a sort of nervous tolerance, for, while Cactus Jack evidently has power, it isn't a broad, sweeping Texas kind of power. It seems to be the sort of power that comes from interest on the dollar invested, the mortgage-foreclosing sort of power.

As for San Antonio, it strikes a man, coming there, looking about, as just the typical American city. The city's magnificence is magnificent. Its squalor, like that in the poor quarters of so many American cities, is something to alarm and frighten you.

You come into the city by car, out of the far west, as I did, from Los Angeles and Tucson—so many millions and millions of acres

59

to half-feed a steer, a few goats and sheep wandering over the barrenness—and there you are, on a flat rich plain, cotton growing up to your shoulders, vast pecan groves, vegetables of all sorts to be shipped north by the carload, the trainload.

The city is half Mexican; nearly all of the labor of that country is done by Mexicans. They are everywhere. As voters they have always been purchasable. Why not? If I had to live as most of them have to live, be paid for my labor as they have been paid, I'd sell anything.

As everyone knows who knows the South, Maury Maverick comes from a family of distinction. There are the Maurys of Virginia, the Mavericks of Texas. He must have gone through something any boy or young man from such a Southern family has necessarily to go through.

Are you going to ride on that, be what is called a Southern gentleman, stay up there on the heights? Knowing, as you must if you have a working brain at all, on what all the distinction you are holding onto rests?

Cheap labor, Negro and Mexican, pounded down and down, ignorance that has gone on for a century, "hill billies," Florida and Georgia "crackers," Mexican "greasers." One-party states— rotten bureaucracies built up, as they must be in any one-party state: The thing that, in the end, must kill all the totalitarian states, either in America or Europe, going on in our South. The nonsense always being carried on about the old South—that unlike the North and the Middle West it was not commercial. The Old South trying to hark back to the Greeks, to justify its "peculiar" institution. As though it didn't take money to buy Negro slaves. If slavery was not the very height of commercialism, what was it?

A young alive man like Maury Maverick, with his alert brain, realizing all that, not wanting to live on "family," be a stuffed shirt.

So this young man goes to Congress, gets there by buying the Mexican vote. There is no doubt of that. But he bought it in a new and legal way. The Mexicans down there were not classified as white men. They were classified as Negroes in the census and other records, federal and state. Maury forced the classification of the Mexicans as white men. That's the way he got them, bought them. He restored to them a little of their self-respect. If you ask me, I imagine they will keep on voting for him till hell freezes. He's got them really bought.

A pretty interesting fact, I'd say, now when we are all trying so hard to square ourselves with the American nations to the south of us, wanting their markets, of course. But also, a little, wanting something else, even understanding, cultural understanding, wanting even to make some amends for brutalities of the past.

The Mexicans and the sympathetic natives sent Maury to Congress, as a Southern New Dealer. But when he came up for re-election the second time, the machine politicians and the special interests managed to gang up on him. They beat him.

I imagine it was the New Deal's fault. They had sent a representative of the National Labor Relations Board down there where the pecan-shellers, in the huge pecan industry, were getting an average of about $1.75 a week.... Mexican women trying to keep families going by prostitution. A mess, one of the ugliest messes in the U.S.A.

I was down there when that was going on, went to some of the hearings, heard some of the rich pecan kings speak of labor, Mexican labor, with sneering contempt.

"You can't do anything with that kind of cattle." The air full of that sort of feeling. At the same time the beauty spots of the city all relics of what an earlier Mexican civilization had built.

So they beat Maury for Congress. He was upsetting the apple cart. He was, they cried, a Red, a Communist. I imagine there was plenty of money spent. They got him. They thought they had him down for keeps. They figured that, because he was a New Dealer, he would probably get an appointment in Washington, or be sent, say, to some other country as an ambassador. And that would be O.K., too. He would be out of their hair.

But Maury didn't do it. He fooled them. He came home, put his name up for mayor in his own home city. He got into a real fight. He is one who doesn't mind a fight. He likes it.

And he won out. They used up all the ammunition they had, hit below the belt, yelled Communism, but he beat them.

And there he was, right away, in trouble up to his eyes.

There had been a permit given for a Communist meeting, not by Maury but by his predecessor. Was he going to revoke it? Was he going to let them meet?

"Sure," said Maury.

"What about free speech?"

"Let 'em spout."

I am sure the man realized, as any man who knows his America must realize, that all this talk about a Communist danger in this country is just plain bunk. That the real reason for all this Red-baiting has its foundation in the fact that, in San Antonio for example, pecan-shellers are now getting $2.50 a day instead of $1.75 a week. That the U.S.A. is a deeply capitalistic country with just a bit of awakened consciousness that our underdogs have been made too underdog, that the real revolutionary danger is in the $1.75 a week, not in Earl Browder or Mike Gold.

So Maury said, "No, I'll not revoke the permit. Let 'em spout," and immediately crowds gathered in the street before the city hall.

They howled. They threw bricks. They threatened to hang Maury to a lamp post but he stood pat. He stood pat in the same way the Little Flower, LaGuardia, did about the Bund meeting in the Garden, in New York. Thinking, believing, that the best way to get the atmosphere cleared was to let them spout.

So that blew over and they tried to get Maury in another way. He had, they said, paid the poll tax for certain union members. It seems that it is against the law to pay another man's poll tax in Texas. In my own state, Virginia, where I live now, both of the old parties do it openly. The Byrd organization does it, and what there is of the Republican crowd does it. In our congressional district, I have been told, it costs a man around $30,000 to be elected to Congress. The money goes into paying up poll taxes. What else?

But in Texas, you can't. Down there they can send you to the penitentiary for doing it. But you can spend money to put on a campaign to get people to pay their own poll taxes.

Maury gave the money—$250—to the Garment Workers' Union, with its lawyer's consent.

The lawyer sold him down the river.

Maury says the union attorney wanted to dictate who should be chief of police in San Antonio.

Maury said, "No."

He said, "They elected me, not you, mayor of this town."

"Do your worst," he said, and the man apparently tried.

"Were you scared, Maury?"

"Hell, yes. I didn't think I'd look good in a cell. I wanted to do things in this town. I'm stuck on my town. I've got a hunch it can be the most beautiful, the most healthful city in America. I'm a Texan. I believe in Texas. I have plans. I want to work. I don't want to be in jail. Sure I was scared."

They didn't get him. He is working.

He said, "Listen, boy. I don't want to be a Huey Long or a Bilbo. I don't want to appeal to anything cheap. I'm no charlatan. I want to work, make this town what it can be. Sure they tried to get me. Maybe if I had been them I'd have done the same. They tried to get me but they failed. O.K.

"I'm not going to be revengeful. Yesterday was yesterday. What about doing one Texas town right? This is an empire, down here. I'm a native of a town I like and I want to make the world like it. And boy, am I going to make it a town!"

He seems to be doing it. He's young, isn't old and cynical, isn't tired. He got eleven millions from the U.S.A. while in Congress to tear out some seventy acres of the worst, the most terrible slums in America. He has driven the big-time gamblers out of his town. He says of the poor little prostitutes, "I'll make them keep off the streets but I'll not arrest and bilk them."

He takes you around, proudly, swaggeringly. He is carrying on the beautifying of the bank of the river that flows through the city. Has got all of the men he can find at work. The merchants, coming to realize that workers getting $1.75 a week are rotten customers, are going over to him.

There was an old Mexican town, called "La Villita," right in the heart of San Antonio—a few old houses, very simple and therefore beautifully built, within walking distance of all the big modern hotels. He is restoring that, making it a part of the new city of his dreams. He is working, half playing, full of energy, a real Texan, not wanting to be a stuffed shirt, not, it seems, revengeful for what they have tried to do to him, trying to keep his head.

He strikes me as American youth, at its best, a man with the courage and energy to try again in another American city what so many men have tried only to meet defeat. It seems to me our one hope—such American youth.

Living in America

Living in America

THE problem of living in America just now and having left, after the business of making a living is taken care of, something extra to go into creative work is largely a matter of reserve nerve force. In my own time and since my own boyhood ordinary American life has changed so much, has been so speeded up, that to walk about nowadays in the streets of an American city, having a certain impersonal quiet place inside, so that life and the drama of life may be taken in and registered, requires, for me at least, a special technique.

However, having that, having it sometime in hand, is there another country in the world where so much can happen that is exciting, amusing, and provocative to the story-teller? The story-teller is not up to the business of changing life or reforming it, he is not trying to entertain, amuse, or lull to sleep, at least not primarily. He is after stories and the telling of stories, and often enough the grim or the tragic phases of life, as they float up to him, catch and fire his fancy as much or more than the milder, softer phases. Why question America as a place for the story-teller or for any other kind of creative workman? If the job is too much for him, if life is too complex and difficult for him to see and feel clearly, that is his failure and not the failure of the civilization out of which he must get his materials if he is to get them at all. And the whole story of the swift, sudden changes in life here, the drive, the rush, the lost sense of values in the

modern industrial world, the necessary loss of sensibilities too—
is that not a story?

What I want for myself, that I may see and feel it all, is just
sufficient reserve nerve force—nothing else. Given that it is my
job as a story-teller to see and feel the story, to take it inside
myself, digest and build my story or stories out of all this rushing,
hurriedly-thrown-together pell-mell of things that is modern
life.

Well, I have set myself that job. And I do not want to join the
chorus of men who cry out against modern life. What has life to
do with the workman anyway? It is his job to look out for himself.
I have little or no sympathy with the man who declares that the
creative workman is unappreciated here. He is too much
appreciated. Favors are flung at him on all sides. Never did so
much second-class work get so much praise or so much
substantial support in any civilization I ever heard about; and as
for good work, I believe it is no longer possible for good work to
pass unnoticed here. The body of our criticism is pretty sound
after all. And I think that conditions for the creative workman in
any of the arts here in America are—as far as the mere business of
making a living is concerned—too good. Those of us scribblers
who have the knack at all of catching the fancy of the big general
public or of impressing them may, if we choose, live the lives of
bankers and brokers. For the poet or the painter the road is
perhaps harder and longer, but why should not the road be hard?
A workman in any of the arts surely gets something from his
work which other men do not get. That, I take it, is why he is a
creative workman. If he cannot get something from his work
which will compensate him for not having an automobile and a
troop of servants, let him go out and be a banker or broker. There
would be a kind of health in that kind of honesty in any event.

Survival comes down, then, to a question of nerve force. Often
I have thought that the whole question of whether any American
workman can go through the long apprenticeship which good
craftsmanship inevitably requires—whether or not he can
manage to make a living while keeping a part of his nerve force
for creative work—is largely a matter of physical stamina.

Take, for example, my own case. I have published nine books
and my work as a writer has received critical attention. My books

do not sell in large quantities. Very well! Until two years ago I made my living by writing advertisements. Now I am trying to live by my pen and by the proceeds of a few lectures delivered during the winter months.

For many years, then, I went on writing, doing on the side other things than writing to support myself. As a young man, and before I became a writing man, I tried to build up in myself an enthusiasm for another kind, perhaps a more conventional kind, of work. I plunged into business, tried as hard as I could to make money. It wasn't in me. The effort only promised to make me a nervous wreck, and so, when I gave it up, I gave up also the notion of money-making. If I did not intend to give people what they thought they wanted, why should they bother about me, was what I had to ask myself.

Being naturally a rather easy-going, lazy sort of man, I quite consciously tried to build up in myself another way of life. For a number of years I had rather rushed about, my speech had become quick and sharp, and I had dived madly in and out among automobiles, rushed into offices, ridden on fast trains, and tried with all my heart and soul to make of myself a good go-getter. It wouldn't work. I really wanted to be a story-teller, a scribbler, I fancy. Then I began to write. But as a scribbler I found my days as a go-getter had set up habits in me that were destructive to myself as a workman. How many stories I spoiled because I tried to hustle them, tried to bang them through by main force! My workmanship went to pieces—the story, the trail of which I had picked up, had not been allowed to mature in me. It was leaky, full of holes, and always for the same reason—the tale had not been felt through because I, the go-getter, had tried to hustle it.

But this hurry, this driving, rushing neurotic thing that was now playing the very devil with the only work I had ever undertaken honestly or had cared anything about was in me. It had become a part of my physical life. I had made it that. Very well, I had to make a change if I could. I began. For months I worked at that job in the city of Chicago. For two or three years I really worked at nothing else. I had to go from one place to another, and I took myself in hand. Was there any reason why I had to be at the new place in five minutes rather than in fifteen?

Surely not. I made myself stroll rather than rush. The old half-

slovenly drawl in my speech which I had rather liked as a boy
began to come back. That helped too. How amusing! Now even in
the writing of advertisements, a job I detested, I did better work;
but the men by whom I was employed were annoyed. One by one
they spoke to me. "Don't! Don't drawl that way! Hurry! Always
try to give the impression that you are going somewhere on a
very important mission," they said. My slow drawling speech also
bothered. I'm afraid I did not much care.

For myself it was working out, I thought, rather well. Now I
saw a thousand things in every street I had not seen when I
hustled along. Hundreds of little by-plays of life I had been
overlooking now popped up everywhere, along the streets, in
offices, in houses. As I could not do much talking when I talked
slowly I heard more talk from the lips of others. Perhaps I began
to learn a little.

I was, I fancy—in the only way I knew how—repairing my
shattered nerves, nerves shattered by the hurly-burly of life, by
the rush of all modern American life. And as I did this, as my
technique for doing it became more a part of me, I began to look
about more, began really to enjoy living. My stories, I thought, got
a little fuller and rounder, they had more body to them.

As for the whole question of whether or not it is possible to
live the creative life in America, here and now, why not? Surely
there are plenty of stories here. And if there is little good story
telling it is not the fault of life. Life does not deeply change
because you ride in an automobile at thirty miles an hour rather
than walk at three; and if it does, and you cannot get at life from
the seat of an automobile, why not get out and walk?

Life in America is, I fancy, just what life has been in every age,
only perhaps more complex and difficult to get at because we
story-tellers try to go so fast. And for that matter, may it not well
be that the stories we try to pick up and tell are really made more
dramatic and interesting by the very speeding-up process
inevitable in our hurried mechanical age? At any rate, there is the
situation. A thousand new sounds, sights, smells, impacts are
whipping away at the nerves in every American center of life.

The American who tries to escape by running off to live, say in
Europe, is putting himself out of it altogether. To get at the story
he has got to stay where the story is. The artist cannot change life.

That isn't his job. He has got to paint it, write, sing it—and to do that he has got to be in it and a part of it, with its rhythm in his blood.

From my own point of view it comes back to what I started with in this effort to say something about the position of the creative workman in American life. If the workman has some reserve force he will pull through and perhaps do some good work. If he has none he will have to find out for himself a technique of building it up in the midst of the clatter. For until he gets it, until the workman gets into a position where the constantly growing intensity of modern life does not use up all of his inner force in merely getting through his day, he will have nothing to give to his work. The creative workman who has nothing to give is, of course, not creative at all.

A Great Factory

MANY men, living in one long house. Rows of small frame houses, all built alike, along the streets of the industrial suburb. Other streets just like it running in all directions. A great city of such streets off to the north. If you took a street car you got down into the business section of the city. Great department stores, big hotels, swell restaurants. Lordy, how many people in this world! How do they all manage to make a living? You could take another car up to the park and on up to where the swell houses were. In your own street—dust, dirt, crying children, toughs in the pool room at the corner. Up there gardens, flowers, green grass growing.

There were two women—sisters—who ran the long house. One of them had married—a fleshy young man who always went about in his shirt sleeves and had a cigar stuck in the corner of his mouth. He ran the pool room in the same street. Some of us went in there on Saturday afternoons or evenings. Harry and I did once or twice. It wasn't a very good place to go.

There were young men hanging about who never worked— better dressed than we were. Get into a game with one of them and, if you were sap enough to lay a bet, he stuck you every time. One of them stuck Harry for a whole week's pay. Harry said he had it coming to him. They were all pool sharks—the well-dressed, cigarette-smoking young men.

The two sisters in that factory labourers' rooming house worked likes mules. Harry and I hadn't much time to be sorry for any one except ourselves but we were sorry for them. They did the cooking in the house, swept and made the beds. It was a huge place—not too clean. Well, it wasn't clean at all. It was said the pool room keeper came home drunk sometimes and beat his woman. I never saw or heard anything of that.

The other sister. Well, you know how young labourers or factory hands talk. Their fancies linger over any woman they see. I was that way myself at that time. Harry may have been. He had a lot of natural reserve. A fellow named "Cal" told me he saw one of the sisters and a man named Slim Beal in a room together.

It was a lie. One day when I was ill she came into my room to make the bed. I could not help thinking of what Cal had said. When I looked at her the idea of her not being straight was absurd.

Trucks in the street outside, dust thick on the window panes. I sat by the open window and had in my hand a copy of George Borrow's *Romany Rye*. A lot of the other labourers in the factory used to call me "the professor".

The tall sister, with the bony hands and the tired sad-looking eyes, began to talk. Her cheeks grew a little red. She was embarrassed because she had got the impulse to talk and it was hard work for her. She told me about a younger brother who had died. It was evident he was the hope of the family. She said that the younger brother liked to draw pictures.

"I do, too," I said, "but I am not very successful. I suppose I'll just be a common workman all my life. I wish I could do something well."

She looked at me, sizing me up. "Of course," she said. It was evident she did not see anything in my looks to make her want to refute my statement. The brother, had he lived, would have been a genius. She knew it quite definitely. He could draw anything—a horse, a ship, a pig, just anything. Show him a picture in a newspaper or a magazine and the next day he would have it down in black and white, as natural as life.

The sister's eyes shone as she spoke of the dead brother. I tried to draw her out concerning her position in the house. "Why do you work here? I bet they don't pay you any too much."

My words frightened her and she went quickly away. It was the only talk we ever had together.

The factory where we worked was a big one. With the man at the next bench I got acquainted quickly. That was Harry. He was the only man there I did get to know well.

He did not belong to the factory or to factory life. Something was all wrong. How I knew I can't say. Harry had a certain air, walked across a room with a certain indefinable swagger. Later he lost most of his swagger.

Back of us both clung a memory of other places, other kinds of life—the life of fields, farms, orchards, small shops in small towns where the factories had not come yet, of nights on country roads under the moon, of rains and snows. "I'll walk out of this damn place when I get ready," I said to myself. I was strong of body. Work in fields is heavy, hard work and the pay is not much but there are no brick walls closing you in. I was in the presence of something tremendous, powerful—but it hadn't got me yet. It hadn't got Harry—yet.

I said something to him one day at the noon hour. His eyes grew bright. We became friends.

He took a room next my own in the great barrack-like place kept by the two sisters. Most of my own thoughts of factory life and what it means to the men in factories, what it does to men, are really his. Later I made my get-away but he stuck, became a drifting factory hand going from city to city, from shop to shop. He may not have been as shrewd as I was. I saw him once, fifteen years later. He had been hurt in a factory and was dying. They were taking the best of care of him. He had, in some mysterious way, kept track of me and sent me word. His opinions of factories hadn't changed much. He died, I thought, rather handsomely.

He thought the industrial age, the age of factories, too big for human comprehension, disastrous to men, but did not put the blame on any one.

Let me return to our life together. We used to go in the early morning down a long dirty street to the factory. Outside

everything barren and ugly. Inside everything clean and shining.
This particular company had built most of the houses in the
industrial suburb. The houses were all alike. There was no
expression of individuality. Well, you can't have artists building
factory towns, can you?

Harry walked beside me, worked beside me, came home with
me evenings. We talked—trying to find ourselves in our world.
On some evenings we walked out beyond the town, on country
roads or along railroad tracks. This was in the winter and it was
often bitter cold, with biting winds blowing. We were young
enough not to mind. It did me good just then to be with a man as
impersonal as Harry. A lot of labourers are always flying off the
handle, talking wild. You see I had to get factory life from the
men's angle. I was one of them.

The factory was something—the walls well built, great light
rooms. The factory stood for something very definite.

There was a row of shower baths where you could go and get
clean after the day's work. Nothing lacking in physical comfort.
The work was easy.

Something more than that—something splendid. Such vast
quantities of goods made and very well made.

The great factory in which we worked was an impersonal
thing like something in Harry, who was to spend his life working
in factories. The steady, even hum of vast machines—beauties
many of them—so intricately made, doing such marvelous
things. Click, click, click. Goods being made, carloads, trainloads,
shiploads of goods. I could get a thrill any time, looking at the
machines. They frightened me, too.

Harry was the son of a country doctor. He had left home
because, in a quarrel, his father struck his mother with his fist. "I
had to leave or kill him." He did not talk much about himself.

We were one in our admiration for the machinery and the
organization of the great factory. Men had done it, the minds of
men had done it. From the angle of production it was almost
perfect. The sound of the machines sang in my dreams all night.
They were powerful, persistent, accurate. They did not tire.
Harry and I agreed often that men in general had little or no

appreciation of what a marvelous thing the modern great factory had become.

It was far bigger than the men who owned it, who ran it, who worked in it. Were we afraid because it was bigger than the individual? We were. We were country-bred lads—individualists. My own individuality has always been the most bothersome thing in the world to me. Take it away and I am nothing. Solve all the problems of my life for me by industrialism, by standardization, and you leave me a dead man. I think I have always realized that. Nothing in the world could ever make me a socialist.

There were radicals enough about. They talked and we listened and on the whole thought them rather off the point.

Harry and I had both come from places where men still worked with simple, crude, rough tools. After he had left home Harry had worked as a farm hand. We had no illusions about labour—as labour. After listening to radical talk I remember Harry's saying, "These radicals are men who think that if they could change the form of government, the social scheme—if they could take ownership out of certain hands and place it in other hands—they would miraculously become good workmen." He thought that what men wanted was to be good workmen. I think so too.

Later, I remember, he somewhat revised that saying. "The reformer is a man who starts with a genuine passion for making life better for all men. The job is too big. A man has to save himself. The scheme the radical has fixed upon becomes in time the expression of his individuality. To give it up he must give up everything. He missed the point. The workman does not consciously call attention to himself. His work should do that. The difference is this—the radical is trying to change things—the workman to make things."

I have a notion that Harry did not get it all. There must be, somewhere back of every reformer, a sense of some divine order. It may be many of them are ready to surrender individuality for the common good. I am afraid I am not.

Workmen and artists are not primarily concerned with the fate of men. They are concerned with things, what they, as workmen, can do to things. I believe that, deep down in him, every man wants to be a workman more than he wants anything else. He wants it more than wealth, success, women, fame, honour.

Men want it as women want children. It's nature.

The great factory—modern industrialism—standardization— stand in the way. Well, what are you going to do about it? Industrialism, standardization have made the modern social scheme possible. They go together. You can't chuck facts. Without standardization you can't have the great factory—you can't have modern life.

You can't have your cake and eat it too.

You will understand that I am trying to speak of something huge and vast, to give as best I can, the feeling of two workmen regarding the great factory they worked in. Although for twenty years now I have not had one political thought, have no scheme for changing anything in the social structure, I am every day more keenly aware that my life is in no way what it would have been if great factories had not sprung up like mushrooms all over America in my time.

I am only saying here what the workman Harry and myself thought of the great factory while we worked together in it. Admiring it, often overcome by a feeling of awe, admiring the men whose ingenuity had devised the specialization of work, the efficiency of it all—feeling that in bringing the comforts of life to men at a low cost in human labour, the great factory had come near self-justification, we could not go with the men of another generation in thinking the machine could solve men's problems. Organization of men in some socialistic state scheme, to make efficiency more efficient, we thought would make things worse.

The great factory—standardization—all that frightened us. I fled from it. He stuck. Modern life has affected me as deeply, getting out, as it did him, staying in.

To return to our talks on winter nights, walking often under factory walls. At night the dark factories seemed like prisons. They are prisons. Some men think life itself is a prison. We helped each other to a kind of acceptance—that is the reason we became friends. I dare say many of our thoughts were crude

enough. I am not presuming to be very certain I have gotten far
with the subject on which I am trying to write. It is a rather large
order.

I am only saying we were afraid of the great factory.

The shining wheels always flying, vast quantities of goods
pouring out, lives of men made more comfortable everywhere,
men employed, the power of the country growing, wealth being
accumulated—in two workmen a feeling of fear. Not of wealth.

What of wealth? I would like to be wealthy myself. Wealth
means to me the opportunity to do as I please. It means the
chance to work always at what interests me most.

The many, in spite of dirty streets, ugly houses—better off in
every way than labourers ever were before industrialism came.
The terror of sheer brute, heavy labour that few men nowadays
know—lifted, at least partly, from the shoulders of mankind.

Realizing that to blame any one rich man or group of rich men
for what evil the coming of the great factory has brought its
foolishness, childishness.

Still buried deep in us the feeling of fear.

Of what? Two boys walking, asking themselves that question,
asking each other.

Did they know of what they were afraid?

Sometimes I think I do now. I have the individualist's fear of
mass production—fear of losing touch. I never walk past a great
factory now without having that fear. I am a man of the west, an
individualist. Self-abnegation is not my strong point.

It may be that I am speaking only from the artist's viewpoint
but I do not believe it. The artist is the man whose whole life is
centered on the problems of not losing touch. I believe that any
man who is a workman has something of the artist in him. The
man who is not a workman is not a man at all.

Fear of losing touch. With what?

Why, with wood, cloth, iron, stone, earth, sky. The line this
pen makes on this paper as I write, the quality of the paper, the
ink, with everything in nature my mind or body touches. My life is
centered here. Life, to me, has always this universal quality. There
is something the machine cannot do for me. When the machine
makes my fingers useless it makes me useless. I am afraid of the

impotency that comes with the losing of the workman impulse.

Delight in the hands, in what the hands do, what the fingers of the hands do to things in nature. Is all that over the workman's head because he cannot express it? I express it in words because I am a workman in words. It is my job to find words to express such hidden fears.

Man's inheritance—his primary inheritance—being taken from him perhaps by mass production, by the great factory, by inventions, by the machine.

The great factory then, for all its wonders, remains a threat to the individualist, the workman. I, an individual, must save, for myself, my own individual touch. The tendency of the factory, of industrialism, is inevitably to place the emphasis on production, rather than on the process of production. That tends to destroy the workman in me. If someone can show me that I am wrong I shall be glad. There are already a great many great factories. There will be more.

It may be that the age of the individual has passed or is passing. Men are always rising up to say that the day of the artist is gone. They have said it many times in the history of man. When the workman, the workman impulse, passes there will be no more artists. I do not want to live in such an age and, being an optimist, do not believe it will come.

It may be after all a matter of emphasis. Now the emphasis is all on production. It may come back to workmanship one of these days.

Prohibition

OLD wine, good ripe beer, aged whiskey. There never was too much of any of it in the country. Always plenty of cheap, hurriedly-made stuff. When I was little more than a boy there was an old fellow, a German, who made good beer in a small brewery in a nearby town. I went there once, with three others, on a Saturday afternoon. I might have been fifteen then.

Until that day I had never tasted beer but once. When I was a small lad I sold newspapers on the streets of our town. That gave me a certain privilege. I went freely in and out of saloons. Farmers and workmen coming in on hot summer afternoons. Drinking the great steins of beer. How cool and delicious it looked. I watched my chance. One hot summer day, when our main street lay all dead and silent, a bartender—he was called "Body Adair"—said to me, "Boy, watch the bar a moment. I want to run to the post-office."

It was my chance. When he had got out of sight I went behind the bar and, selecting the largest glass I could find, filled it with the foaming stuff.

Walking out from behind the bar I put my foot on the rail. I lingered over it a moment. Well, I was a strong, heavy-armed labourer just come in from the hot fields. I imagined such another standing beside me. "John," said I, "do you think it will rain?" Saying which I lifted the heavy glass. "Here's to you," I said. What a bitter disappointment. The stuff was bitter. I spat it out quickly and going into an alleyway poured out what was left in the glass.

Oh, that first disappointment. How was I to know then that I was to become a devout drinker and in the end a man sold out, betrayed by his own country. No one dreamed of prohibition in those days. There was a prohibition party just as there is an anti-cigarette party now. I tell you fellow citizens be on your guard. Anything may happen in a democracy.

On the Saturday afternoon Bob, Herman, Vet and I, driving along a dusty country road to the brewery. They were all somewhat older than I, had all been there before. I remember that there was a table outdoors under a grape arbor. The German had tried to bring a touch of the old country into our Ohio.

Thick slices of rye bread with home-made cheese. Four, five, perhaps even six glasses of beer drunk during the long afternoon and early evening. It was my initiation. I may even have been a little drunk. Oh, the joys of intoxication. Almost everything in life worth while to me has taken the form of intoxication. I have been drunk with wine, with good food, with sunshine, music. Good painting makes me drunk. Beautiful women... I shall never, I hope, get over that intoxication. Anatole France declared all women beautiful. How absurd. Had the man no sense of selection? I have always suspected he was at bottom a little coarse.

Bob, Herman, Vet and myself reeling a little perhaps as we walked in an old apple orchard back of the German's house. The brewery was just across the road. His wife had got dinner for us. She charged twenty-five cents. Money counted for something in those days.

I remember that Vet and I were at the time after the same girl. We had hardly been on speaking terms but the beer had mellowed us. We drew away from the others and walked arm in arm under the trees. "Well," declared Vet, "as for Mabel, let her go to hell." He did not mean just that but, under the influence of the beer, I knew what he did mean. He meant that men are men, that men have their own problems, aside from women. "We have got to stand together." Vet said. "You bet we have," I answered.

Something warm and close. Two boys feeling each other as separate things, queerly related. Later as a man trying to make his

way in the world and finally as a writer and a story-teller, trying a
little to understand people enough to tell their stories somewhat
fairly and sympathetically, I have had that same feeling and have
lost it again and again.

There was Vet and I walking, let us presume a little drunk,
under the trees. For the first time I seemed to see him quite
clearly. He was the son of a small town carpenter and wanted to
be an electrical engineer. We dismissed girls and women and
talked of the problems of our two lives. I remember that, as he
talked, I forgot my own problem thinking of his. It is a good
feeling. In all my life I have never got it often enough.

A man—that is to say, myself—growing up and slowly
learning to discriminate a little in drink. Education is, of course,
necessary. There has always been too much coarse drinking in the
country. When I was a boy in a small town and later in the cities
where I lived men drank their whiskey with what was called a
"chaser". A drink of whiskey and then, quickly, something else to
wash the taste out of the mouth.

Why put anything into the mouth that does not taste fair and
fine?

At first, when I used to go to the city, I was a labourer and often
discouraged. I drank some terrible stuff purely for the effect. Once
later, in the city of London, I drank terrible stuff for another
reason. I was on a bender down in the east side of London and had
picked up a half dozen weazened little old cockney women. I
drank cheap English gin with them and listened to their talk
while they called me "dearie" and "darling". I was sick in bed later
for a week but it was worth the price. They were charming
women, very witty and clever—the sharp biting wit of poverty
and the streets. I could not refuse to drink what they drank.

Ripe beer, old wine, aged whiskey. It went far to make life in
America worth living. The much abused saloon was something
too. In the old days when I went into a strange town and did not
know what to do with myself I lit out for a saloon. Men gathered
there. We drank and talked together.

You must understand that a writer has exactly the same
problems that confront other men. If you think we go each

morning to our typewriters and, sitting down, begin to reel off
stories you are mistaken. Writing stories is work, a very subtle,
delicate kind of work too.

Long sterile periods come. There are months when I am like a
field in which nothing will grow. Before I knew much of life and
of what went on in other men (God knows, I know little enough
now) I used to think that these sterile periods came only to
myself. I used to grow desperate about it. Perhaps I was at the
moment too much concerned with myself. The tune would not
get itself played.

It was then, at such periods of my life, when drink did most for
me. As it was between the boy, Vet, and myself so it was between
myself and others.

As I drank along—having naturally, I am quite sure, some
sense of selection—being not too coarse-fibred—I began to be
more and more discriminating in drinks. A man learns slowly—
at least I do. As I emerged from the ranks of labour—did what is
commonly called, "rise in the world"—I had naturally a little
more money to spend for drink. *Champagne* I never cared for—it
was always—as we drank it in America—a pretentious, fakey
kind of drink, the symbol of senseless lavishness—but some of
the other wines. I shall not try to make a wine list. Names are
almost forgotten now—and I am not a sadist.

What I am trying to say is that it is as important to have good
taste in drinks as in food, women, men friends, music. A man
works all his life trying to build something up and it is destroyed
by ruthless vulgarians.

Examples in point.

I have seen a man, who lays some claim to being a gentleman,
carry his own flask into a house where he went as a guest. He had
once been poisoned by bootleg whiskey and had become afraid.
To my amazement others in the house did the same thing. I was
so ashamed for the host and for his guest that I left. The others
did not seem to be so affected.

There is a certain ruthlessness in life, characteristic of many
reformers and industrial millionaires that is, to my way of seeing
life, the very height of vulgarity. How ruthless to pass a
prohibition law. Surely those who brought prohibition upon us

were not themselves drinkers. What right had they to decide?

Millionaires, rich and successful authors, fashionable portrait painters—these people may yet, I presume, occasionally enjoy drink fit to put into the mouth. Reformers, not being sensualists, or sensitive, do not want or need it.

It is we poor men of talent who must suffer most.

Prohibition is the triumph of vulgarity. Once I had some discrimination in drinks. It is going. I must sink down into a sloth of bootleg stuff or become a teetotaler. Vulgarity on all sides. What am I to do?

The point is—and really I must try to make my point clear—the point is that I cannot lose my taste in one direction and retain it in another. If I am vulgar in one particular I am vulgar through and through. All this talk about a man being a good judge of prose but having no feeling for poetry, having taste in foods and none in drinks, in music and not in painting, is sheer nonsense. You are vulgar or you are not vulgar. You like coarse things or you like fine things.

The point not very clearly understood is that in passing our prohibition law we have in reality struck at the slowly growing culture of the whole country.

It is not stupid to think that, because coarse men use drink coarsely, no man shall drink? As well say that because some men have indigestion no man shall eat, because there is bad music played we shall have no good music.

Well enough I know that my voice is a feeble one. What I say will have no effect. However I feel this inclination to speak up. It has seemed to me, from the very beginning, that this whole matter of prohibition has been put on the wrong footing. We should begin to find out, sometime, that people are not changed by laws. You do not make men moral or immoral that way.

Anyway, being moral or immoral has nothing to do with the matter.

Men continue to drink. It is all a question of what we shall drink. It is a question of taste.

Drink is the great equalizer. I dare say that, unlike food, it is not an absolute necessity to the continuance of human life.

But who wants just to live? If I cannot put some flourish into my life what good is it to me? Too much greyness in an industrial civilization. I do not want to be grey. If I were a bird I would want to wear the most gaily-colored plumage I could find. I want to sing occasionally, shout, link arms with other men, tell them nice little complimentary lies about themselves, have them do the same to me.

I want to dance, make love, get drunk when getting drunk will loosen me up.

Being as I am, the kind of man I am, I dare say I will do these things in any event.

I will get drinks all right. Plenty of men offer me drinks. Almost every day I get letters—"Come to my house. I have something good here."

Mostly optimistic lies, a forlorn hope.

We are all sunk into the vulgarity of second rate drinks. We go deeper and deeper. Nothing has ever so discouraged me about democracy. Nothing has ever so stood in the way of the growth of good taste.

Nothing has ever struck such a blow at comradeship, as between man and man.

Prohibition—the triumph of vulgarity.

In a Box Car

DO you want to know how men happen to kill each other? It is because they are irritated beyond endurance, sometimes by the other man, or women, sometimes just by the circumstances of their lives.

I was a young fellow then and out of work. It was winter, during a period of hard times and nearly all of the factories were closed. I was beating my way from one town to another and had crawled into an empty box car. There were many tramps abroad that winter. The crews of freight trains paid no attention to us but as long as we were quiet let us ride where we pleased.

No one paid any attention to us. We were just driftwood. What did it matter?

Three of us were in the box car and it was a bitter cold day. None of us had overcoats. Of course we could not build a fire in there. The door of the car was open. No one bothered to close it. When you are cold as we were a bit more cold makes no difference.

The other two men in the car were standing near the door when I climbed in. The train was slowly getting under way. They did not speak to me and I did not speak to them.

Soon the train was moving faster. I cannot even remember the name of the town we were leaving. I had tried to get work there without success. It was somewhere in the Middle West.

Well, I moved back into the car and sat down on the floor. What is life worth? It may have been that I had a touch of fever. The two men near the door were of middle age, blue with cold, ragged and dirty. I think now they must have been dopes. One of them was a large, heavily built man and the other was thin and tall. Both wore half grown beards. You are always meeting such men when you are out of work and drifting about. They have a fixed, determined air about them. They hate each other and, in fact, hate every one.

The two in the car were silent for a long time. We had got out of town and were groaning along through the country at a fast rate. I heard some member of the train crew run over the top of the car, over our heads.

It is an odd sound, when you are half asleep. I remember thinking of my childhood. When you are very cold that way sleepiness always comes upon you. They say it is an easy way to die and perhaps it is. I may have been asleep and dreaming.

I was dreaming of one of my younger brothers running over the roof of our house in an Ohio town on a Spring day. Everything was quiet in the house. I even thought I heard my mother moving about downstairs. She would be cooking something—cookies, perhaps. We were a large family when we were all at home and Mother was always cooking.

And now I thought that the fragrant smell of cooking had come floating up the stairs to where I lay. Do you remember how cookies baking in the oven smelled when you were a boy? I felt warm and comfortable. Perhaps I was in bed with some childhood illness. I had always enjoyed such times when I was a child. It gave me a chance to lie in bed and read. Although we were poor there were always plenty of books in our house and Mother always managed to get materials to make cookies. Where the books came from I do not know. Father borrowed them perhaps. Everyone in town knew he was fond of books. They said he was a smart man but he could not make much money.

At any rate there I was and I was awakened from my dream by the two men in the car who had begun quarreling.

I straightened myself up, shivered and looked at them.

The men who are called "dopes" always have something

determined in their characters. Well, they have an object in life—
to get the "stuff." They are always seeking it. If they cannot get it
in one town they drift on to another. It is because there are so
many "dopes" that there are so many desperate crimes.

It isn't because such men are brave. It is because they are
determined. They go from place to place seeking. They must have
money but do not care for money. They cling together but do not
care for each other. They are like Prometheus bound to a rock.
Wild birds are biting at their vitals. Such men carry about inside
themselves always, except when they have got some of the stuff, a
terrible, gnawing hunger.

It will not let them alone. The hunger is like drops of water
falling from the roof of a cave, down under the ground. Silently,
persistently something is being worn away. Cowardice is being
worn away. When there is a hideous crime done somewhere, look
for some such man. Look for a shrinking man with a pale face and
trembling hands. He will have a queer determined look in his
eyes. Sometimes his face twitches in an odd way. If you speak to
him he will whine and fawn on you.

He will be slick in getting out of it. He is like a rat cornered.
Watch his eyes. If you are a jailer do not take chances with him.

The two men on the train were talking. They were quarreling.
The question about which they were quarreling was an absurd
one. Was the city of Buffalo larger than the city of Toledo? What
difference did it make to them?

I saw their faces twitching as they glared at each other. They
still stood near the open door. "Well, I lived in Toledo for a long
time," one of them said. It was the larger one. "I was married
there. Later I went to live in Buffalo. I know what I am talking
about."

"You lie."

"You are a dirty liar yourself."

One of the men suddenly thrust out his hand. I dare say he
intended nothing. As I was sitting in the darkness, back from the
door, and they were in the light by the car door, I could see
everything very clearly. The man who killed another man did not
specially hate him. He did not care whether or not Toledo was

larger than Buffalo. Perhaps he had been several days without a shot. I even fancied I could see a queer, wavering light in his eyes. I dare say I made that up.

He was just hungry for his dope. Thank God it was not my kind of hunger. I was hungry for food, a warm bed, a job. I wanted to get on. I dreamed of some day getting up in the world. Then perhaps some woman would want me as I sometimes wanted a woman. I used to go about the towns, when I was out of work, looking at pretty women, dressed sometimes in fine furs. I did not envy them the furs, the grand houses they lived in, the carriages in which they rode at that time. I envied the men who were with them, on whom they smiled.

I was hungry myself all right but not with the hunger of the men in the box car.

One of them had tried to fight off his persistent gnawing hunger. He thrust out his hand as though to push it away.

What he actually did was to push the other man, the tall, thin one, out through the open door of the car. As he fell I saw him clutch at the side of the door with his weak, trembling hands. He actually did hold on for a moment but his hand was cold. He hung and then fell.

I was sitting so that I could see his body bouncing along beside the train. The ground was stony there. Then he lay still. The fast moving train whirled us out of sight of the body. The second man was leaning out of the car door watching.

Well, that was that. He came back into the car and sat down on the floor near me but he did not speak to me. He began to cry. He was crying like a sick child.

Of course with me the question was one of getting away. As it turned out, none of the train crew had seen the body lying beside the tracks when the caboose passed. A farmer found it later the same day. I heard about it in the next town where I got off the train.

It seemed to me we were a long time coming to a town. The train was running too fast for me to get off. It is awkward, getting out at the door of a box car from a moving train. It requires a special technique—and when your hands are cold. . . .

The question in my mind was this—well, there was the fellow sitting between me and the open door. If he happened to think. I am sure now he was crying because, although he had killed another man, he had got no satisfaction from the deed. He had not specially wanted to kill him, was just filled with weak excitement. Killing someone meant nothing special to him.

On the other hand—if he thought.

But such fellows do not think. What is life or death to them?

I remember that once he looked at me as though to say, "Well, who are you? What are you doing here?" He was a heavily built man. In a struggle such a man would have an advantage. If he pushed me out the door, killed me as he had killed the other fellow, it would make no difference to him.

He would have the advantage of not caring.

Did he care to save himself by doing away with me? That was the question.

I have never been so absorbingly interested in another man's mind. But perhaps he had no mind. Hunger may have eaten it away.

He was sitting on the floor of the car, crying in an odd, hysterical way, not from remorse. It was because the hunger inside him would not stop. I remember watching his eyes. They did seem alive—in his pale, dead-looking face. I had determined that if the look in his eyes became—what shall I say? If the look in his eyes became normal, if it became human...It would be human now for the man to try to push me through the car door, get me out of the way. I had seen what he had done. There was no one else who knew.

My chances lay in the fact that he did not care. I watched my chance. When the train began to slow down as we approached another town, I got up. I even made some silly remark. "It's going to snow", I said. He did not answer. He was not crying now. His face was twitching. To get to the car door I had to pass quite close to him. It would be quite possible for him, by catching hold of my leg, by tripping me...

He did nothing. To get out at the door of a box car when the train is moving it is necessary to drop to the floor. Then you squirm about until you get your legs out. You let yourself down as near the ground as you can, holding on all you can with your hands. Then you start your legs moving and drop. If you are lucky or know how to do it, you land right side up.

Domestic and Juvenile

SO this was the domestic relations court.

This was in a Southern city.

The judge was a small man physically. He smoked cigarettes as I did. He heard some four or five cases and then adjourned court for ten minutes while he took a drag.

We sat in this court room and smoked. We threw the butts out a window into the street. People wandered aimlessly about in a large outer room. Now it began again.

In the street there was a great noise. Someone raced the engine of a Ford. It made so much noise that I missed one of the stories of domestic difficulties being told by a young woman in a torn raincoat. She was nervous and upset. She was excited.

I did not miss all of it. I missed, let us say, six sentences.

They were precious sentences however. "Damn," I said.

This judge was all right. He was a small nervous man. Most of the people in there seemed nervous. The judge slouched in his chair. His face was prematurely old and wrinkled.

There was something very boyish about the man. He threw a leg up over the arm of a chair. He slid down deep in the chair, almost disappearing. Now and then he looked over at me and smiled, a half-tired boyish smile.

Everyone liked him. People did not take this judge as seriously as they have taken other judges I have known.

He had surprisingly little dignity. On his desk were a lot of
papers. Warrants or summons, or whatever papers are issued in
such cases were piled before him. Once he took the whole pile and
threw it into a waste paper basket.

There was a clerk of the court, a woman. She had nice eyes.

There were three or four deputies.

You know what deputies and court attachés are like. They are a
special kind of human being. They have heard too much of
domestic difficulties. They are unmoved. You can't help
wondering about such people. How are their own domestic
affairs arranged? In most courts the judge is a very dignified man.

Well, your judge is an educated man. He has been to school, to
college. Every judge has his own style—like a United States
Senator.

The court attachés take on something of the style of the judge,
but they are not up to it. If he is witty, they try that. You know
what a policeman is, trying to be witty.

Or the judge is heavy and learned. That puts the policeman up
against it too. He also grows heavy and stern. It results in a kind
of heavy stupidity, verging on brutality. Given the least excuse he
becomes brutal. It seems to be his only way out.

As for the domestic relations judge, in that court, in a Southern
city, he was a lovable man.

That throwing of the court papers into the waste paper basket
wasn't a flourish. It was accidental.

Two men and a woman rushed to pick them out, to assort
them, put them back in order on his desk. He was very contrite.

"I'm sorry. I didn't think what I was doing," he said.

The court room was quite small but there was a big waiting
room outside. People were sitting out there, men, women and
children.

There were people who have domestic troubles.

They were white and black. As I said, this was in a Southern
city.

They sat on benches as at a railroad station.

They were afraid, worried, nervous.

You know how people are when they have been summoned
into court.

They were afraid out there but when they were brought into the court room, where the judge sat hearing their stories something happened. They began to smile, they squirmed, they felt a bit silly.

He got them all right. He did something to them.

I had just been reading Mr. Bertrand Russell on marriage and morals. He had given me a picture of a new kind of civilization.

Suppose women really got away from the moral taboos laid on them by men. What would happen then?

The father cutting less and less figure in the lives of children. God knows he cuts little enough figure now.

So the woman becomes everything—in society.

The state becomes the father.

What is to happen to the man? I presume the poor cuss will work. He will be like the worker bee, going out to get honey—or money, bringing it home, keeping it up until he drops.

In these domestic relations courts the father seldom appears. Two women have been quarreling.

Or there are boys who have been stealing.

Cases.

Item.

Five young boys, ranging in age from eight to twelve, tried to break into a movie house, through a rear door. They had no money and wanted to see the show.

Item.

A colored boy of fourteen. He was selling whiskey to the boys of a white school. The superintendent of the white school caught him. He had three half pint bottles of moon in his pocket.

The colored boy was from a colored school. He had been bragging to other colored boys there. "I'm going to be a big bootlegger when I grow up."

Item.

Two white people. They were both dopes. This case was quite hopeless. There was a man who was married. His wife hadn't come to court but his mother-in-law came.

It was a warm day but the man and woman were both white and trembling, as with a chill.

The two women wanted the man to go to work and support them but he said he couldn't. He was right about that. There he sat, white and trembling. No one would give that man a job. What was to be done? The two women had talked themselves into the belief that this judge could make the man work, make him fit to work. The judge whispered to me. "Unfortunately we have no lethal chamber."

There were no doubt young medical students who could do something with the three carcasses, the wife, the husband, the mother-in-law—all hopeless dopes. The medical students might find out something, cutting them up.

Item.

A young boy. His father had divorced his mother. Or perhaps she did it. She worked in a store, had a good job.

She was at the head of a department in a big store.

Her son was in high school. He belonged to the football team. The team had gone somewhere to play another high school team.

They changed their clothes in the basement of a high school building.

The boy on trial here wasn't a regular player. He was a substitute.

So he slipped into the school building and went through the other boys' clothes. He got nine dollars and eighty cents, a lot of soiled handkerchiefs, six packages of cigarettes and two watches.

He went away then but they caught him two hours later.

He still had some of the swag.

The judge asked him—"Did you ever do this before?"

"Yes. I never got caught before."

"Do you know why you did it?"

"No."

"It might be a good thing you were caught."

"It might be. Whatever I have to do, if I have to serve a sentence, I might as well be at it."

The judge to me—"At what age did you quit stealing?"

"I don't know that I have quit. I still steal something every now and then."

"So do I. I suppose everyone does."

Item.

A negro man came in. He told his story. He worked hard, he said. He worked all day. And when he came home, he worked too, aiming to please his wife. He was a peace-loving man, and he only aimed to please his wife.

Well, he came home in the evening. His wife was pretty lazy. She sat there in his house, a big broad-shouldered, deep-breasted yaller gal.

So, he worked in a barber shop, shining shoes, and he came home.

That morning early he had got up and had got his wife up. They were going to select the coal for the winter.

He told how he escorted her to the coal yards. He was a regular Chesterfield about it. It was a ceremony. The coal was in big bins. Coal comes in various sizes. So this brown man was very particular about pleasing his wife but just the same, as he testified, she looked at him with infinite contempt in her eyes. Some women are like that.

The picture was, however, nicely etched. In the early morning they were in the coal yard. The brown boy was escorting the yaller gal about, from bin to bin. As he told the story you got, somehow, the picture of him, brown and courtly in the grey light of early morning, escorting the yaller gal from bin to bin.

"Look it over carefully, darling. Git jes' what you want. I only aim to please you, my darling."

So then he went to work. He shined shoes all day.

His wife had stayed in the coal yards for a little while, picking up the best coal, as he had shown her how to do. And then she had taken it home.

Well, he came home in the evening. His wife had gone to bed. She was in bed all day.

"Alone?"

"I don't know judge."

She had gone indolent during the day. There she was, when he came home, the big lazy yaller thing.

They did not have any electric lights in their house. They had but one lamp. There wasn't any supper prepared.

There wasn't even a fire lit in the stove. The coal was on the sidewalk, out in front of the house.

The negro said he was afraid to leave it out there. He wanted the lamp to light his way while he carried the coal he had collected into a shed at the back.

She was putting on her stockings. She also wanted the lamp.
"What did you do then?"
"I argued with her. I used persuasion. I reasoned with her."
"And then?"
"I chastised her, jedge."
"How?"
"Well jedge, I got my two legs around her neck like this. I was sitting in a chair. I jerked her down there.
"I had her head in there, between my legs, like this."
"Yes."
"Then I clamped my legs together like this."
"Yes."
"I'se strong in the legs, jedge."
"Yes."
"So then I took off my belt.
"The back side of her was sticking out jes' nice. I took off my belt. I lammed her good, jedge."
"Pretty good technique, I call it."
"What's that, jedge?"

The next was a curious case. There was a young man who might have been a poet—he might have been twenty-four—who was already a habitual drunkard.

His mother had sworn out the warrant for him. When he got drunk he grew rather violent. He had come home on the night before and had made his mother's house hideous with curses.

A curious argument had started between him and the judge.
"But can't you quit drinking?"
"I don't know, perhaps I could, judge. I don't know."

The young man twisted his lips in a queer nervous way as he talked.
"Why don't you?"
Silence.
"Well?"
Silence.
"It's pretty rough. Your mother having to come up here and have you arrested."
"She didn't do it."
"What?"
"I say she never did it."

"Yes she did. Her name is signed here."

Turning to the woman. She was small and fat. There was a puzzled look in her eyes.

"There she is. There's your mother. She had you arrested."

"No, she never did."

"But I say she did."

"She didn't."

"She signed that. She came here and complained. She is sitting there now."

"But she never had me arrested."

"Something in her told her to do it. She came here. She lodged a complaint. She had you brought in here."

"She is a good woman, judge, but she is muddle-headed. Now you see what a mess she has got us in.

"Just the same she never did it. Not her. I know her. She never did it. She isn't that sort."

"He is always like that, judge. I can't make him out. He is my boy but I don't understand him.

"He puzzles me, he worries me. I can't sleep at night thinking about him.

"I've never been able to make him out."

"He gets drunk. He raises the devil. He swears terribly."

"What does he swear about?"

"About life, judge. He just swears about life."

The judge:

"Well, my boy, I'll tell you what I'm going to do—can you quit drinking?"

"I can I suppose. A man has what is called 'a will'. He can use that I suppose?"

"I'm going to give you three months.

"If you go straight, O. K.—otherwise the workhouse for you.

"I don't mean for taking a drink. I mean for getting drunk, coming home, raising hell there, swearing like that.

"Where is your old man?"

"He's dead now."

"Are you the only child?"

"Yes."

"Well there it is—if you don't do it the workhouse for you.

"Do you think it's fair? Do you think I am being fair with you?"

"I think it's fair for you."

"What do you mean?"

"I think it's fair for you, being judge. It lets you out."

"I think it's nice, your sitting up there and saying it."

"I think you think it's fair.

"Well."

"You have got a friend sitting there with you."

"Yes."

"I think he thinks it is all right. That is what people are like."

"I think you think—'well, I'm putting it up to him.'

"What do you think your mother thinks?"

The young man's lips kept twitching. He had a queer look in his eyes.

"I think my mother came down here. She lodged a complaint. She had me arrested."

"I think she did it and that she didn't do it. That's what I think."

And so there I was, in the court of domestic relations. The judge kept hearing cases, he passed sentence, he laughed at couples and sent them home.

When he could stand it no longer he adjourned court. He and I smoked cigarettes. He threw the butts out of a window into the street.

The cases kept coming and coming. There were plenty of cases.

"It just goes on like this, day after day?"

"Yes," he said.

He had a puzzled look in his eyes. It was not unlike the look in the eyes of the woman who had her son arrested for getting drunk and swearing at life.

Look Out, Brown Man!

IN Georgia, Alabama, Louisiana, Arkansas, Texas, Mississippi, and even in Indiana and Ohio, the big shuffle-footed Negroes' Negro man, the so-called "bad one," goes about on the alert now. He has to be careful. These aren't good times for a Negro man to be too proud, step too high. There are a lot of white men hard up. There are a lot of white men out of work. They won't be wanting to see a big proud black man getting along. There'll be lynchings now.

Such a Negroes' Negro man doesn't always remember to be polite and courteous to whites. He isn't slick and fawning. He's not a white man's Negro. There are wenches like that, too—thick blood in them, heads held high. You'll see one of that kind occasionally on a country road in Georgia, a fine proud one. Such a carriage she's got, such a swing to her hips.

Look out, brown man!

You'd think, if you listened to Northern people talk, or to professional Southerners in the North, that all Negroes were alike. I've heard them say, "Why, I can't tell one Negro from another." Might as well say, "I can't tell one field from another, one mountain from another, one river from another." Some can't.

They say, "It's different down South. The Negro knows his place down there." They mean to say he always goes fawning, taking off his hat to any kind of low-grade white, getting off the sidewalks. Why, you'd think, to hear them talk, that Southern Negroes, particularly in the far South, were just dogs. Not very high-class dogs at that. There is a kind of dog that always goes about like that, his tail always between his legs.

As though any decent Northern or Southern white man, or woman, would want a Negro man, or woman, to be like that.

There are whites that do want it. Second-, third-, and fourth-rate whites they are. They are in the ascendancy in a lot of places in the South now, have been in the ascendancy ever since the Civil War. Before that they were there of course, but they were kept under. Why, you can find as many loose-lipped, boastful, slack-eyed, second-rate whites in the American South as in any place on earth. Who do you suppose does the lynching down there, in the dreadful ugly little towns?

The cheap ones got into power in a lot of places in the South after the Civil War because the whites with class to them got killed in the war. Or they lost all they had. The first-rate families in the far South are surprisingly feminine now. I mean there aren't any men left in some of the families, just a few high-class women hanging on. They don't do any loud talking about killing Negroes—the Southern people with class to them, men or women. I think the real Southern people, of the old South, always did understand the position of the Negro pretty well. There was a situation. The South had something on its hands—"our peculiar institution," the statesmen from down there called it. It was peculiar, all right.

You had to assume that all Negroes were natural servants, that they liked being in a subordinate position in life. They gave love and devotion to the whites, expecting nothing.

I can't see why a Negro should be any different than any other man about all that. A man does what he has to do. How many whites are there in subordinate positions in life, doing what they don't like to do, being pretty polite about it, too?

I can't see this sharp difference between the impulses and desires of Negroes and myself. I think decent Negro men and women have the same feelings I have. They have, under the same circumstances, the same thoughts, the same impulses. I've been about Negroes a lot. I've watched them—that's my specialty, watching people—I've talked to them.

"But you can't understand the thoughts and feelings of a Negro," men say. I've asked a good many Negroes about that. "If you can get on to yourself a little I guess you can get on to me," the Negro says.

"Why," someone says, "you've got something primitive here." Sure you have. You've got the difference of a few thousand years out of the caves and forests. How old is the human race anyway? How much difference do a few thousand years make? And anyway we haven't any pure-blooded Africans here—not any more.

I know this—that the people with some class to them, both men and women of the South, never have talked so big about the difference. These people always did recognize a certain position they were in and that the brown men and women about them were in. It was a difficult position. Slavery never was any good. It wasn't any good for the whites or the blacks either. Most of those who talked so big about the glories of slavery never did have any slaves. The intelligent, human white man of the old South did the best he could with life there, as he found it, and the intelligent brown man did the same.

They got to a kind of friendship, too. Don't think they didn't. Once I was walking with such a white man in a city of the far South when a loose-lipped, cunning-eyed brown man came shuffling up to him and asked for money.

"I'se in trouble, Mr. White," he said.

"You are, eh?"

"Yessah, Mr. White."

"Well then, where is your white-man friend? Why don't you go to him?"

"Because sah, I ain't got no white-man friend."

"You ain't, eh? Well then, I'll tell you something—the Southern white man who hasn't a Negro-man friend and the Southern Negro man who hasn't a white-man friend isn't any good.... You get out of here. You make yourself scarce."

That is about the attitude of the intelligent white or brown man or woman in both the old and the new South, as far as I have been able to get at it. The trouble is there are not enough intelligent whites and browns. Which race has the best of it in that, I don't know. That's one of the things you can't find out. There are all kinds of shades to intelligence. You don't find it all in books, I know that.

You have to think about the Negro with a little intelligence, a little sympathy. You have to consider his position in our civilization. You have to remember that not so many white men and women are anything so very special. Hardly any of us are anything so very special really.

You have to think of what the Negro has done in his position, how well he has handled it, both in the North and in the South.

Then you have to remember also that there are Negroes who are not white men's Negroes. I dare say there were proud men, fierce men, fighters and strutters among the tribes in the forests over there in Africa, too. The blood of these men must have come down, some of it, into some of our blacks, some of our browns.

I, for one, can imagine how such a man feels sometimes, when he has to knuckle under. I'm a white man and I've had to knuckle under to second-rate white men myself. I've had to laugh when such a one laughed, listen to his dull yarns, pretend to be impressed when he talked like a fool. I've done it. I've sat in advertising conferences, out in Chicago, for hours at a time, listening to some big windy man talking nonsense. I've sat there smiling, being polite, nodding my head, looking impressed.

I remember one such advertising conference when I sat like that for four hours. I was fingering a heavy inkwell that happened to be on the table before me. I wanted particularly, I remember, to bounce it off the head of a certain vulgar fat man who kept several of us there the four hours that day while he talked about himself. He was telling us what a big man he was, but he wasn't big. It turned out just as I thought it would. What he wanted us to do for him, and what we did, over our protest, broke him. I'm glad it did.

The whites in America have got the Negro into a certain position in our civilization. We present-day whites didn't put him there. We are in rather tight times. The Negro, because of his long subjugation, because he has known, has been taught by the circumstance of his position, a lot about sliding through such

times, will get through the present situation better than a lot of
whites. He will know how, will have been taught by life how to do
it.

That will make a lot of second-, third-, and fourth-rate whites
jealous and sore. There'll be lynchings now. You watch. There'll
be women insulted.

You'll be surprised, if you watch it, how few first-class white
women will be insulted. Most of the women insulted will be the
slack wives or daughters of slack second-rate whites, and in this
situation the fawning, polite white man's Negro will get through
all right.

The fellow who has to look out now is the Negroes' Negro.

Don't strut much these days, big boy.

Walk carefully now.

Some of us understand how you like to strut, how it is in your
blood. A good many of us don't mind an occasional strut
ourselves. Why, most of the strutting songs, to which we strut,
when we do strut, we got from you.

We'll be your friend, if we can, big boy, but it's going to be
rough going. There'll be lynchings now. It is a time to walk softly.
If you have any intelligence, brown boy, Negroes' Negro,
remember that it has been by remaining friends with the
intelligent people among the whites, by having an understanding
with them, that the browns have got along with the whites as
well as they have.

Why, I am talking to Negroes now.

Bear this in mind, Negroes' Negro. There are a good many of
us whites who are, more than we like to admit, in the same
position as you. If your people have been slaves, so have ours; if
you have been in a subordinate position in life, so have we.

There are a good many kinds of slavery in this life.

More brains, white man and brown man, for God's sake, more
brains!

Look out, big brown boy, the lynchers are loose.

The Cry in the Night

THE man, the young mill superintendent, and I, went into the mill. There was a little hallway and we stopped for a moment in there. I had the feeling we were staring at each other.

There would be that question in his head:

What does he want here?

Men and women are coming into factories. They are escorted. Such factories as the huge Ford plant at Detroit make a specialty of escorting people through.

They come in, farmers from their farms, town people, merchants and lawyers. Society women come. They walk through in their soft fluffy dresses.

They are in a world of which they know little and sense less and still they are impressed.

The workmen and the workwomen at the machines stare up at them.

Why, there is a world, a life here, of which those who come thus into the great rooms know nothing. The machines are doing something.

The machines are weaving stockings, they weave cloth, they shape iron. Shoes are shaped in machines.

The visitor sees before him a great machine. Inside the mill all is in order and outside, often, all is disorder. In a certain cotton mill town in the South at the end of a peculiarly disorderly street, I saw piles of old tin cans along a roadway as I drove down to the mill. There were weed-grown fields and women and men were shuffling aimlessly through the street.

The morning was a dull rainy one. The wife of one of the owners of the mill had taken me there...

Inside the mill I saw a Barker-Coleman Spooler Warper.

It was a machine just introduced into that factory, an extension of the thought, of the imagination, of some man, a machine that threw many men out of work.

The factory superintendent at that place told me it cost twenty thousand dollars.

He said that its introduction into the mill did away with the labor of a certain number of hands.

That statement did not at the time impress me much. The machine is pushing men aside. That is going on everywhere. "Let it," I said to myself that morning.

I stood before the machine. It was a mass of moving parts. Its movements were as delicately balanced as those of a fine watch.

It was huge. It would have filled to the last inch this room in which I now sit writing of it.

But can I write of it? I cannot say how many parts the machine had, perhaps a thousand, perhaps ten thousand.

It had Herculean legs.

It unwound thread from one sized ball and wound it onto another. The white balls of thread moved about, up and down along hallways of steel. They were moving at unbelievable speed. As the thread wound and unwound, the balls moving thus gayly along steel hallways, dancing there, being playful there, being touched here and there by little steel hands directing their course, so delicately touched...

So delicately directed....

Bobbins being loaded with thread...I dare say bobbins being loaded with many colored threads...

Perhaps some silk, some rayon, some cotton.

> *I may, for the time, have stepped
> outside the province of this par-
> ticular machine.*

I remember a woman, a mill owner's wife or daughter, tall and delicately gowned, standing near me. I remember two mill girls, one with a mass of yellow hair. No, it was just off yellow, with streaks of gold in it...

Her fingers were doing things rapidly, with precision. I did not understand what she did.

I remember thinking rebel thoughts, to me new thoughts.

I must have stared at the woman who brought me there and at an alert blue-eyed superintendent.

Thinking of artists, striving blunderingly, as I am doing here, to express something.

No accuracy to their movements—if they be writers no words coming from under their flying fingers with such beautiful precision.

There, in that machine, what seemed at first disorder in movement becoming a vast, a beautiful order.

Why, a man goes a little daft.

A thousand, perhaps in the life of such a machine a hundred million, white balls, each containing to the hundreth part of an inch, the same yardage of slender thread...

They dancing down steel hallways, every hop, every skip calculated, they landing at little steel doors, never missing...

They being touched, handled, directed by fingers of steel.

Never harshly to break thread that I could break easily between my two fingers.

Thread flying, at blinding speed off one spool and onto another.

These handled, something done to these. In this shape, this form, they are serving some obscure purpose... in this vast modern passion of goods making.

I am describing this particular machine in a room far away from it, in a quiet room, no technical description of the machine before me, the accuracy of my description mattering nothing...

An impression sought, something beautiful, something in movement beautiful.

Something in tone beautiful, in sound beautiful.

Why, there is power here. Here is the almost god.

A crazy new grace—

Steel fingers jerking—in movements, calculated, never varied...

Great arms moving...
Materials touched with such delicacy of touch as I can never
know.

I remember standing in that place, that time. I shall never
forget that.
I remember thinking of men of my time, thoughtful men,
earnest men, who would have destroyed all machines.
I remember there had been such thoughts in me.
I think it must have been the vast order in the mass of steel
parts, all in movements, that had caught and held me so.
I, all my life, a lover of artists and their work... men working
at least toward order.
Thinking—"these men who designed and built this machine
may some day be known to be as important in the life swing of
mankind, as the man who built the Cathedral of Chartres."
Whispering to myself—"They may be the real artists of our
time.
"We in America may be, unknowingly, in one of the great
forward-thrusting times of the world."
Thinking also of that woman standing there beside me as I
looked at the machine, it in some new way exciting me...
A sardonic thought. I am sure I said no rude words to the
delicately bodied, delicately gowned rich woman who brought me
into that mill.
I thought suddenly, staring hard at her.
"Hell," I remember thinking, "you are a woman delicate and
lovely, but you will never find you a lover who will touch that
body of yours with the delicacy and strength with which those
white balls of cotton are being touched."
Thinking:
"Is blood necessary, is flesh necessary?"
"We humans are but little bundles of nerves. Our nerves betray
us.
"We think we think.
"In the machine we have made a thing infinitely more
masterful than ourselves."

It was a moment of pure machine
worship. I was on my knees before
the new god, the American god.

Myself not hysterical, not made hysterical by the wonder of
that particular machine...
I have felt dimly the same vast order sometimes in the stars,
walking at night on some country road.
I have felt it in rivers.

I have felt impotence too. This is not a feeling individual in me.
I challenge any painter, song-maker, word-arranger, any poet, to
go stand where I stood.
A Barker-Coleman Spooler Warper in a cotton mill will do. It
is enough.

Why, if he, the artist, had made it...
Let him stand as I did, not having made it, never in his whole
life having made anything that moved forward, doing its work,
with perfect order...
Never having loved perfectly, created perfectly...

Let him be a workman at such a machine.
The man, the workman, does little but start and stop it.
It works outside him...
I, a man, can go blunderingly into blundering other lives.
I can fail because you who read fail also.
Your whole life is a story of failure.

As for myself, all of my success as a writer has been in telling
the story of failure. I have told that story and told it well because I
know failure.
The machine does not fail.

I ask you men who read to follow me.
As yourself...

"What will it do to me, as a man, to stand, pulling a lever, let us say, to a machine that does not fail?

"Can man actually stand, naked in his inefficiency before the efficient machine?"

Men, you know it cannot quite be done, not yet in any event. We know this—impotence comes from the fear of impotence. In our machine age can we help fearing?

Why, I was in an American Cotton Mill at night. There was a mill superintendent with me. I think I ought to tell you, who have not been in such a mill, either in the daytime or at night, a little of how cotton from the farms is made into thread and then of how, in the great loom rooms, it is woven into cloth.

The cotton mill is a complex thing like all modern mills. It has been built up slowly from small rude beginnings. Here is this cotton, brought into the mill in its bales. It comes from the fields.

There is a story there too, the story of Southern cotton fields, but it cannot be told here.

In the mills the machines begin to handle the cotton. They roll and toss it. Now it has begun to move forward in the mill, a moving snowy mass.

As it moves forward the machines caress it, they stir it—iron fingers reach softly and tenderly down to it.

The cotton has come into the mill still impregnated with the dust of the fields. There are innumerable little black and brown specks in it. Tiny particles of trash from the fields, bits of the dry brown cotton boll, cling to it, tiny ends of sticks are enmeshed in it.

The cotton gin has removed the seed but there are these particles left.

The fibre of the cotton is delicate and short.

Here is a great machine, weighing tons. See the great wheels, the iron arms moving, feel the vibrations in the air now, all the little iron fingers moving. See how delicately the fingers caress the moving mass. They shake it, they comb it, they caress it.

Every movement here is designed to cleanse the cotton, making it always whiter and cleaner, and to lay the delicate fibres of the mass, more and more, into parallel lines.

Why, this cotton is already on the road to becoming. It is becoming goods. It moves with roaring speed toward that end.

Long months spent making this cotton in the fields. All the danger of bad weather, boll weevil, drought.

Hope coming, despair...a farmer's whole family spending months making a bale of cotton. See how nonchalantly the machines eat it up.

And now it is clean and has begun to emerge from the larger machines in a thin film. You have been in the fields in the early morning and have seen how the dew on the spider webs, spun from weed-top to weed-top, shines and glistens in the morning sun. See how delicate and fragile it is.

But not more delicate or film-like, not more diaphanous than the thin sheet now emerging from yonder huge machine. You may pass your hand under the moving sheet. Look through it and you may see the lines in the palm of your hand.

Yonder great ponderous machine did that. Man made that machine. He made it to do that thing. There is something blind or dead in those of us who do not see and feel the wonder of it.

What delicacy of adjustment, what strength with delicacy! Do you wonder that the little mill girls—half children, some of them—that the women who work in the mills—many of them I have seen with such amazingly delicate and sensitive faces—do you wonder that they are half in love with the machines that they tend, as modern boys are half in love with the automobiles they drive?

The mill superintendent's voice went on, explaining things to me. My nerves tingling.

The reason they run the mills at night it seems is this—well, all this machinery costs tremendously. Suppose you have an investment of a million dollars in machinery.

A million dollars, it seems, cannot stand idle. It must work, work, work.

Men like myself, who will never understand finance, cannot comprehend this. If someone gave me a thousand dollars, ten thousand dollars, a million dollars, I would lay the dollars aside in a heap, I would think of them as so many dollars lying there, waiting to be spent.

But it seems money isn't like that.

Money is power. Power must be used. The mill costs too much.
It cannot stand idle.

Idleness would destroy it. The cost of the money that brought
the machinery would consume the machinery.

There is something very complex here too, a thing called
finance.

The machinery must run, run, run. It must work, work, work.
People must run the machines.

Night does not matter. Time exists during the night too.

I think it is time now for women to come into power in the
western world, to take over the power, the control of life. Perhaps
they have already taken it. There is plenty of evidence that they
have.

To be sure there are all sorts of women, but we should not be
confused by that fact. That there are plenty of silly women in the
world means little. The world has always been run by leaders in
any event, and it seems to me that the new leaders must be
women...

Because, as I have already tried to point out, the woman, at her
best, is and will remain being untouched by the machine. It may, if
she becomes a machine operator, tire her physically but it cannot
paralyze or make impotent her spirit. She remains, as she will
remain, a being with a hidden inner life. The machine can never
bring children into the world.

"Nor can women," someone says, "without the assistance of
the male."

Well, there is the rub. There is where our hope lies. If these
machines, brought by man, so casually into the world—they, the
machines being what they are—such amazing, such beautiful
manifestations of man's imaginative power—they at the same
time having this power to destroy man, if these machines are ever
to be controlled, so that their power to hurt men, by making them
impotent, is checked, women will have to do it.

They will have to do it perhaps to get men back, so that they
may continue to be fertilized, to produce men.

There is a cry going up out of present-day men to the women
but there is a cry coming from the women too.

I heard it that night when I went to visit the factory.

The machines in that factory were doing their work. I was caught up fascinated by what was going on in the room into which I had come, as I have always been caught up, swept out of myself, by what I have seen and felt in modern factories.

I was in the factory that night and thoughts went on in me. Perhaps I had gone a bit daft. The machinery in the great room was going at terrific speed. The night also helped to make it a strange world into which I had come.

I had gone to stand by myself on a little raised platform, the young mill superintendent having left me there, when an odd thing happened. There was an accident. The lights in the great room in which I stood suddenly went out. The room was plunged into darkness.

There was no stopping of the machinery. It was as I have explained, a room in which cloth was woven. The machine in there went on weaving cloth. How long they could have continued to do it, I don't know.

In the factory that night, when the lights went out, I stood trembling on the little raised platform to which I had climbed and tried to stare down into the roaring darkness below. There were people, workers, men and women, down in there. The darkness in the mill lasted but a few minutes.

I have already told of how voices can carry through the terrific roar of the mills. The voices find the little crevice in the sustained roar. There were voices that night.

It began with a woman's voice. She laughed hysterically, I thought. It was a young girl's laughter. "Kiss me," she cried. Was she calling to the machines? Machines do not kiss. She laughed again. "Kiss me while the lights are out," the voice said. A male voice from far across the room answered, wearily I thought.

The male voice was not much. "Who? Me?" it asked wearily. "No, not you."

There was a little chorus of male voices.

"Me?"

"Me?"

"Me?"

"Me?"

(hopefully)

"No, not you. None of you."

"I want a man," the girl's voice said. It was a clear young voice.

There was an outburst of laughter from many women—ironic laughter it was, down there in the darkness—and then the lights came on again.

The mill was as it was before. It roared on. Men and women workers in the room were staring at one another. "The women often do that sort of thing," the young mill superintendent afterward said to me.

"Why?"

"Oh, they are making fun of the men," he said coldly enough.

I Want to Be Counted

I AM intensely interested in this meeting and have come up here from my home in Virginia for that reason.

First of all I have a simple desire to stand up and be counted on the side of Theodore Dreiser, John Dos Passos and the other men and women, mostly I think writers, thinkers, perhaps poets and dreamers, who had the guts to go on this trip down into a little Kentucky mining town. I have been in mining towns myself, I know what most of them are like.

In the mining town in question there had been an attempt to organize a union. I believe the Supreme Court of the United States has said men have a right to form unions, even a communist may run for Congress or for the Senate, or for President—legally—I believe.

A few years ago I was on a visit to France—not considered, I think, an unenlightened country. Even then there were communist deputies sitting in the French house of Deputies.

But in Kentucky they are afraid of unions—so they fight them. They shoot men who join unions—hunt them like rabbits. Now I do not know who owns the mines at Harlan, Kentucky. It is some big company.

There are men in that town, county officials, lawyers, doctors, preachers, store keepers and workers. The workers are, I daresay, quite miserable. I do not need to go to Harlan, Kentucky. I can believe that. I have been in coal mining towns myself, in England,

117

in France, in America, in the North and in the South. I was myself
from a small town of the middle-west, a farming town. I
remember when, as a boy, I first saw, from a train window, a coal
mining town of that county. I remember the shudder that ran
through me. There were men and women living like rabbits in
dirty holes. I remember how the sight frightened and startled me.

So nowadays everywhere workers are out of work. They are
poorly paid.

It is so with all workers in all trades now. With the industrial
workers it is worse than with any other sort of workers.

Why? It seems to me very simple. Nowadays, because of our
human mechanical genius, the building up of the modern
machine, you can manufacture five times, ten times, in some
fields perhaps 100 times as many goods per man employed as you
could 25 or 50 years ago.

So nowadays, if you want to cut wages in any plant, any
industry, if you want to lengthen hours to speed up the work,
keeping the workers always keyed up to an intense pitch,
breaking down the nerve force, breaking by persistent speeding
the spirits of men and women, it is easy. Are there not thousands
of men waiting for jobs outside the factory gates?

I am a worker in a factory, you come to me. Being my boss, you
tell me. "You will have to take another cut. Your hours will have
to be lengthened, etc." There I stand by my machine. I turn my
head and look out a window into the street. There are all of those
other men and women standing down there in the street by the
factory gate, unemployed men with families. Do I take what you,
my boss, choose to give me? I usually do.

This happens not only in industry. In my own country, in the
South, in Virginia, I am told there are farm laborers now glad to
get work at 50 cents a day.

I remember what a man said to me a short time ago. I was on a
train and talking to this man. I knew him. He was a large
manufacturer. "You are a writer, Anderson," he said. "You write
stories and novels, books, etc.?"

"Yes."

"Well," he said, "I could not do that. I could not write any
books. Do you want to know why?"

"Yes, I would like to know."

"Because," he said, "I could not go on talking like that—what it would take you a whole book to say I could say in two words."

I was telling a friend about this. "Sure, he could," my friend said. "He could say, 'You're fired.'"

So you have got labor driven into a corner now subdued, defeated.

Occasionally something breaks out—a strike. Were you ever in on one? The experience is something never to be forgotten. There are these men, the workers, in a machine age, all controlled by a few men up above—far, far up above, by men who perhaps never visit the factory. Oil controlled absolutely by men who never drilled an oil well, soap controlled by men who never made a pound of soap. The same with food, all kinds of foods, with steel, with textiles. Do you think that farmers, who raise our food, have any control over the food they raise? It is to laugh.

You workers are caught down under there. Suddenly, with your fellow workers, you strike. Something runs through a shop. A surprising number of our strikes nowadays are like that. They are operatic, unexpected, often uncontrollable.

A kind of tremor runs through a plant, or mine. There are cries and shouts. These little individual units the individual workers, lost down there in that amazingly beautiful and terrible thing— the modern world of the machine—these units, so tied, so bound to the machines, suddenly fly off the machines.

Why, it is something uncanny, something to the onlooker a little strange.

There are these units, tied thus to the machines. If you go nowadays much into great modern factories, you cannot escape the feeling that men and women in industry are in a queer new way tied, bound, to their machines. They seem to have become a part of the machines.

It is, I say, strange to see them fly off thus, separate themselves even temporarily from the machines. It is even pathetic this little struggle of individual men and women to free themselves a little, go again toward one another, touch, feel for each other, in this strange new machine world we have made.

Men come out into the light, into the open. Words long suppressed come to the lips, hand touches hand.

"You here, Jim, and you, Fred, and you, Joe? You are going to stick, to fight?"

"Yes, by God."

"And you—Maude and Helen and Kate."

A strange new sense of brotherhood, of sisterhood.

"Do you think we have a chance?"

"Yes. Yes."

Hope, fight.

"What the hell can we lose? Our lives? Hell, they've got our lives."

Light coming into dull eyes, hope into brains dulled by long years of toil. Men are marching now. They are singing. The strike is a marvelous thing. Win or lose it is a marvelous thing.

There is this sense of brotherhood come back, shoulder touching shoulder, at last in these lives a period of aliveness and of hope, of warmth, of brotherhood in struggle.

Ask any man who has been to war. Did he get anything out of it? Ask him. Did he get new hatred of his so-called enemy?

Never. I'll tell you what he got, if he got anything. He got flashes of a new sense of men—the sense of brotherhood. He got that or he got nothing.

Why the strike is like that to workers. In these days usually it doesn't last long. The same brains that have organized all of this big strange new thing in our world, modern industry, have also organized the means of crushing these outbreaks.

That is a machine too. The machine that crushes these new hopes. How deftly, how powerfully, it is organized. It has organized the press, the schools, the churches, the preachers, pretty much the whole middle and professional classes of lawyers, doctors, merchants, salesmen, newspapers, newspaper reporters, editors of newspapers. It has pretty much got them all.

As for the politicians. It is shameful to mention it to a crowd of intelligent people, it is so obvious—I mean the organization, the control of our modern so-called public men, by the machine, by money, by the money brains that control the western world now.

And all of this for what?

Who is served by it? I mean by this modern crushing organization of modern society? Has it been built up to serve an aristocracy men and women of blood lines, an intellectual aristocracy—an aristocracy of taste, of refinement? Are there gods nowadays walking the earth who must be served by all of the rest of us, by the common man or woman, by his brains, by his

talents? Are these new gods, specially refined, intelligent, kind
and thoughtful beings? Are they themselves even served by it?
Are they made happier, are their children better off, are they
better off?

Why they are caught and held by the machine as we are.

Are they special men, specially endowed by some strange god?

Why no—none that I have seen.

Who is served?

A refiner of oil.

A maker of steel.

A soap maker.

A hog killer, out in Chicago.

A weaver.

A money changer.

What, all of this for these men?

Money brains.

Soap brains.

Wheat brains.

Shoe brains.

Clothing brains.

This beautiful new majestic thing in the world, the machine,
now crushing millions of people under its iron heels, this thing
that sprang out of the brain of men, out from under the cunning
fingers of men—this thing all for these men.

Soap brains.

Wheat brains.

Coal brains.

Shoe brains.

Money brains.

Is that what our people came to America for? Was it for this
we built all of our railroads, cut down the forests, opened up the
land, conquered the sea, conquered the air—that these men, with
specialized kinds of brains, meat brains, oil, soap, shoe, iron, coal,
money brains . . . was it all only to set up a new kingdom for these?

Why, I will tell you something. There is something wrong. We
men and women of our day are in a strange, an odd position. Do
you know what I think is wrong? We are, all of us, men and
women living on one world while we think and feel, most of us, in
an old and an outworn world. We are living on one world while

we try to think and feel in another. Do you wonder there is confusion?

There is a new world. It is here. It is a machine world. I do not believe there is anything wrong with the machine. Often it is beautiful, a powerful, a strange and lovely thing in the world.

It has got out of our hands. We are not controlling it now. It has really frightened us, unnerved us. We are in a time of transition now, men and women passing out of one world into another. Beyond a doubt, before we again get into the clear, out of the fog of fear and hatred we are now in, out again into an open road where we can go forward, if it is in us to go forward, before that, beyond a doubt new forms of government will have to be made, new kinds of cities built, there will have to be new kinds of agriculture, new kinds of control in every department of life.

Well, and so, what of it?

Are we afraid? Is that what makes us so cruel to one another just now? Of course we are afraid!

We are afraid of one another. Millionaires are afraid, workers are afraid, merchants, doctors, lawyers, school teachers, preachers, newspaper writers and publishers—almost without exception we are all afraid. Fear is what is ruling now in Harlan, Kentucky.

This meeting is being held here today to voice a certain protest. Something has happened in the life of a certain community in the State of Kentucky. It did not happen because it was Kentucky. It might have happened in California, in Florida, in Maine. The ordinary man or woman who lives now in Harlan, Kentucky, is not a different sort of man or woman from one who lives in Chicago, in New York, in San Francisco, in Kalamazoo.

There is just a town in Kentucky, sunk yet in an old world, living, thinking, breathing, feeling in an old world and by an odd chance confronted suddenly by a new world. That is all.

And there is something else. There are certain individuals here confronted with something too. There is Mr. Dreiser here, Mr. Dos Passos, and these other men and women.

Now look—this is what happened. There were all of these cries, rumors, tales of brutal things being done down there. There was a strike. Why no one in America is alarmed much by communism in Russia. That is far away. Our newspaper cartoonists have fixed it all nicely for us. We can think of Russians, of the Russian people as something strange, as far away, as not quite human.

The Russian is a great bewhiskered brute. He is dirty and heavy. He scratches himself and out jumps a Tartar.

But what is a Tartar?

Oh, he is a kind of a wild and lousy cowboy on a horse who dashes through streets, tramping children underfoot.

All a little savage, a little wild, a little crazy.

This in spite of Turgenev, Chekov, Tolstoy, Dostoevsky, Gorky, Gogol, Russian painting, Russian dancing, the Russian theater, all tremendously civilizing influences—all coming out of Russia.

Well, it's all right, I guess. Does not the average European think of us Americans as all rich, all riding in high-priced automobiles, throwing money about, living in palaces? You ought to know how true the picture is.

So there was all this ugliness down there in Harlan, Kentucky. Newspaper reporters going down there, to find out if all the stories told were true, were beaten and driven out of town. The mine owners had got their hired gunmen in there. You ought to know about that in New York. Chicago knows about it. There was apparently a reign of terror.

Well, what about it? Were the working people of that community being terrorized, thrown into ugly little jails, beaten, was Harlan, Kentucky, really being made into a kind of Siberian penal camp, under the old Tsars?

It was a fine question. Would some one go out there and find out?

Mr. Dreiser did not want to go. Mr. Dos Passos did not want to go. Why, I know this type of man. I'm one of them myself.

I know what these men want. Mr. Dreiser is a story teller. He is a man who had never sought and does not want the limelight. He wants to wander about talking to people, to workers, to millionaires, to merchants. He wants to go talk with women. He is a story teller. He has a tremendous searching constant hunger in him to find out about lives.

It gnaws at him, bites at him, will not let him alone.

Dreiser has been that way all of his life. He wants the truth
about people. He is tender about people. When something hurts
some one it hurts him too. He doesn't want to be that way. It
would be much more comfortable for him if he was indifferent,
self-satisfied, could take life merely as a game, play to win.

Why this is a grand chance for me, as another American
writer, to say something about my friend Theodore Dreiser. I
myself began writing after Theodore Dreiser did. I guess you all
here know what has happened to American writing.

It is like this. As soon as a man here, in America, shows some
talent as a writer they pounce down on him. They want to buy his
talent.

They usually do too, I'll tell you that.

So they offer him money, position, security.

All he has to do you see is to corrupt slightly everything he
does.

They want to make a clever man of him, a cunning little
twister of words and ideas, soiling his own tools, going crooked
you see, selling the people out.

Oh, it's nice, some of the implications of being a successful
writer in this country.

You don't even have to lie. You can just keep still. Shut your
eyes.

So Dreiser wouldn't do that. He had a curious hunger for truth.
He was in love with truth. They say he is an immoral man. By the
gods, it's true. He has been blatantly, openly, immorally in love
with truth all of his life. He has fought for her, coaxed her, put his
hands on her, raped her.

He hasn't let the magazine editors run him, the publishers tell
him how and what to write. He hasn't writen any leg shows for
the movies. Most of his life he has been poor. Long after he was
famous he was poor.

And what did that mean? Let me tell you what it means to
American writers. I know.

Let us say that the average young American writer comes from
a poor family. Most of them do. I don't know why. They are lucky
if they do. They may get a little real education that way. My
Heavens, if the average American millionaire knew what, in
accumulating his millions, sweating it out of working people,

scheming and lying and cheating often enough to get it, if he knew what he was doing to his own children, to his own sons and daughters, how he is cutting them off from real contact with life, from real education, dwarfing them (the daily newspapers ought to tell him that story but he won't see it) if he knew he would be the first man to throw his millions into the river and go Bolshevik. . . .

Why there is something in being of the proletariat too. I was one once. I was a common laborer until I was 24 or 25 years old. I swear I would have been a better artist, a better story-teller now if I had stayed there. I might then have had something to say here as coming up out of the mass of people, out of the hearts of common everyday people, out of poor farmers and poor factory hands, always growing in numbers in this country. I say that if I had stayed down there, never tried to rise, had earned my bread and butter always with the same hands with which I wrote words I might have had something real to say with the words I wrote.

Mr. Dreiser has stood out against this, against the corruption of American writers with money, with promises of social distinction, with all the subtle promises that can be given such men. He has stood out. He has been honest and fearless. He was the first downright honest American prose writer.

Do you think that has not meant a lot to the rest of us? It has meant everything.

So there is Mr. Dreiser. He is naïve. He has never had success enough to make him smart, make him clever. Why I have been called naïve myself. I remember coming to New York once, some years ago. It was after prohibition so I was invited to a cocktail party. I went.

A certain well-known American critic came up to me. He staggered up. Well, he was drunk. "I don't like your work," he said. "You're too naïve."

"Oh, yes? You think so?"

"You are naïve. You believe human life amounts to a damn. It don't amount to a damn," he said.

And so there was this Harlan, Kentucky, situation. The eyes of the whole country had become focussed on that little spot. It had become a little ugly running sore, workers being beaten, women thrown into jail, American citizens being terrorized, newspaper men trying to investigate, being shot and terrorized. When you have got a disease inside the body it has a nasty little trick of breaking out in little sores of that sort.

So it was thought some one—a body of men and women of more or less authority—should go down there to investigate, to find out the truth, if possible. Why, Mr. Dreiser did not want to go.

And here let me step aside a moment to say something. I was recently, since this Dreiser thing came up, at a certain American College. I had gone there to talk about country newspapers.

So I was in a room afterwards with half a dozen young American men—fine young fellows too, two or three of them on the college football team, one of the famous teams of the country, and we were talking. The boys spoke of Mr. Dreiser.

"Why did he go down there?" one of them asked, and another answered, "Oh, I guess he wanted some publicity."

Ye gods. Even in the young. Refusal to believe any man can do anything for clean reason. Taking it for granted that men of the artists' class are also business men, thinking always and only of money, publicity, what is called fame. A man of Mr. Dreiser's world reputation, and an honest artist, being put instinctively on the footing of some little publicity grubbing movie actor. It makes your flesh creep to think of it. We pay through the nose for our glorious American money civilization, now don't we?

When it comes to Harlan, Kentucky, Mr. Dreiser and the others who went down there with him went as a last resort.

Others were publicly asked to go. There was a call sent out. Men of prominence in the educational world, college heads, statesmen, so called, humanitarians. There was a long list of big names.

Not a man would go.

They all got sick suddenly, or they had appointments, or their sisters got sick, or they had a cousin coming to visit.

It was a hot spot, you see. They all wanted to keep nice and cool.

And then too, the word had gone out that some one might get hurt.

But there is something more than this. We, in America, are in a queer time. It is a speak-easy generation.

You will find this sort of thing everywhere now. They will talk to you in private.

Why, there are some men like that judge down in Kentucky, that prosecuting attorney down there. I know a lot of such men.

Sometime ago I was in the South, in another town when a strike was going on. It is always the same story. The company whose plant is being struck employs what they call a detective agency, to guard the property. I'll tell you they do a lot more than guard it. They are strong-arm men, thugs, racketeers. It is the business of these men to make trouble.

Why? I'll tell you why. Once you have made trouble, set off a few sticks of dynamite, the soldiers may be brought in.

It's easy after that. Now you get an injunction against picketing, against parading, against what they call, "unlawful assembly." It's a line-up, isn't it? The United States Government, the courts, the whole middle-class, the newspapers, the churches, the state governments, county government, and to round it off these hired gunmen—all of these against what? Against a few miners with their blackened eyes or a few pale, consumptive cotton mill workers.

In this court to which I went a few tired men and women, confused as such people always are when confronted with what we call "the majesty of the law," in that big strange room—I'll never forget their confused faces—so they were being tried for what was called, "unlawful assembly." They had gone into a vacant lot. They hadn't any permission to go into this vacant lot. They were gathered together there, huddled together, talking.

If I remember correctly they even had resisted arrest. A woman had, I believe, scratched the deputy sheriff's or a soldier's cheek. Some frightened mill hand had cursed. So they had been dragged into court. A jury had tried them. While the jury was out in that case the judge went into his chamber. I followed him in there. I had been curious about this thing. I introduced myself. We had cigarettes. We talked. Why I believe Theodore Dreiser who is accused of what is called criminal syndicalism, is also accused of being a communist. He isn't, any more than I am. He couldn't be if he wanted to be. They wouldn't have him. As I understand it the Communist Party is a working class party. Mr. Dreiser belongs to another class, the class to which I have the honor of belonging— the artist class. Why, I do not know nowadays whether it is or is not an honor to belong among us. As a class nowadays, we have become as weak-kneed, as money-hungry, as afraid to speak out as most of the men of the press, the church, the courts and the schools.

If you think Mr. Dreiser a communist, you should have heard the conversation in that judge's chamber that day. You see the door was closed. We were alone in there. That judge thought the coming of communism absolutely inevitable. He said so.

Then he went right out and sent those men and women to jail for unlawful assembly. There you are.

You find it among college professors, preachers, school teachers, men in the offices of big companies, you find it everywhere.

I do not know how many newspaper men and women I know personally. A good many. Perhaps fifty, perhaps a hundred, perhaps two hundred. But this I do know. In private conversation, over a drink, in a speak-easy almost to a man they are what is called radical. The profession, everything considered is miserably paid. A clever advertising writer will make four times what even a first-rate reporter makes.

But the radicalism is usually all private. It is private almost everywhere. It is under the rose. In public—in the public prints— well, you know what happens.

It is characteristic of our whole American attitude just now— that is what I am trying to say. We are a speak-easy country. That is what makes me glad for Theodore Dreiser. That is what makes me glad for these young communists. Why, a friend of mine down South asked me recently—"What is the difference between a Communist and a Socialist?" he asked me. I couldn't tell him the technical difference. I didn't know. I am myself a story teller, not a political economist. "I don't know," I said. "I guess the Communists mean it."

So there you are, Mr. Dreiser and these other people have had the nerve and the manhood to go down there into Kentucky, where there is apparently this reign of terror. They went openly and only after other men and women had refused to go. What they found there I will naturally leave for them to tell. They went there and asked questions. Mr. Dreiser made no speeches. He doesn't make speeches. He wanted, the others wanted, to call public attention to what was going on. He wanted truth. And then too, he spoke aloud in a speak-easy country. He said in public what millions of Americans are thinking in private.

For that he is accused of criminal syndicalism.

So that's what criminal syndicalism is? I am glad to know. Now I know at last what is the matter with this country. We need less speak-easy citizens and more criminal syndicalists.

And they say Mr. Dreiser is immoral. He has loved women. Isn't it terrible? When it comes to Mr. Dreiser's immorality—Do you remember the story of Abraham Lincoln and General Grant? Why, there it was. It seems General Grant drank whiskey. So that upset the preachers. A delegation of them went to Abraham Lincoln. They told on Grant. "Horrors. He drinks whiskey."

"What kind?" asked Abraham, "what brand? I'd like to know," he said. "I'd like to give it to some of the rest of my generals."

Why, that is all I have to say here. There is this accusation of criminal syndicalism now standing against Mr. Dreiser. They would like to take him to Kentucky, try him down there, throw him into prison. Well, I have just this to say. That if they can do it, if they do it, it will be the shame of all decent American writers if they do not to a man go out at once and commit criminal syndicalism. They ought to find out how it is done and go and do it. They ought to go to jail with him.

It is time for writers, college professors, newspaper men, for every one who has the public ear to speak out. As for the communists, if there is any little vestige of freedom left in the country they should be allowed to speak and agitate too. They may have found the true solution to our economic difficulties. I don't know.

I think the writers of this country ought to quit pandering. It is a troubled time, an uncertain time. I think we writers ought to quit thinking so much of money and fame and social position and safety and line up with the underdogs.

That's why I'm here. I don't like public meetings and public speaking. I'd rather be in a quiet hole somewhere, bent over a desk or going about quietly, talking to people.

I'm here because I think that Mr. Dreiser has got a rotten deal. What he has done has been twisted in some places into something it wasn't at all. I think the press, the pulpit and all of us are to blame. As I said before, I think that if they can take Mr. Dreiser out there to Kentucky and try him in that court for criminal syndicalism then we ought all to begin committing criminal syndicalism as fast as we know how to do it. I don't believe we ought to be satisfied or condemned to live all of our lives in a speak-easy country.

To Remember

I T'S silly to forget it—what America is. It's so easy now. Adrift again. It's an American passion in me—to go, look, see. In me there is an undying love of automobiles. I should be a tester for some big factory. I'm a wonderful driver. In my hands a car goes more miles and easier, with less wear and tear on the car, than a car in the hands of any other man I've ever seen or ridden with. The voice of the motor is the voice of my beloved. Every year the cheap cars get better, lovelier in outline, more sensitive to the touch, more enduring. The cheap car I have now has been run thirty-five thousand miles. The car actually likes it. It likes me. It still sings gayly along the road, and when it gets dirty I run it into some wayside creek, at a ford, and wash its face, hands and body. At some places now, out in the Middle West, gas is down to eleven cents.

The cooking gets a bit better. All of this talk by the doctors, the ones who write the syndicated stuff in the newspapers, the family doctors, even in the small towns now ... no more beef steak and fried potatoes for breakfast, even in Tennessee ... diet's the thing now ... a long life, if a discouraging one ... eat more fruit and vegeatables ... it's all beginning to take effect. The ham sandwich and the hot dog are going. Yesterday ... where do you think? ... that's right, in Southern Illinois, I got a great plate of finely cooked vegetables with a glass of buttermilk for fifteen cents. The waitress says to me, she says, "That's right. That's the sensible way to eat."

For me there is no definite good life, either in the city, or in the small town, or on the farm. With the car I continually mix them up. It's any amount cheaper and nicer than the attics we poets used to live in. A man may write on a flat stone, under a bridge, near Paducah, Kentucky...(There is a swanky big hotel in Paducah—called The Irvin Cobb—huge painting of Cobb in the lobby—prices a bit high for a modern novelist—art also, however, gets on.)

Touch with people picked up on the road. Keep always a vacant seat for the chance adventure. Confusion. They all apologize for being down and out. It's an almost universal American impulse. "I am an American and should have risen in the world. This is the land of opportunity." They all want to explain how it happened; they didn't cut it, didn't make the grade. Not one I've seen in this present drift—and I've seen and talked to plenty—as yet really blaming capitalism, the machine, our American overlords, anything much but self. "I should have made it. It's the land of opportunity all right. It's all my own fault." Oh, sweet Americans.

Is it sweetness or colossal stupidity? I don't know. It's a bit discouraging to one who, like myself, is always getting hopped up and writing fervently, even feverishly—*The Revolution, The Revolution.*

The main point of this drifting that I so love—I tell myself—to remember (may the gods not let me forget) the land itself. It's so gorgeous, so big, so infinitely varied. Mountains, valleys, rivers, strips of forests coming down to look at roads, little creeks, prairies, pine forests, beaches facing oceans and lakes, rich land—plenty of rich land yet...the vastness of it...the gorgeous swank and richness of it...

...to remember how utterly silly it is to have depression here—down-and-outs apologizing for being alive...how fast they learn to whine...whining and apologizing for being alive, even as they walk—homeless and hungry, like as not—across the face of it.

Will we ever have sense enough to take what is so obviously spread out so temptingly before us here? To remember it could be done?

Delegation

YOU get caught. It isn't as though you thought you really knew anything about government. You know you don't.

There is, however, this thing going on. Suppose you happen to be a man like myself, a born wanderer. You drift from town to town. Nowadays, if you have a small car, it's easy. You keep seeing and talking to men, and often to women. There are always places to go in a town. There are often meetings being held, or you can go to a part of town where workmen congregate in the evening. They're glad to talk. You keep finding out things.

But all of your thoughts do you no good. Thoughts don't seem to help. You see men and women everywhere defeated. They don't want so much—a job to do that is at least a bit interesting, decent food, clothes and shelter, the chance to play a little. What gets you in a time like this is the terrible humility of men. Someone says to you "Come on. Let's protest," so you do. You sign things, serve on committees. You protest. You send telegrams to governors and judges.

I went with some three or four others to make a protest to the President. That was Hoover, then. It was when the ex-soldiers came down to Washington and camped there, demanding the bonus. You will remember how the government got after them with machine guns and soldiers and bayonets and tear gas and drove them like sheep down across Maryland and Pennsylvania. It seemed a shame.

Some earnest fellow got after a little bunch of us highbrows and worried us and teased us into going down to Washington to protest. I think they had telegraphed the President and asked him "Will you see them?" and that he had wired back "No." I can't be sure about this. We who do the protesting are seldom taken into the confidence of the men who run such affairs. The Communists, for example, go in deep for mystery. I am a little uncertain as to whether I ever met a real one.

Anyway, I came into New York and went to the Pennsylvania Station, and there were three others. There was a kind of manager of things. He kept running around and saying that a lot of newspapermen were coming to interview us, but none came. We got on the train and sat in the smoker. There were two men we took to be real revolutionists sitting opposite a friend of mine, who is a writer, and myself, and we spent most of the time trying to prove to them by arguments that if they would only let us alone, let us stay at home and write beautiful and stirring prose, we, in our own subtle ways, would correct the wrongs and the injustices of the world a lot faster than they ever could by chasing around and worrying presidents—or by nagging us into doing it. You can see how it is. You seldom get a sock in the jaw sitting at home and writing beautiful prose.

And then, bang, we were in Washington and at the White House offices. There were a lot of police and soldiers and any number of bright, alert-looking newspapermen. We stood there in the White House offices, in a big outer room. It was a hot day. I forgot to say that at Baltimore our delegation had been joined by a colored man. He was the editor of a Negro newspaper, a modest, nice fellow. Someone had got up a manifesto, and we had all signed.

Men kept running up to us, newspapermen, some of whom I knew. It was the President's birthday. The newspapermen told us about other delegations that had come, the Girl Scouts with a bouquet of flowers, a delegation from the Chamber of Commerce with a cake, etc. I was thinking "Suppose he does see us. He won't, but suppose he does. Would there have to be speeches made?" The truth is that I felt as I usually feel when I go into a bank to try to borrow some money. When I get like that, my back always aches. Think of me protesting for soldiers. I'd make a bum soldier.

I do not know how long we waited, perhaps an hour, before we were shown into a big room. There was a youngish-looking man sitting at a desk, and beside him sat two very fat, important-looking older men. They didn't pay any attention to us, so we lined up against a wall. Instinct may have led us to do that. I wondered how the others felt. As for myself, I think I felt much as a young man feels when he goes to speak to her father about it.

Then I noticed something. There was that youngish man, the President's secretary, sitting at the desk, and right away, when I looked hard at him, I got onto something. "He is just as scared, he feels just as uncomfortable as we do," I thought. It was a grand thought and turned out to be true. I have seldom had a thought that gave me such comfort.

The man got up from his desk and the two fat, important-looking men left the room. They stopped at the door and looked back hard at us highbrow Reds, and I had another thought. "Gee," I thought, "who knows? They may be Secret Service men." I have always wanted to have a Secret Service man after me.

We were alone in the room with the one man. A marvelous thing had happened. The man facing us, this big official man, was as upset as we were. It seemed to me he was actually scared. As he advanced toward us, the sheets of paper held in his hand trembled. He had gone a little white. When he began to speak, his voice trembled.

First he made us a little speech. He told us we were in the wrong. "I am not speaking for the President," he said, "or in my official position as the President's secretary. I speak," he said, "as a fellow-American and a fellow-craftsman."

After that he lectured us. I can't remember all he said. It was something about upholding someone's hands. He read the speech from the piece of paper he held in his trembling hands and afterward our spokesman also made a little speech. He tried to tell the man what we represented. He may have been wrong. I am not sure that we represented anything much.

I don't think that is the point. We had been asked, pleaded with, to go down there, and we went. When we got there, we felt silly, at least I did.

Then this thing happened. That man, that President's secretary, was so obviously afraid of us. It seemed wonderful to me. We went out of the office and down a street, and a newspaperman I knew, a man named Buck from my old Chicago days, came and put his arm through mine. "Do you want some beer?" he asked, and I said "Yes." I made my friend, the writer, come with us. Afterward I read in the newspapers that we were followed from the President's office to Communist headquarters. It is a mistake. We didn't know there was any such place. We went to a speakeasy and had some beer. It was a hot day.

Afterward we came out, just the two of us who had come from New York. We walked along a street. "Well, that's that," my friend said. We were walking under some nice trees. They have nice trees along the streets in Washington. "Yes," I said, "that's that, but did you notice that we scared that guy? We gave him indigestion," I said, and my friend wriggled with delight. A look of the most beatific pleasure spread over his face. "See," he said, "so you noticed it, too."

The Line-up

THIS curious performance takes place twice a week. It is good theatre. We went into a big hall and there were already some two thousand men assembled. I saw no women, and there were no women prisoners in the New York police line-up that morning. Perhaps the women had been quite innocent during the half week, and perhaps they do not do it to women.

The walls of the long hall were painted a warm gray, and we sat in a mass at the back, in a dim light. The policemen were in civilian clothes. The Police Commissioner, once a General, wears the red button of France. He made me think of Frank Crowninshield. There was the same masculine gentleness. The New York Commissioner of Police has style.

The police, in their civilian clothes, looked like any crowd of rather well-set-up citizens. They were surprisingly young and good-looking. I wonder if all this stuff about the brutality of the police is also romance. I have always been afraid of the police. There may be a criminal sleeping in every man.

So we were assembled at the back of the hall, a solid mass of humanity. The Commissioner came in with two or three guests and they sat apart. I heard him introduce one of the men to another as "Governor." "I'll bet he's the Governor of New Hampshire," I thought. I don't know why I thought that. There was a man who sat alone, in a high pulpit-like place. He was silent. A reading-lamp shone down on the white pages of a book and he wrote in the book.

137

At the end of the room there was a sheer wall, also painted a warm gray, such a wall as would be good to hang paintings against, and a narrow bridge led across it. The prisoners walked across the bridge. A man stood silently there. He made a signal, and one of the prisoners stopped. He was under a strong light, the only strong light in the room.

Two thousand police, looking intently at you, try to fix your face in their memory. The light was so arranged that the face of the prisoner seemed to jump out at you. At his back there was a white board with figures on it. It marked the prisoner's exact height. It was just such a board as they put along the banks of rivers to mark the stages of the river in flood.

Intense silence in the room. A voice spoke. This was the best theatre of all. The voice seemed to come out of the sky, as though God spoke to the prisoner. There were no men walking across the bridge for minor offenses. All were felons.

Voice: "John Harley ... arrested at Fourteenth and Broadway, by Officers Grady and Hines ... taken in the act of attempting to pick a woman's pocket. What about it, John?"

Each prisoner took it in his own way. There were Negro men and white men, pocket-pickers, stealers of automobiles, killers, thugs, highjackers, racketeers. There is this odd thing you find out about the world of crime. The man who steals an automobile, gets caught and sent to prison, comes out and steals another automobile. He doesn't begin to pick pockets or hold men up. He steals automobiles. The man who has killed a woman kills another, the dip keeps on dipping, the racketeer racketeering. It's discouraging. There are certain of my own traits I would like to change. As you watch the line-up you are inclined to throw up your hands.

"What about it, John?" The man in the darkness, some place up above, asked his questions in a clear voice. The voice was not unkindly. It did not attempt to bully. It was almost friendly.

"What about it, John?" John's eyes move nervously about. From where he is standing, his face flooded by the strong light, he can see none of us. It is as though he stood in some space between worlds. He decides to plead. "I have a wife and children. I needed money, had to have it."

"Have you ever been arrested before, John?"

John wets his lips with his tongue. After all, this is cruel. There is a queer sort of impersonal cruelty.

"Yes. I was arrested twice before." He hesitates. "Well, maybe three times." There is a period of silence and then the voice reads off John's record... arrested eleven times... eight convictions... has served time in Sing Sing, in the Ohio State Penitentiary. John was a veteran. He is man of fifty. A silent man, down below, makes a signal and John walks away.

Into darkness, no doubt to another long period of darkness in some prison. He will be an old man when he comes out again.

Others come, blacks and whites, defiant ones, some who attempt to be slick, some who squirm, some who arouse pity in you, others who arouse fear. There were two young men the likes of whom I had never seen before. There was something in them altogether depraved and fearless. In your heart you knew that if you wanted someone killed these two would do it at a reasonable price. One of them, the slicker, more glib one, did the talking for them both. They let him talk.

"We were just going along the street."

"Where did you get the gun?"

"I saw it lying in the gutter. I picked it up."

"It was still smoking, wasn't it, Ed?"

"Yes. It was in the gutter. We were just walking past. I picked it up." That pair also off into the darkness.

They kept coming and going. It was as though some terrible realistic painter was hanging pictures on the warm gray wall, under the light. "Here you are. This is a sample of what you can be, you humans! Take a good look!"

You get all sorts of notions in your head; remember books you have read about crime and criminals. You come out of the place, walk along the street. There is a sudden realization of something, of crime always going on, there, behind the walls of that building, in the next street, in the bright sunlight, in the darkness at night.

As I was coming out of the building I spoke to one of the sub-commissioners of police. All of the police, assembled for the line-up that morning, had got, as I had, a jump of the heart at the sight of the two young killers. Their appearance under the light, under the voice, had been the high spot of the morning police drama. "There should be a lethal chamber, shouldn't there?" I said to the sub-commissioner of police and he looked at me, I thought with wise eyes. "Yes. But who would say who was to go into it?" he said. I thought his eyes were a bit too shrewd as he looked at me. "Sure. Sure," I said, hurrying away.

Give a Child Room to Grow

OLDER people are always hungry. They really want each other. Something in our lives builds a barrier between us. The child is naturally innocent. I think his is the innocence of an animal. How much better we treat a puppy than we do a child. It may be because the puppy develops faster and also quickly learns to escape by running away. It is absurd to pay more attention to a child than to an older person. Innocence is all right but it is also rather a bore. A little of it goes a long way.

There are the people, that is to say older people, in any house and a child comes among them. What a breaking down of all reserve and dignity. The child is grabbed, kissed, played with, worried. Such speeches made: "Oh how sweet! how sweet!"—this got off just the same when the child is, as any child must be often, dirty-faced, irritable, certainly not at the moment sweet. It seems very like hypocrisy.

At first, you are inclined to say to yourself that it is cheapness on the part of its elder, that he wants the attention of the child in order to feed his own egotism; but later you begin to see that it is a deeper thing. I think it must be because of a queer emptiness in all of us. Oh, how deeply all of us want the kind of affection that is only to be got by the development of the greatest of all gifts ... understanding.

But it is slow difficult business to come to understanding. We are slovenly and lazy. How dumb we are, how stupid, not only

141

about the child but about each other. Often I think there is
something very evil in us that wants to hurt. "Oh God, give us a
bit of maturity, give it, give it" should be our prayer, day and
night.

It is, for example, obvious that it is all-important that the child
be given knowledge as fast as possible and what more sweet,
more important knowledge than the learning that you must earn
love, must deserve it a little. What empty words about love, the
stars, the mystery of the universe, always being said to children. I
wonder sometimes that we, as a people, ever achieve the wonder
of one of these children grown into a poet. Why there could be a
very sweet, very great dignity and reality to this innocence of
childhood. I have never been in a house with a child without
feeling this reality. It comes always when, for some reason, the
attention of the older people about is taken away. It may well be
that, even in the youngest child, something is really trying to
grow. When the thing I am now speaking of happens to a child it
has about it the same wonder that is connected with all growing
things. A very beautiful and wonderful thing comes into the
child's eyes. See how still it sits. The older people in the room are
chattering. They are moving about. Is this unfolding mind trying
to understand?

Rush to it, grab it, break the beauty of the moment. It may be
that this beauty is too much for us. We can't stand it.

Who was it invented the absurdly romantic notion that
children and puppies instinctively like certain people and not
others? Abraham Lincoln was adored by all children... The Pied
Piper of Hamelin.

I should never say the word *love* in the presence of a child
when I do not feel love. I should myself try to preserve a little
dignity in the presence of the child in order that the child may at
last get at least an inkling of personal dignity. The simple fact is
that I am interested in the child as I am in any other wonder in
nature. The child is not mature, cannot be. It wants a very great
deal of letting alone. If I were to handle, maul, kiss, squeeze,
fondle, pile things around the roots of a tree, or a plant just
coming out of the ground, as I do these things to a child, could the
tree live? The constant wonder is that children do survive. How
many older people are carrying through life the terrible scars of

childhood? As we grow older, see these scars in our own children, now grown, we do begin to realize a little what we did to them in childhood, but this does not seem to prevent the same thing being done over again to the first child that comes into our house.

Here They Come

ONCE practically everyone in America at all interested in
sports knew the trotting and pacing horses. When one of the
champions was to appear at one of our state fairs, J.I.C., Maud S.,
Nancy Hanks, Dan Patch, the people turned out as they do
nowadays to a big college football game. Men and boys hung over
the fences along the racetracks.

"Here they come!"

The trotters or the pacers were in the homestretch in an
exciting race. Some of the drivers were shouting wildly while
others sat with grim tense faces, holding the reins over their
steeds.

The horses themselves, as they swung into the full rhythm of
their stride, seemed to flatten. Heads were thrust forward,
nostrils distended. There was the ringing sound of hoofs on the
hard earth. A little grey mare was creeping up inch by inch on a
big free-legged brown gelding. He was a high-stepping, long-
striding one. She was at his flank, at his shoulder. There was the
wire just ahead. Would she make it?

"Here she comes! Here she comes! Ha! She has made it!"

Almost every boy and man hanging over the fences along the
homestretch at the big mile tracks, at the state fairs where the
fastest sometimes came, at the little dusty half-mile tracks at the
county fairs, knew his horses. He could recite for you the
bloodlines of his favorites. In every American town there were a

few men, owning a few good ones, colts they hoped might come on, get into the big time. It was the sport of the small-town man, the farmer. A few city men went for it but on the whole it remained the sport of men who lived close to the horse. General Grant loved the trotters as did the first of the Vanderbilts. The big-timers went to the Grand Circuit meetings at North Randall, near Cleveland, to Goshen, New York, Meadville, Pennsylvania, Kalamazoo in Michigan. It threatened to blow up, come to an end with the coming of the automobile.

Unlike the running tracks, harness-horse racing never was a sport for big-time gamblers. A quite different crowd was attracted and is still attracted. They are a hearty suntanned outdoors crowd, these harness-horse men.

It was a horse age, when almost every man you knew owned some kind of horse. The country doctor drove a horse along country roads to visit his patients, the lawyers and judge went horse-drawn from town to town to attend court, the livery stable was the hangout of the young sports of the towns. Men and boys knew the bloodlines of horses as now they know the various makes of automobiles.

It seemed a dying sport but it never did quite die and now it is coming to life again. Go in the winter to the Old Glory horse sale, held in New York City, where the yearlings from the big Hanover Shoe Farms and from other big breeding farms are brought in for sale. They will be coming up also from many big and little breeding establishments, buyers there from small towns all over the country, a few rich men, many of the small-town well-to-do class, what we have learned recently to call "the middle class." They will be also at the big Indianapolis sale and at the fall sale of yearlings from Walnut Hall near Lexington during the Lexington Trots, in late September.

They are in the show-ring at one of the big sales. There is a man on a pony leading a yearling around the ring. The pony goes at a furious gallop. The man cries out. The colt is on a halter, at his galloping pony's heels. The man shouts. He gives wild cries. He cracks a long whip over the colt's head.

"You see—he is bred right, eh," he is saying to the colt buyers. "Look how naturally he sticks to the trot or pace."

"He is a good one, boys. Buy him and own a winner."

It goes on and on, man's love of the horse. The automobile threatened to kill it, wipe it out, but didn't succeed. For a long time, after the automobile came, when the barns that used to stand back of almost every house in the towns began to be torn down or turned into garages, it looked as though a special breed of horsemen, the drivers and owners of trotters and pacers, might die out and what many men had thought the noblest and most beautiful of all forms of sport, be forgotten.

Forgotten also the time when the rich city man, living but a few blocks from his office, still felt he had to own a good one or a team of good ones, the time when you could see a horse race almost any day, down through a residence street of an American town or city, when after a snowfall, horsemen of the towns got their best ones out for a sleigh race down through the main street. No red and green stoplights for them. A country lawyer, a saloonkeeper, a doctor, each up behind his own fast one, the main street cleared of farmers' teams, men and boys standing in crowds on the sidewalks before the stores, all business suspended for the time. The quiet-seeming country doctor has become like a wild man now. He is holding the lines over a big gelding that has been to the races and won't break no matter how much noise the doctor makes. He plans to throw that little mare the lawyer is driving off his stride, and so wild cries come from his lips and he slashes his long whip back and forth over his gelding's head.

It is fun, horse fun, man's fun. The country doctor as he drives visiting his patients from house to house along country roads has trained his gelding not to be annoyed by his cries and his whiplashings. The big gelding knows the game. He half turns his head waiting for the little mare to go into a "break."

Even the preachers indulged in it sometimes, although a preacher had to be careful. If he went off to one of the big sales and bought himself a yearling and had the fun of training him, seeing him get a little more and a little more into his stride, if he began to dream of seeing his horse in a race at county-fair time, he had to take him to a professional horse trainer and driver.

"Jim, you understand that, as far as the public is concerned, he is your horse. It wouldn't do for me to send a horse into a race and if you do send him in, it's on your own. You understand?"

"Sure I understand, preacher."

"Preacher, he sure looks like a comer to me."
There were farmers who got what was called the "horse
craze." Such a one sold his farm and moved into town. He bought
some colts and opened a training stable. He trained on the half-
mile dirt track up at the town's fairground. He might be a young
man whose father had died and left him a good farm and
everyone said he was a fool to let a good farm go for the horse-
racing game.

However he had a dream. He had his heroes. He dreamed of
someday becoming an Ed Greer, known far and wide as "The
Silent Man from Tennessee," a Walter Cox, a Budd Doble. The
trot and the pace were American insitutions like baseball, highly
technical, fast, exciting. Almost every man along the main street
of an American small town knew the fine points of the game. It
had its heroes, known to all, its Babe Ruths among race-horse
drivers, its Jimmy Foxxes, its DiMaggios. The fast trotter had
been an American development and all the world champions had
been born and trained here. When the Europeans wanted to get
really good ones they had to come here. The Czar of Russia and
the Grand Dukes sent their buyers. Buyers came from the kings
and princes of many lands. Some of our famous drivers and
trainers went to drive and train in Europe.

It was a time when all men were close to the horse. It was true
that the run was the faster gait, the gait a horse naturally took
when pressed to extreme speed, but the American always did love
technique. Look what we have done to football and to baseball. At
the trot or pace, there is something controlled. You are held
within a certain definite technique, as when a poet writes a
sonnet. I remember when one day I took a young man, a horse
lover, son of an old-time trotting-horse man, to see a trotting
race, at a time when the harness horse seemed on his way out.
The young man did not understand or see how skillfully one of
our well-known harness-horse drivers tooled his horse through
the stretch, pressing him to the last possible inch of speed at the
gait and not overpressing to throw him off his stride. The boy
could not understand because he knew only the saddlers and the
runners. I wanted to weep not only for my friend's son but for all

sons born in an age when what had seemed the finest
developments of the horse ever known was passing out.

But it has not passed. Now it comes to life again. Now we have
the Hamiltonian, named for old Hamiltonian 10, whose blood
runs down through almost every horse, trotter or pacer, going to
the harness races today, a big forty-, fifty-, sometimes even sixty-
thousand-dollar race. It is a big race, in a sense we Americans
understand, big money involved, and it gets attention. The big
city newspapers send their sport writers to the race, the city men
turn out, whole pages in the sports section of the big city
newspapers are devoted to the race, a Peter Astra, the
Hamiltonian winner, Kentucky Futurity winner, owned by an
Ohio small-town doctor, gets his picture in the city newspapers.
Go among the people at Goshen on the day of the Hamiltonian
and you will find a vast majority of the crowd still small-towners
and farmers. It is their big day. The best of the new ones, the
coming champions, will be there. It is their kind of horse racing,
the kind they know and love.

And now harness-horse racing is adjusting itself to the
modern age. It is not only that they step faster and faster every
year, dozens of good ones down now well below the two-minute
mark, great horses, like the Greyhound and Billy Direct stepping
miles that would have seemed unbelievable to the men of the
horse-and-buggy age, a new one like Peter Astra likely, before he
retires to the stud, to go faster even than the Greyhound or Billy
Direct, new men, Doc Parshall, Sep Palin, Vic Fleming, Ben
White, to take the place of the Coxes, Greers and Dobles of
another day, but there is also a sharp stepping up of the getaway
going on.

It was the scoring for the start that too much annoyed the
modern harness-horse racegoer although it did not annoy the
people of the horse-and-buggy age. The horses went up to the
head of the homestretch and turning scored down for a fair start.
There were numbers drawn and the pole horse, on the inside of
the track, was to lead the way. If another horse scored down ahead
of him or a horse went into a break, leaped into a run, it was no go
and had to be done over again, sometimes, five, ten, even twelve
or fifteen times, the starter scolding the drivers, we in the crowd

sitting patiently, each driver trying to get the advantage of the start, sometimes a driver fined, it all, we felt, a science too, the drivers striving to outwit the starter, but to the modern race-goer, knowing horse racing for the most part only at the running tracks, it was all too slow.

Starting machinery is being introduced now, to get the horses off quickly. Bigger and bigger crowds are coming again to the harness races.

And there is something else. The man who owns a trotter or a pacer can, if he has the gift, if he loves the feel of the lines held over a good one, get up behind him himself. It isn't at all necessary, as with the running horse, to turn him over to some slip of a boy. All the thrills may come to any man, a horse lover, who can feel himself, as the harness-horse race driver may, a part of the horse at speed, controlling him, handling him, timing him to get out of him the last inch of speed. The harness-horse man can, if he wishes and has the courage, the nerve, the gift of the hands holding the reins, get up there himself. It is this fact that is drawing them back. The little owners are again going to the yearling sales. Horsemen, who can afford to own big stables, the Harrimans, the Dunbar Bostwicks and other rich men are buying fast ones. They can get up there themselves, know the feel of the horse, know in their own bodies the curious accord that sometimes grows between man and horse. Women who have the horse passion can do it. In '37 at the Lexington Trots, held in late September, a slip of a girl of eleven, Miss Alma Sheppard, daughter of Lawrence Sheppard, trainer at the Hanover Shoe Farms, took the three-year-old trotter, Dean Hanover, out on the tracks and with him smashed the three-year-old's records, doing the mile in 1.58½. With the modern bike sulky the weight of the driver doesn't matter too much. He isn't up there on the horse's back. What matters is something in the driver's hands, in his head, in his nerves. He doesn't have to hand the game over to a boy, stand aside. He can get up there, behind his horse, the racing flanks of his horse, his pride and joy, between his legs, be in it, a part of it.

This is the fact that, in the end, will surely more and more bring horse-loving men back again to the harness horse and to harness-horse racing.

Little People and Big Words

O N my farm in Virginia is a man who has been there, as farmer, for twelve years. He works hard, trying to make the farm pay its own way. I live there in the summer and wander around America in the winter. I meet a good many people of the so-called artist class—authors, musicians, poets, painters. Mostly, I have found, they are very sour on life.

They think that civilization is going to pieces. Things are not right with our country nor with the world. I gather that of course none of this is their own fault. It is the fault of the people, they say; the people, who are too dumb.

I think all this would be of no importance except that from these men and women come the books and articles that people read. So they influence the thinking of others.

These writers and poets and painters seem to be in a terrible hurry. I find that they do not have much time to make acquaintances outside their own circle. So they can never understand the people of whom they complain. The people are "the masses." They dismiss them with a word.

Not long ago I was walking with a friend along crowded city streets. For an hour he talked of himself, of what a terrible problem life was to him. Civilization, he said, was falling into chaos. Why? He used vague words, "People are too stupid." He spoke of "the people," but he did not mean the hundreds of individuals who passed us as we walked, for he was not aware of them. His ears were filled only with the sound of his own complaint.

We passed a boy and girl and I heard her saying: "You don't want to worry. There've been things worse than this before. We're going to come out all right. Why, if things were all right all the time, we'd never appreciate it!" I saw her smiling at him. The boy's frown changed and I saw him smiling back at her.

"These dumb masses," my friend said, making a sweeping gesture. He had seen nothing but what he had been thinking in his head. "Like cattle! How can you make them understand?"

Another friend of mine is a young poet. I took him with me once to spend an evening with a certain family. They are what is called "middle class." They had heard that my friend was a poet, and so they were a little overawed. For a while conversation did not go easily.

A boy of perhaps 20 came by to visit one of the daughters. He stood waiting for her and he seemed embarrassed, talking too loudly and saying things he did not mean. After he and the girl had gone out together, I was told that they had been sweethearts from childhood, but that lately the girl had been attracted to an older man with a successful business. The mother favored the older man, but the father liked the boy. The girl's sister favored the boy too. "She wouldn't be happy with Tommy," the mother said. "I don't want to see any more unhappiness."

The girl's sister got up and excused herself; she was smiling, but I saw that her face was strained. "I shouldn't have said that," the mother said. Then I learned that the man this other daughter had been going to marry had suddenly gone insane. She was herself nearly half insane with grief. But she had been sitting there with us, covering up her grief, smiling, talking, trying to come back to normal.

"She'll get over it," the father said. "It's hard for her now, but she won't let it beat her."

When we left, my friend the poet asked me what I saw "in dull middle-class people like that."

These are the words we hear—"the masses," "the middle class," "the capitalists." Thousands of men working in the great factories, one word, "the masses," makes them all the same, pigeonholed and dismissed. The people who use the word do not see the lines on their faces; they are not aware of the ideas, the problems the emotions that make these thousands of faces, these thousands of lives each one different from the other, each with its own strivings and ambitions, its sorrows and joys.

"The people are stupid." But there is no such thing as "the people." There is instead the individual. He can be put into this "class" or that "class," but he does not know it. He remains himself, a man or woman shaping his life, living an adventure, striving for happiness, for decency. He knows so well that he will die for it, if need be. The good fights have never been fought and won by those who use the big empty words and find "the people" dull.

I used to talk with a woman who worked at a machine in a factory. Her husband was dead; there were two children at home to support. She was not a machine that guided another machine. Her children were going to school; she read their schoolbooks and taught herself through her children's minds. She talked of the machine she worked at. "It is a wonderful thing," she said. "My boy knows how it is made, and he taught me. Some day he is going to make a better machine. I think that is the idea of America. It says, 'Here! There are things to do, things to make better. No one is holding you back. You go out, all you young ones, and learn, and work, and make things better.'"

She was a part of "the masses." Her life was not dull. Her life was joy and adventure.

I spoke of the farmer on my place. He has been struggling for years to improve the half-worn-out soil of my farm. He gains a little, year by year. That poor soil is a living thing to him, a sick thing that he is nourishing and helping back to health. He is a man of few words, but occasionally he talks of what he thinks about.

Once in a while when I have been listening for too long to the big thinkers, I go out to the barn where he is perhaps milking a cow. I talk with him and my mind clears of the big words I have heard, all the complaints and questionings. "This is 'the people,'" I think as I listen to him. "This is what is so ordinary and commonplace." And I wish that I had my friends with me, to listen too. The farmer is talking to me of his life, of the soil he nourishes, of an idea that came to him out in the fields the other day. Then he talks of the people in the neighborhood. The son of the family down the road has come back from an agricultural college, and he has a lot of new ideas. His father pretends to be dubious, and they argue, but behind his son's back he says to the other farmers, "You ought to come and listen to my boy." And the young man nearby, who married the girl no one thought much of, the girl he found in the city; well, it seems he broke his leg and couldn't work, and this girl got out and did the work, and took care of him too. It seems she is a fine girl, after all.

The farmer tells me all this. He makes me aware, if I had never been aware before, that each individual's life is a world of its own. It may be a very little world, compounded of things that would be of no importance elsewhere; but it is separate, it is individual, it has its own color and adventure.

That is the answer to those who say "the masses," "the classes," who use the words that mean nothing. They do not see beneath the big empty words to what is right next to them, to what is all around them, to the individuals who are "the people," to the adventure of their days, the ever-varied texture of their lives, the dreams and hopes that, slowly, they work to make into reality. The words are dead, empty and bitter; "the people" are unaware of them, for the people are alive.

The Times and the Towns

New Orleans, A Prose Poem
in The Expressionist Manner

C ADDY Smith's got her some new gloves—brown ones.
Well, you take a tall one like that and she scatches a lot.

Want a drink?
When you go in the place what you say is—"give me
Commercial". Then you'd better watch out. If he pulls the
woodside tap it's OK. Look out for the riverside tap. That's
slop—pure slop. They hand a lot of that out. It's these tourists.
That's what you got to give 'em. You can't take chances. O'Leary
took a chance and where is he now?
You take a town like New Orleans and it aint never been
boomed none, to speak of.
They used to have bugs down here, so thick you had to cut your
way through. Did you ever have the bone fever? They used to
have sewers right in the streets. They got 'em moved now. It's a
good town all right.

Them millionaires run in herds. You got to get 'em headed
your way. We aint ever had no good cowboys down here.
A town like now Los Angeles, or Miami or this Coral Gables is
a turning round place. You can't stand the gaff. You go in. Then
you turn around and come out. What t'ell.

Drifting slow music, quickening now and then—sometimes.
On Decatur Street, down by the French market, they been singing

a song called, "shake that thing", for months now. A lot of songs start down there, near the river in New Orleans. Then they go North into the big time. Soda clerks and bank clerks get to singing. Then the road houses up North get busy.

Songs get worn out pretty fast.

You take a song now, or anything that starts in New Orleans. It has to go North doesn't it? There aint anything but water and swamps South. You can't do nothing on water.

If you want it warm you can get it as warm in New Orleans as any place in this world. You tell a lot of them boomers that. But wait—maybe it aint very good propaganda. Maybe they want it cold. I don't like it cold myself but some do. Some say blondes is usually cold. I wonder.

Its cold here sometimes all right. You never see so much rain. Everybody huddled in doorways. A lot of people get the wrong idea of New Orleans. "The city care forgot." They don't like that stuff much up to the Chamber of Commerce. They want you worried.

A lot of young people, male and female, get all fired up about books they want to write, pictures they want to paint. They come down here and get rooms. Such a lot don't do a town no good. They got sore because no one pays any attention to them.

Why should they? People been doing that to New Orleans a hundred years now.

This New Orleans civilization aint no intellectual civilization.

Its bedrocked in ships, in song, in the Mississippi River.

Its a way down south town, this town is.

The South always did hoe its own row—off'en Canal Street, in New Orleans. Little towns South don't change much, side streets in New Orleans don't change much.

It would make you sick if you're the up-and-coming kind. You never saw such paving, politics pretty rotten, I guess. You never smelled such smells, saw more dirt, shiftlessness. Good gravy!

On Burgundy Street in New Orleans, during carnival time, a brown girl sitting back of an old heavy wooden blind. Headline out of a northern newspaper tacked on the blind outside. "Kip's gone back to Alice." It's a pretty wide-open town all right.

Carnival went off good O.K. The Mayor was dead and Ring Lardner came down. Prominent citizen falls off a float. Lots of northern money in town. The antique men on Royal Street did good.

Niggers cut loose better than ever. Gangs of them in all the little side streets, singing, dancing, joy in the air. They ran into houses and pulled out other niggers—sometimes by the hair.

"Shake that thing. I'm getting tired of telling you to—shake that thing."

A few whites wandering aimlessly in the black streets—wanting to dance.

On Canal Street the big show going on. A pretty good show this year, they tell me.

On side streets, hidden away, something you maybe won't see again in this life.

I'm going to tell you it won't last long. New Orleans is a swell town. It can be put on the map and it will be too. Its in the air now. Better invest some money down here.

Better get to New Orleans some carnival time soon. Beat the boomers here if you can. Bring some money with you. A lot of us down here need money. We'll like you better if you bring it down.

The end of New Orleans—the old town, the sweet town, is already in sight.

As I told you, right at the beginning, Caddy Smith's got her some new brown gloves.

A tall girl like that has to scratch a lot. I told you that.

What I didn't tell you was how nice her eyes are.

You got to find that out for yourself.

Chicago—A Feeling

FEAR. Something huge—not understandable. How can I write of Chicago without putting myself in? How can I write of anything without putting myself in? My egotism is my weakness and my strength. I was little more than a boy when I first went to Chicago. There are streets thirty miles long—perfectly flat. Buildings and houses you dream about—distorted dreams.

You must see the background. It lies where the long tongue of the Great Lakes reaches farthest down into the land. A low black swampy place—a wind-riven land.

To the east, reaching up, Michigan. To the west Wisconsin, Minnesota, the northwest.

To the south land, flat like a billiard table—fat land. No such corn-land anywhere else in the world. Innumerable droves of fat sleek hogs, eating the corn. Cattle off the dry western lands, coming in lean and bony, getting fat and sleek, eating corn.

Carl Sandburg, Edgar Lee Masters, Clarence Darrow.

Railroads coming—all the real railroads—mills, factories.

Men, men, men!

At first when, as a boy, I went to Chicago, nothing to do but get drunk as often as I could. It was too big for me—too terrible. Could people live in such streets, in such houses?

They could and did. I could and did.

At first I was a labourer. Then the shrewder side of me came to the fore. Men have always liked me first rate when they came to

161

know me. It may be because I like men. I began to sell men things—write advertisements, sling ink. Thousands, untold thousands, doing it. Some getting lots of money, others not much. I never got such a lot.

Hope—hopelessness.

If you have only seen the famous Michigan Boulevard, the North Shore, Lincoln Park, Jackson Park you do not know Chicago. Why talk?

There is the huge northwest, the west, the south.

Millions of people of all nationalities packed in close, packed in among slaughter houses, factories, mills.

Long stretches of vacant lots. Five, six and eight storied apartment buildings, standing in the midst of acres of black weeds—wind-riven—a lot of them.

Brutal murders going on. Everything unfinished.

Other cities getting all puffed up with feelings of civic virtue when they think or speak of Chicago.

Leopold and Loeb.

Nonsense.

I remember nights when I walked the streets of Chicago—half drunk, hopeless—swimming in a sea of ugliness.

Then suddenly—a glimpse of the Chicago River—that great sewer. A sewer nothing. You wait. The Chicago River will some day become one of the lovely rivers of the world of cities. It is unbelievably beautiful sometimes—from the bridges—the gulls soaring above, the strange, lovely cryptogramic, chrysoprase river—cries, oaths.

Something vital in Chicago. So many people in one great flat place where a real city had to be. A huge place—unformed. Not in the least like New York, Boston, Philadelphia, Baltimore.

Besides it Cleveland and Detroit are villages—grown suddenly to look like cities.

Railroads everywhere, boats crowded in the narrow river, smoke, dirt—a climate so terrible in its extremes of heat and cold that only strong people can survive—to really be alive.

Chicago has been from the first—will always be, while the land lasts—a real city. It is a real city, like New York, London, Paris.

A real city does not care too much what you, a mere man, think of it. "Here I am. Go to hell."

Los Angeles, Cleveland, Seattle, such places give themselves
away too much. They are whistling in the dark.

A city has to have something back of it. Land, a lot of it. Rich
land—corn, wheat, iron, rivers, mountains, hogs, cattle. Chicago
has back of it the Middlewest—the empire called Mid-America.
Corn, hogs, wheat, iron, coal, industrialism—a new age moving
across a continent by railroads, moving unbelievable quantities of
goods across a vast place, in the centre of which stands Chicago.

Through Chicago. You'll be routed that way—going most
anywhere.

Chicago being what it wants to be, what it grew to be. Chicago
unformed. Who can tell what it will be?

There is something terrible about the making of every great
city and Chicago is still making. When is is made it will not be
another New York, Paris, London. It will be Chicago. Here I am.
Go to hell. It was the city of my own young manhood—when I
first began to comprehend, faintly, what differentiates the great
city from the overgrown town.

Cities are almost as distinct, as individuals as nations, trees,
hills, people.

Chicago is terrible—it is at moments beautiful in a way you
only understand when you have lived there a long time.

When you have been drunken and hopeless there, when you
have been sick of it to the marrow, when you have accepted
Chicago, then, at last, walking hopeless, endless streets—yourself
hopeless—you begin to feel its half wild beauty.

Then at last the city you have so dreaded and feared has done
something to you that makes it—no matter where you afterward
live—your city.

I was a young man in Chicago, almost a boy there. There I saw
the first woman who rejected me—felt what men feel when they
are so rejected. There I first made ink flow, sang my first song.
There after many efforts, I wrote a sentence I could bear reading
the next day.

There I first heard sounds of men's voices—related to streets,
houses, cities—saw my first real actor walk upon a stage, heard
music first, saw painting.

I wrote a song once, long ago, I called the song *Industrialism*,
but what I really had in mind was *Chicago*.

"In the long hours of hate,
In the never-ending days,
Over the fields—her black hair flying—
My mistress
Terrible
Gigantic
Gaunt and drear

I've got to die—you've got to die. We do not fancy your thin hands
that reach and reach into the vase.
Where old things rust.

Death to you now.
Thin dream of beauty,
You be gone.
Our fathers, in the village streets, had flowing beards and they
believed.
I saw them run into the night—
Crushed.
Old knowledge and all old beliefs
But your hand killed—
My mistress
Grim.

Awake and shake thy dusy locks.
Come drive the soldiers to their toil
A million men my mistress needs, to kiss
And kill

For her desire,
Tonight—
Arise."

When I visit any other great city of the world I am a guest. When I am in Chicago I am at home. Something loose, unformed, undisciplined alive in Chicago is in me too. It is a little what I am. I am more than a little what Chicago is. No man can escape his city.

I am not proud of it. Chicago will not be proud. It is a real city— my city.

Take it, or leave it.
There it is.
And, God helping me, here am I.

The Far West

DEAR Monte: Memories of Joaquin Miller. He went to London, they say, and smoked two cigars at once. As I understand the matter he had cigars stuck in both corners of his mouth. Also he wore big cowhide boots and a wide western hat. He went to literary dinners in London outfitted like that. It made his everlasting reputation. The English thought he was just lovely. Nothing helps a writer over here like getting a London recognition.

Do you remember, Monte, when we were both advertising writers in Chicago? When the president of our agency got drunk he used to shake his long finger under our noses and declare Joaquin Miller the greatest poet that ever lived. He always recited *Columbus* when he was in his cups. You will remember how his voice trembled and sometimes, when he was a little more than ordinarily lit, the tears would come into his eyes.

"Sail on, and on and on," Oh boy!

I understand that in San Francisco they get twenty-five cents for showing you where the poet sat when he did it. I may be wrong. It may be fifty cents. I didn't go.

Bret Harte lit out for London too. I can remember seeing pictures of him when I was a boy. He dressed very carefully and looked like a very proper old English gentleman, sitting in a club. For some reason, on the coast, they do not make the fuss over Bret Harte they do over Miller and Stevenson.

167

R.L.S. is their chief pride. They mark down every bench he sat on, every tree he leaned against. "Here leaned Robert Louis Stevenson. May his soul rest in peace", etc., etc.

I have been on the coast for a year and a half now and have been intending writing you for a long time. Now I am on a train cutting out for New Orleans. There is a man from the Middle West has the berth above me. He has heart disease and dared not stay on the coast for fear there would be an earthquake. He's wrong. They don't have earthquakes out there. Ask anyone on the coast.

The man says California is in for a big boom again. Ten years ago he went to Florida, near Miami I think, and bought a farm. He hung on and hung on and in this last big Florida boom cleaned up. He took the money he got and bought land in California. In the long run, he says, people will be less scared by earthquakes than hurricanes. Hang on and on and on. He says the American people have got to go somewhere, have got to be on the move. They'll surge back westward pretty soon now. Where do you think the man on the train lives while he is waiting to make these clean-ups? In Chicago. He told me so himself.

At first, just after I saw you and when I lit out for the Far West, I was around the desert states. I went to Phoenix and Reno and Goldfield and Virginia City. We went from a place called Carson City in Nevada to Goldfield in a car. There were two men with shares in mines to sell, a dentist, a doctor and myself. They took me because I was a writer. You know how it is. If you are a writer, business-men, fellows who have mine shares to sell and real estate men will take you anywhere. They think you'll write about your trip. "It's publicity," they say, "there's nothing like publicity."

The ride down over the desert was something never to be forgotten. What looks like just a long dip between two hills is thirty miles across. You come to little towns—not a soul living there any more—empty houses standing just as they were when the miners walked out—mining machinery lying about.

There is a place that used to be a saloon and hotel. The stage coaches stopped there. The mining men in the car with us talking of old times. They used to haul the ore from Goldfield over the desert hundreds of miles to get it to a railroad. At Goldfield the ground rotten with gold. When the miners left the job at night— three, four, even five hundred dollars concealed in their pockets. They called it "high-grading" the mine owners.

Jim Corbett, Jack Johnson, Tex Rickard, George Winfield of Reno. A dozen other great names of the western flush days murmured in my ears as the car went at thirty miles an hour over the desert sand roads—seemingly getting nowhere. When we had at last achieved the top of a hill, towards which we had been flying for an hour, there was another, just like it and also thirty miles away. Imagine the long roll of the sea, wave tops thirty miles apart. You've got it.

Occasionally, during the day, we stopped the car and got out to stretch. At one place, I remember, we came to a house standing in the very middle of one of the long dips. Sage brush and yellow sand. Not a tree in sight. A man lived there who writes cowboy stories. There was a fenced space back of the house and five cows in it. I gathered that they, and the lonely life out there, were for the sake of local colour. He did not tell me so. What he did was to reach under the house and pull out a bottle of whiskey. Apparently he wanted us to stay. When I was introduced as another writer he looked at me with questioning eyes. I had never heard of him or he of me.

Into my ears always being poured the tales of the past. Rawhide, Bowie, Virginia City, bad men with guns, vigilance committees, streets of mining towns filled with millionaries, two hundred thousand lost at faro in an evening. What the hell! Who cares?

The states of Nevada, Arizona, Idaho, New Mexico without enough people left in them to make a respectable suburb for an eastern city.

Everything happened so long ago. I'm not an old man. It happened when I was a boy and when I was growing up. That day on the desert in the car all the men of our party whispered me the same story. "When you go on west, over the mountains, to San Francisco and Los Angeles, you'll hear big tales. You'll hear what men have done out there. Where did they get the money to do it with?" Men standing on the desert and waving arms toward dimly seen distant mountains. "They got it out of these hills, every cent of it. Then they left us flat."

All the men of the desert states clinging to the notion that, if someone would make just one big strike, it would all happen over again. They have to cling to something I suppose. They can't farm.

Goldfield—the strangest American town I ever visited. We got there in the evening and put up at a big hotel. There had been a fire,—half the town swept away. It would never be rebuilt. Most of the houses empty anyway. The hotel, a huge ruined place that had once housed hundreds of millionaires, where crowds gathered for world championship prize fights, with a bar as long as Hinky Dink's in Chicago when we worked together in that town, tiled dining room floor—a good many of the tiles fallen out—the hotel housing perhaps three guests.

A few men standing about in the big lobby. They were dressed like stage mining men. I had a hunch the movies were responsible for that. Not a man of them had put a pick into the ground for years.

Waiting for easterners with capital to invest. Our party created a little furore. When I was shown to my room on the third floor it seemed to me that empty rooms were stretched away for miles and miles in all directions.

Later I came down into the hotel lobby and was buttonholed by mining men. The dentist and I escaped. It was dark and we walked aimlessly about and got into a street of prostitution. Worn out old prostitutes waiting to buttonhole. Two or three of them came out of a house and stood staring at us under a street lamp. "My God—easterners." Hope in old bleary eyes. The good days come again. We might be investors.

It is what I have been wanting to write to you about, Monte— my impression of the Far West.

Time, space, everything a little out of proportion for me.

I get it that everything that has happened out on the coast has come in long surges like the crests of the hills you run toward— out on the flat sage bush deserts. Everywhere else in the country things moved more slowly. The east was settled slowly—people coming over in sailing vessels in the old days. When we were boys in the Middle West old people used to talk about the trip over. It took thirty days sometimes. They settled in New England and the eastern states and their sons came on out into our country. They were all farmers, looking for cheap land—a place to settle down in, to stay in. In the South the same thing happened. Cotton raising with slave labour was hard on the land. All right. Plenty of new rich cheap land west. Down South you hear stories of the grand trek westward, into Mississippi, Alabama, Arkansas, Texas. The old baron and his family on horseback or in carriages, long lines of wagons, slaves, cattle, pigs, even chickens working their way westward, often not more than four or five miles a day.

The west coast far away—outside the picture. Spaniards and Mexicans lived out there. Read again Dana's *Two Years Before the Mast*.

Then the gold rush. That brought in the young blood with a bang. It's a pretty dull book and full of bad jokes, but Mark Twain's *Roughing It* does give a good picture of what life was like out there then. I read it again while I was on the coast.

What you get is a sense of the rest of the country as something too far away. How can they help that feeling creeping in? Even now, on the best trains, you get the feeling. It's like going abroad. The desert is like the sea. Imagine what it must have been like to the crowd that surged over it looking for gold. If they went by sea it was just as far, just as difficult. The dream in every man's breast to get out there, dig out a few millions in gold and get back east— "back to the states", they used to say.

In Los Angeles an Italian boy was shining my shoes. "How's things in the old country?" he asked. A questioning look in my eyes. He explained. "New York's the old country to us wops out here," he said.

That first masculine surge of people into the country passed and there was a quiet time. Then they found and put on the market another kind of gold—golden sunshine.

That got of course a different kind of crowd—more respectable—not so full of pep. It got the old ones, the sick ones—people who wanted to retire, people who wanted to sit all day in the golden sunshine. It isn't exactly the finest kind of people to bring into a country, small retired merchants from the

Middle West, retired farmers. They live in bungalows. You know nothing grows out there unless you bring water to it. If you can get the water anything will grow. We, of the East and the Middle West have this notion—put into our minds by the advertisements—of a sea of roses stretching away in all directions as far as the eye can see. What stretches away is brown sun-burned hills—more beautiful than seas of roses could ever be, I think.

The ugly thing is the bungalows dropped down all over the hills. They are the ugliest things the brain of man ever dreamed and all filled up with retired people. Nothing to do. Lord what a life.

San Francisco is something. It is a really beautiful town with its sweet hills and its cold crisp air. Often heavy fog rolling in from the sea. The bay there is the most magnificent thing I've seen in my wanderings.

I went up north to Portland and Seattle. Rain, a cold fog, great hills, great trees. The people seemed too small. They hadn't touched it yet and I could get no sense of them. I guess they haven't been there long enough. I like an old country, old houses, old streets. Chicago, when we lived there together, was always too new for me. I like a country into which people have come because they needed to come to make a living, where they intend to stay. Then I like to get there after they have stayed. I presume all that northwestern coast country needs staying with.

Down south it's something else. It was all rather grand to me. Los Angeles seemed a gaudy madhouse. All the strange hopeful people of the Middle West who had money enough must have gone there looking for paradise. No lack of energy down south. The days roll up with endless sameness. Every day in Los Angeles is just like circus day in the small Middle Western towns. That's where they've got the sunshine, the movies, the oranges. That's where they know how to sell town lots. Every day when I was in Los Angeles I woke up thinking—"Today it will blow up, deflate." It didn't. I half believe it never will. Such a mad town you never dreamed of. Wide streets, more automobiles than you ever saw, even on Fifth Avenue, in Hollywood—really a suburb—

people going about dressed as Christ, Julius Caesar, Ivan the
Terrible. In Los Angeles, women dodging out of doorways. One
of them hails you. She looks like a New England school-
mistress—lean, energetic, determined. "Is that woman going to
solicit me? I'm lost", you think. She's only an agent for a real
estate company. You're all right after all. She wants you to go on a
free excursion, ride in an automobile, have lunch at her expense.

Los Angeles taught Florida how to do it and when it looked as
though Florida might outdo the land of sunshine they discovered
oil. The city seemed to me the top, the very peak of everything
industrial America means. It is sanitary, it is alert, it grows and it
sure does advertise.

And after that, to top things off, I went to Tia Juana.

Flash men of all the world, gamblers, touts—all the old worn-
out racing men come to life again. I saw old sports I thought were
ready to die when I was a sport myself—some twenty years ago.
The easy picking had brought them back to life again. I can't write
about Tia Juana. It would take a book.

After that the train for home. Home for me means most
anywhere east of the deserts. I could never feel at home out there.

I'm in the desert as I write. It stretches away like the sea. It may
be just the desert between the coast and the rest of the country
that makes it seem so far off.

Well, I started to give you my impressions of the Far West.
There it is, I cannot think of it without thinking of the deserts and
the mountains. When I was a boy the school books called it, "The
Great American Desert". It separates the Far West from the rest
of the country, separates the Far West from us. People out there
deny the feeling but I'm sure they have it. They feel out of the
circle, too far away. It leads to an overvaluation of the East and
Eastern men. As I said in the beginning things get out of
proportion.

It wants something that will, I presume, come. Los Angeles is a
city built for the automobile, whereas all of our Eastern and
Middle Western cities were built for the horse. It may be the
whole Pacific Coast is but waiting for the airplane to come into its
own. There are no deserts and mountains in the air.

Just now the Far West wants something to take away the feeling of being too much outside. The whole west coast civilization may be but a thrust into the future.

It is outside all right. That shoe-shiner in Los Angeles expressed something that—whether they are ready to admit it or not—the whole west coast feels.

"How's things in the old country?" you'll remember he asked.

And then the explanation.

"New York's the old country to us wops out here."

It isn't only New York.

Everything east of the mountains and deserts becomes the "old country" when you're out on the coast.

Small Town Notes

PEOPLE everywhere are up to all sorts of little subterfuges to get through life. City people are not so different from people on farms or in small towns. Few people can be, in themselves, beautiful or feel any beauty or splendour in themselves. They have to create a role for themselves and then try to play it. Most people are drab. There is no colour. They lead drab lives, wear drab clothes, live in drab houses, make drab marriages. There is a kind of terror in the contemplation of drabness coming on.

If you live in any small town you see people often. In the city an endless procession of new faces. In a town the same faces seen day after day.

There is a lawyer in a town in Illinois who is getting old. He belongs to the church and leads outwardly a quiet, orderly life.

In secret he has in his desk, in his rather shabby office, a number of pictures of young and lovely actresses. Sometimes, when there is no one about, he takes them out and looks at them. It is rather heart-breaking to think of the man, who is now so old that his hands tremble, sitting in that place and running through his photographs. I shall never forget the shabbiness of his office, seen once on a summer afternoon as I sat waiting to speak with him. Everything in his office is sharply remembered and will be remembered as long as I live. By an accident he had left a drawer of his desk a little open.

Not that I wouldn't have opened it had I known what was there. I am altogether unscrupulous in my desire to know such things about people.

2

My own father was a small town man. He came into Ohio from North Carolina when he was a young man. It may be that his family, like so many Southern families, was ruined by the Civil War. I never have looked much into his past.

I am a little afraid it will not be as exciting as my fancy has made it. I would rather leave it as it is, as my own imagination has built it up.

It is very likely that my father's marriage was like most marriages. Any marriage must grow, at times, almost unbearably tiresome to both people involved. How could it be any other way?

It happens that I know something about my own father that is terribly revealing. All of his life he was a great reader of books.

At one time, in his early life, he got hold of a little book of verses. The verses were written by a woman. He kept them by him all the rest of his life.

He had never known the author, had never seen her. She lived in Cincinnati.

When he was a young man and before he married, father went once to Cincinnati to work. He may have hoped to find the woman. He had learned the harness maker's trade and worked there through a winter as a bench workman in a wholesale harness establishment.

This is what had happened.

You see he had got hold of the book of verses at a time when he was young and, I presume, eager for love. He wanted high romance. The verses were written by a Miss White and had been privately printed. Miss White must have been a rather neurotic young thing—if she was young.

Father had got hold of the book by accident, at a very impressionable time in his own life, and as the book called out very loudly for a handsome and noble young lover to come to Miss White out of some far, mysterious place, father had dramatized himself as coming.

It is nothing. How many times have I done the same sort of thing myself.

You see I have to thread my way rather carefully through this tale. It is all built on a single incident. Years later I found that little book of verses hidden over the sill of the door in a woodshed back of a house in which we once lived. I watched and once saw father go into the woodshed and close the door. I went and looked through a crack. Such an odd expression on father's face. There was something touching in the tender way in which he handled the book.

When father went to work in Cincinnati there was, in the same city, a family of some standing by the name of White. There was a Miss Ethel White who was quite lovely. The name of the woman who had written the book was "Ethel White."

Of course father got the two confused in his mind, wanted to get them confused. The Miss White in Cincinnati once had her picture in the society columns of a Cincinnati paper. Father cut it out and pasted it in the front of the book.

The Whites of Cincinnati lived in a grand house on a grand street. The young harness maker may have gone up that way sometimes to walk on Sunday afternoons. He may have seen Miss White drive up to her house in her carriage.

She was young and lovely and I am quite sure the woman who wrote the verses was not. When women are young and lovely they do not need to write verses.

Later my father got married, of course, and had a large family of children. He was in business for a time and then the business failed. Down he went on the social ladder. He became a house painter.

He clung however to his book of verses. It was on the sill over the door in the woodshed for a time and then it disappeared from there. Father was carrying it about in his pocket. He had handled it sometimes when his hands were covered with barn paint. The pages were badly soiled. After a time he did not read it. He merely liked to touch it with his fingers.

3

It is quite possible to see and feel life as you would a novel. The most adaptable man gets close to but few people. People everywhere are essentially lonely.

Now that I have come back to live in a small town I realize it all anew.

When I was a boy I lived in just such a town as I am in now. Well, that was a Northern town and this town is Southern.

Except the negroes, they are the same kind of people.

I remember as a boy I used to go about distributing newspapers. I was even then curious about people. You know how a boy likes short cuts.

I went through alleyways, climbed fences. The town became like a play to me. The drama unrolled slowly.

In the spring, fall and winter it was already dark when the train from Cleveland came in, bringing my evening papers. It took only a few minutes to run through Main Street and leave my papers there.

Then I began my trip through the streets and alleyways of the town.

What things did I not see. There is material for a hundred novels and stories stored away somewhere in my memory.

I became something of a jack-the-peeper. There was a woman working in a kitchen and talking to herself. People talking aloud to themselves leave a strange, uncanny impression on the mind.

There is something coming up out of the unconscious mind—listen.

On such occasions I used to creep close to the kitchen doors.

It may be the woman in there was just scolding. She thought some injustice had been done her.

She was having an imaginary conversation. "Now, I tell you, I have stood all I will stand. I work and work. What do I get out of life?

"Here I am, doing that man's cooking. I mend his clothes. He comes home here, eats his supper and then lights out up town."

The woman was thinking of the days of her girlhood. She had become a drab creature. On every street, of every city, long rows of houses and apartments filled with drab women. In towns the same sort of thing.

Drabness going on as a quality in life.

The drab woman does not think of herself so. The wife of a railroad section hand, working in her husband's kitchen, is thinking of her girlhood.

Sometime, for at least a night, say at a country dance, she, a young woman then, felt beauty and youth in herself. She clings to that.

And there was the time when she got married and was first made love to.

That may have turned out badly.

She clings to what she was. She is indignant that beauty did not stay in her.

She must blame someone.

After hearing such a woman talking to herself in a kitchen— standing by the kitchen door to listen—I slipped away.

In the darkness of the little street outside I met the labourer coming home, heavy footed. I hid behind a tree.

And there was the labourer also talking to himself.

The labourer goes into his house and sits heavily down to read his paper. I creep back to see what happens. The man and his wife merely eat in silence. If they have children, the children are frightened into silence.

4

There was a school teacher who never married. She lived with her mother in a little house at the edge of town. I used to go with my papers out to the end of a street and then cut through fields to another street and there, on a spring night, I saw the school teacher walking about in the fields.

She frightened me a little when I came upon her and afterwards she was afraid of what I might think of her.

She was afraid I would think she had gone into the field to meet some man.

One evening she kept me after school. It was hard for her to say what was on her mind. I was sitting at my desk in the schoolroom and she kept walking up and down. Tears came into her eyes.

She told me she had once met Christ in the field. First of all she made me promise to tell no one and then she told me that one evening—it was a spring evening she said and she had gone to bed. She said it was quite late. She was restless and could not sleep.

Suddenly she heard a voice calling her. The voice told her to get up and dress and go into the field. She said she did that and then something, a kind of inner voice, told her to lie down in the field.

She said she did lie down and that it was a bright, moonlit night, but at that moment a cloud passed across the face of the moon.

She closed her eyes and Christ appeared to her. She had always been hoping it would happen again but it never did. She said Christ was young and was dressed in a long white robe, and that he stepped so lightly that his feet barely bent the grass, and that he came quite close to her and touched her with his finger.

She opened her eyes then, had to, she said. The touch of Christ's finger had given her such an odd feeling. It had thrilled her through and through.

When she opened her eyes she saw the figure for a fraction of a second quite plainly and then, like a flash, it was blown away.

The Man at the Filling Station

A N odd place for him to be living. It was two or three miles out beyond the edge of one of the factory towns that are sprinkled over the flat prairies which cluster about Chicago.

So many railroads come into Chicago. They come from the East, the West and the South, around the end of the lake and across the flat places. In the evening when you walk across that flat country you see trains constantly coming and going, far away. On a summer evening the sun goes down red and hot over the edge of the floor.

In the winter it is desperately cold out there and on summer evenings the sunset is never quite clear. There is always smoke hanging in the air in the distance.

There is a factory building out on a flat low place, with swamps all about. No other building for a half mile. Then another mile of vacancy and you come to Bill's place.

Crowds of labouring men come out of the factory in the evening. They huddle together by a street car track. The street car seems to come from some far distant place like Africa or Asia. What I mean is that it seems to come as from across a long flat sea.

It is a sea of green swampy land with occasional yellow stretches of sand.

They have built cement highways through the swamps and across the flat low places. Motor cars filled with men, women and children come out of Chicago, and out of the terrible factory and mill towns about Chicago, and run across the flat land.

They are going East and West and South.

At night there is a flare of light against the sky from the steel mills at South Chicago perhaps.

A flare of lights against the sky and the sense of a great city, somewhere near at hand. The darkness of the long lonely stretches seems full of shadowy people sometimes.

You get to thinking of Chicago. People are always passing through there going east or west, north or south. It is a place of hundreds of thousands of unknown insignificant people. All great cities must be like that.

Bill was one.

I knew this man named Bill who had a gasoline filling station out there along one of the roads.

He sold gas and oil.

Then prohibition came. He did a bit of whiskey and beer selling.

I had got me a car and used to go out that way—to see the sun go down—to see the trains moving in the distance.

Back of Chicago the open fields—were you ever there? Trains coming toward you out of the West—streaks of light on the long grey plains.

If you go farther South or East or West the cornfields begin— huge long rich fields of corn. I used to get thoroughly sick of Chicago and drive at night until I could see the cornfields in the moonlight beside the road. Then I felt more at home.

On a farm at least a man is connected with something. He is connected with his piece of land. He has plowed there, cultivated, put seed in the ground, harvested.

There is his house and his barn, near the road, where the cornfields begin.

The house is white and the barn red. There are fruit trees near the house—a pig in a pen nearby.

You feel the man in the house, a little permanent, a part of something.

Bill had his red and white gasoline filling station, that was spick and span, and back of it hanging over the swamp was a little house, not so spick and span.

The foundations of the house were stuck down into the soft mud. There was no place for Bill's children to play but in the cement road in front.

Bill was a large, loose-jointed man with dark, romantic eyes, a tiny brown moustache and a loosely-knit strong body.

By the front door of his house back of the filling station and attached to the wall of his house was a glass show case.

It was such a show case as you see in small town stores.

While I was having my car filled one evening I went to look into the show case.

A Confederate ten dollar bill, a mummified mouse, a butterfly pinned to a card.

Some bullets from the World War, a Masonic button, a woman's cheap breast pin, a German picture postcard.

More of such junk. Heaps of it.

There were men standing about. They looked at me with suspicious eyes. Perhaps they were the customers who consumed Bill's bootleg whiskey and beer.

Bill's wife was surprisingly young and handsome. She looked like a gipsy. Often I used to see her sitting on the doorstep of her house, her legs spread wide apart, her hands on her hips.

Her children cried and fought in the road in front of the filling station. She paid no attention to them. She seemed to be staring into the West, to where the sun was just starting to go down.

Bill did that himself sometimes. Gradually I got acquainted with him.

One night I came to the filling station quite late. It had begun to rain and I had been running my car slowly for miles along the flat road. There was a light in Bill's house back of the filling station. The filling station itself was dark.

I stopped my car. Bill and his wife were having a fight. Just as I came up he struck her a blow. He knocked her down.

When he did that he came out in the road to me. "Well?" he said. Then he looked into the car and saw who it was. His wife was lying on the floor in the front room of his house. He had knocked her down there.

She got up and came and sat in the open doorway with the light at her back. She put her hands on her hips and spread her legs apart.

"Come, get out," Bill said to me. I pulled the car to the side of the road. I was in a mood and so was Bill. God knows, I may have been in love just at that time.

My notion of this adventure is mixed up in my mind with some idea of unrequited love.

A kind of aching hunger inside that sends you driving a car across flat places at night. And nothing for the hunger to feed on.

"Let's take a walk," Bill said.

We walked for miles straight across the flat land along a smooth flat road. The wind blew and it rained little spatters of rain. It may have been twelve o'clock at night when we got started.

Then Bill began telling me of his adventures. There was nothing very exciting. As a young man he had been to Mexico, he said. He said he had been a cow man in Mexico and in the Panhandle of Texas.

He spoke of Mexican women. "They are all right and easy to get," he said. We walked on in silence for a time after he said that. "God," he cried suddenly. The word came with a little explosive bang from between his lips.

Then he spoke of helping to build a railroad somewhere in Southwestern Missouri.

We just went along like that and Bill talked. When we came back from our walk out of the darkness and the rain, I pointed to the show case by the front door. "What's that stuff you have in there?" I asked. "Oh, it's just stuff. It's junk. I just picked it up. Everything's junk," he said.

He said he wanted to show me some snapshots he had had taken of himself when he was out West. He had scores of them. There were snapshots of Bill in Mexico, one, I remember, of him drunk—two Mexican women clinging to his arms.

There was one of Bill and an Indian woman standing together by a farm-house door. There were pictures of Bill on horseback, in cowboy togs—Bill leading a horse by a halter—Bill astride a horse driving cattle.

Bill standing on top of a mountain with his hat in his hand, the wind blowing through his hair. While we looked at the snapshots Bill's wife stood silently back of us looking over our shoulders.

I prepared to leave. Bill followed me to my car.

"Where did you get this woman?" I asked.

"Oh, in one of the factory towns out here," he said, pointing.

"I am having my kids by her," he said.

That seemed to Bill to explain Bill and so I drove away.

When I drove away, at perhaps two o'clock in the morning, Bill's wife was sitting on the doorstep of her house with the light shining over her shoulders. Her hands were on her hips and her legs were spread apart.

They may both have been waiting up—say, for a truck to come and bring them a new lot of their bootlegger's supplies.

Let's Go Somewhere

DEAR Charles:

It is a terribly serious lot of questions you have asked me. "Is the South to be industrialized?" "Am I trying to escape industrialism by living in the South?" "What am I up to down here?"

You must be careful, Charles. If you are not more careful you will be speaking to me of "the psychology of escape."

Only a few weeks ago I dined with a lady who spoke of "spiral evolution." My head snapped back. Do you know they even talk that way in the South sometimes nowadays. Young, intellectual negroes do it. Perhaps I am trying to escape the age of words. I have a dreadful fear of being psychoanalyzed by a psychoanalyst. On some nights I dream of these birds. One has got me cornered on West 8th Street in New York. I squirm and squirm but cannot escape. I tore a bed sheet to pieces trying to get away from one.

She was a female psychoanalyst, too. You understand this was in a dream.

The South! Your letter has stirred me, of course. Why, man, Virginia is not of the South, nor is North Carolina, Tennessee, Kentucky, Missouri, Oklahoma. If you want that you've got to go far down.

I do not know about Florida, have never been there yet but am going soon. Once, in Paris, on a cold bleak day Fred Frieseke, the painter, showed me some things he had done once when he was

far down somewhere on the Florida coast. He, that is to say
Frieseke, had been doing a lot of paintings of young girls and
women, as full of innocence as a picnic is full of bread. I wonder
why innocence tires me so. After ten minutes of it my bones
ached.

So Fred Frieseke got out these other things. They wouldn't sell,
he said. He knew that when he did them, so he had done them for
the pure fun of it. There was one, I remember sharply, of a stretch
of sand road. The sea was somewhere in the distance and there
was an old negro man struggling up along the road. A sense of the
vastness of seas and yellow sand stretching, and this old black
man in the midst of it—going God knows where. Something felt,
put down, a painter's job well done for once anyway.

So you want the South too, Charles. You want the warm sun,
cockroaches on the wall and in cracks, birds floating in a hot still
blue sky, that amazing, never-to-be-forgotten song of insect life
under your feet. At any rate I understand your mood. Chicago,
New York, Cleveland, Detroit, all of these cities are like clenched
fists. New Orleans and Mobile are like open hands. They will
never industrialize these cities quite. Life is too languid.

The sun shines down there, the rains are warm.

Mobile is a city few people know about. It is a sweet city. The
land up above is all red and three strong rivers come racing down
and pour into the bay.

The rivers wash the red earth down into the bay. I have seen
the bay of Mobile like blood. I tried to make a painting of it so, but
I can't paint much. You, who are a painter, know that.

> "There is a fountain filled with blood
> Flown from Emanuel's side."

I dare say Palm Beach and the other big swell places, down along
the Florida coast, are all right but a writer or a painter, who is any
good, as you and I are, can't get together the money for them.
Some day a very rich man or woman will invite me down there
and I'll go too. I want to see how much money they spend, how
bored they are, what fine clothes the women wear. No one loves
fine clothes on a woman more than I do, when I don't have to pay
for them.

Of course industrial America is going to spread out everywhere. In the long run there will be factories in every town. How they are going to use all the goods they make I don't know, but folks can use a lot. Waste is an art, too. I should be a frugal man myself because I so love to go my own way, not be under too many obligations—but you should see the things with which I am cluttered.

The factories and things and more things. All the bare bones of life quite gone. Things get all mixed up. Women now can spend more money, being two thirds naked, than their mothers were able to spend covering up everything from the eyebrows to the toes. It's a talent.

But, my dear friend, you ask me if I want to escape the industrial age. Why not? I belong to the artist class, as do you. Thank God, it is a small class. James wrote me last week.

He said he had got all het up on the industrial age, working men, etc., etc., and had gone Bolshevik.

Then he said he got to thinking—suppose, he thought, I had to listen to Max Eastman reading poems to street car conductors, on strike, or Floyd Dell discussing love at a radical forum. You know, women's place in the industrial scheme, something like that.

The thought threw him, he said, into something near convulsions. He got what he called "crowd fear" and fell right out of the Bolshevik class.

"I've come home," he said. "Let's go walk in a city and swear at tall buildings." He said he wanted to swear and laugh and love the world. We'll probably go some place together soon.

The South and the warm sun.

Memories.

If you want to see and feel something beautiful in this world go some time to New Orleans. Well, evening is coming on—say in early March or April. Go into the old city, to the Pontalba Building. There are two of them. Take the one that faces down river. Go to the top story and get out through a window into the balcony. They call it a gallery down there.

Very well, be there, Charles, as the evening falls, and the light begins to fall—grey and golden and red and purple and blue. A man who can paint still-lifes, as you can sometimes.

Who can feel the wonder and glory in an old empty bottle, a

basket of apples, a kitchen knife and a loaf of bread—a man like you can stand up there and see the tops of ships in our great American river, and see the buildings men loved when they built them, and Chartres street, and the very essence of the South, and be glad and go to bed afterwards and sleep praising his gods.

Tears in the eyes, for once anyway, because inanimate things can be so lovely.

Wharton and I were once in a little shaky cabin far down Mobile Bay. We used to build bonfires there on the beach, outside the house—not because it was cold—it was hot all right—but because we both liked the sun and the flicker of the reflection of the dancing flames—come through the windows—on the walls.

The walls were of old grey wood, unpainted. We had little enough furniture, I'll tell you that.

There wasn't an antique piece within a thousand miles that we knew about.

And so the cockroaches used to come out—as big as my thumb—and walk across the grey wall. It was the South all right. The cockroaches liked the light too. We had them named.

"There goes Clara," said Wharton, and sure enough it was Clara. What a charming slender brown cockroach she was. Such legs. Such eyes. She made a little dry shuffling noise—her feet on the grey wall lit by the dancing flames. So there was Clara, and Tom and Joe came out and pursued her.

Then Isabelle came plumper than Clara, and Clarence and Jake and Martha and Cicero. They loved to dance and run in the firelight and Wharton and I sat in the darkness and saw our share of love and life.

There were cockroaches in the kitchen too. We used to leave the dishes unwashed and the cockroaches did most of our housekeeping. They ate all the bread crumbs off the floor. We hardly had to sweep at all.

Why I like Ohio, Charles. I was born and was a boy there. When I travel from New York to Chicago, as I do sometimes, my heart always gives a little jump when I cross the State line.

I love it and I have written about it and I have paid my debt. I was twenty years in its factory towns and in the cities of the North.

I have love for Chicago too, where I lived, and its winds and the reach of the lake shore.

And men there—not artists specially, but advertising men, scribblers, as I was once, and distracted salesmen selling carpet sweepers and newspaper reporters and insurance agents.

And New York, with its clean sea winds and its smart women. That is a town.

O, I love the women of the northern cities, with their style and their graceful figures, like beautiful automobiles. I love to see them walk and ride in their expensive cars and wear their lovely gowns—if I only don't have to buy them.

But, Charles, I have, through my mother, a touch of the Wop in me. It is in my eyes and in my hair and in my tummy. It works in me like yeast.

I like some dirt, the sun has made pure, and some leisure and warm places and men.

I like the South—you had better come, Charles.

I like the little lumber camps down in Louisiana—the bayou country—Weeks Hall's place on the Teche—and the low wet country over toward Florida; and Georgia, with its red hills, when the peach trees bloom.

And negroes and sweat and sun.

And mules in the sandy roads.

The roads at evening when all the negro boys and girls get out in the big road and walk and sing and talk and make love.

Soft voices untouched yet by our intense neurotic age. No neuroticism in the skies, in the trees.

They kept telling me I am trying to escape, that I am running away. It may be true. I saw a boy once step on a rattlesnake and shall never forget his white, frightened face nor how he ran. He was trying to escape too. He had, I should say, an escape psychology, spiral evolution—there was a kind of spiral movement to him—and the Lord knows what else.

That I was not born of the South was not my fault, Charles. I did not manage that. I am only writing you because I am thinking of something.

If you want to go somewhere, Charles, bring your paint brushes and come on. We'll head South—the sun over our shoulders.

Come on, Charles, let's go somewhere South.

Country Town Notes

IT seems Mayor Maxwell of Marion, Virginia, and the town council of this fair town recently went Bolshevik on roller skating. Roller skating became for the time and in the minds of the city fathers almost a capital offense. The Watkins boys had a roller skating rink here. Where they came from, we don't know. They were tall young fellows who looked like mountain men to us. Had they confined themselves to roller skating and raking in the shekels, everything might have been all right.

But it seems they were up to other things—poker playing, for example. One of the Watkins boys got caught engaged in such a game.

This is said to have been the first poker game ever played in the history of Smyth County, Virginia.

So Mr. Watkins was up before His Honour. "So-and-so many dollars and sixty days in jail," His Honour said—"and you don't need to go to jail if you close the skating rink, get out of town and take your rink out with you."

Which was all right and might have been justice. Justice is a thing we know little or nothing about. Often at night we awaken out of a deep sleep, trembling from head to foot for fear justice may be done us.

But to return to our tale. Having soaked the Watkins boys, His Honour and the town council did not stop there. There was a called meeting of the council. They had all become afraid the Watkins boys might transfer their license to run a skating rink to someone else.

You see there had been a slip-up when the Watkins boys got this license. They had got it too cheap. Who knew they were going to rake in all those shekels—who knew that our young blades and ladies were going to flit, night after night, through the mazes of joy—enticed by that tall Watkins, who, Heaven knows, could surely skate—who knew that nickels, dimes, quarters and halves were to fall like gentle snowflakes into the Watkins till? Of course no one knew.

The town, it seems, had gone skate mad. It was a disease, an epidemic. Much good silver was being diverted into these strange coffers—as one might say. Why we even felt this bitterly ourselves. People who might well have been sitting at home, reading our papers and absorbing wisdom, light and mental grace, were up there twining and intertwining themselves around that hall back of that long Watkins.

And to about the worst music we ever heard—we will say that.

We will say more. The town council said more. The special meeting was called by His Honour, but His Honour was not there.

He was at home; he was sick, but his spirit reigned. The council said that the Watkins skating rink license could not be transferred to anyone on the earth, above the sea, or to anyone in the water's under the sea.

But was justice thereby done?

Ah!

Let us pause now and consider this matter. Let us walk under the night skies and think. We are strong for justice for everyone but ourselves. We do not want any justice in our own dish.

We don't want to roller skate either. We never learned. We hate to fall down. We hate to have a certain part of our anatomy bruised. We hate to lose that grace people are accustomed to see in us.

But was justice thereby done?

There are people involved in this whole matter who, by the action of our town council, are hurt, bruised, the joy of their lives taken away—their young hopes crushed.

For example, there is Colonel Stardust Collins.

Here is an exemplary young man, a bachelor—handsome, young, of unimpeachable character. He works in a bank and sleeps upstairs over the bank.

As anyone ought to know, working in a bank is confining, sleeping upstairs over a bank is confining.

A man needs exercise, he needs joy, association with his fellows, both male and female.

And so, for Colonel Stardust, the coming of the Watkins brothers was a joy. Who has not seen the Colonel, in the waning light of a summer evening, walking through the Rialto, his skates in his hand; who has not seen him also in the stress and storm— as one might say—of winter evenings?

It is said that the Colonel bought himself skates of silver; that he bought himself a season ticket. As a matter of fact by this action of the town council and an irate Mayor he is out $23 and no cents.

But that is not all he is out. Colonel Stardust says—and we think he speaks with sage wisdom—that roller skating never did bring a moral blight upon the souls thus engaged, least of all upon himself. He says that, as a matter of fact, it kept away sinful thoughts. "While skating," says the Colonel, "my mind was full, not of sinful thoughts but of pure ones."

"I thought of birds mating in the spring, of sea gulls on lonely rocks in ocean, of lambs gamboling on the green."

"Not gambling, you understand, with dice or cards, but with their legs—just as I skated."

And so the cry for justice goes up. We think the town council ought to give Jerry Collins his $23 and no cents. We think they ought to take the last, slightest insinuation of sinfulness, by thought or deed, off his name. We think they ought to backtrack this much.

The town thinks so, Wolfe's boarding house—where we eat— thinks so, the Rialto thinks so.

Will the town council act?

If it is not done we think a mass meeting should be held.

It is the man who knows nothing at all of writing who gives most advice to writers; the woman who has never had a child is most likely to speak, or write, about child raising; I think, in all fairness to them, that it will be admitted that 'most all the bitterness—well, say against the old saloons—came from men and women who were never in a saloon.

Whether they were right or wrong, is another matter. I am thinking of myself writing to farmers, trying to give them advice. The whole thing is a bit absurd.

I was born and raised in a small town, just such a town as Marion, Virginia. My father half ruined himself with drink. He had been born what is called "a gentleman," but had no head for business. Like myself he liked to take life with a certain flourish. I mean, to put the hat on the side, rather than the top of the head, wear a brightly-coloured tie, carry a walking stick.

Poor man, he never did get over loving women, and I dare say I never shall. When a woman makes herself beautiful I am grateful to her. I like to see her walking, beautifully gowned, through the streets. Really, I do not want her to pay any special attention to me.

I am grateful to her as I am to the man who saves a lovely old building in a town, rather than tear it down to build an ugly, although perhaps more efficient one.

I like men who are manly and frank, women who carry themselves with grace and beauty. My conception of what is nice in life is my own. I stand on it.

Only last Sunday I was walking in Marion with Mr. Funk, the prosecuting attorney. We passed two negro children. They had nice faces and skins that would have made a painter mad with joy. O, the loveliness of the coppery browns and reds in the negro children's faces! I had no way of knowing whether or not Mr. Funk saw what I saw. Probably not. I have thought about painting all my life. I wanted to be a painter but did not make it, so became a scribbler.

My father's drinking made our family poor, often we suffered extreme poverty, but afterward, a long time afterward, I did not blame him. Life was dull to him. Drink, I think, inflamed his imagination. He used to sing and tell marvelous stories to us children when he was drinking. Sober, he was often dull, sad and heavy. In his cups he gathered us about his knees. He would read some old tale and expound it. He read *Robinson Crusoe* and some of the Shakespearean comedies. He imagined himself *Falstaff*, although he was a lean, not a fat man. He walked up and down the floor. There was no butter in the house. For weeks sometimes we lived on corn meal mush. "Man does not live by bread alone," he said. It was hard on mother to be sure. We were, however, a family of boys. "Women do not understand the needs of us men," he said, with a flourish of his hand.

How many charming memories I have of the man. One night we went swimming in a pond. It was called "Fenn's Pond" and was at the edge of town. We went there on a rainy night.

So there we were at the pond's edge in the darkness. Black clouds raced across the sky. Father was a strong swimmer. "It is nice to swim naked," he said, "that is why I brought you here tonight."

"If you feel yourself tiring," said he, "put your hand on my shoulder."

And so, stripping ourselves and leaving our clothes on the bank in the rain, we plunged in. I remember his broad white shoulders gleaming in the darkness, his strong man's arms flashing out. How small and weak my own arms seemed.

And now we had reached the further shore and had drawn ourselves up on the wet grass. This was in the summer and the rain was warm. We lay there a long time.

In his grand eloquent way father spoke of the sky. It was, I thought, very black but we could see places where the black was denser. It stopped raining. "The sky is not black, it is deep purple," said my father.

He called attention to the deeper purple of the water. Near the shore, where we were lying together naked on the grass, it was actually black.

I remember also the lightning playing across the sky, the rumble of distant thunder.

Again—I am a newsboy on the streets of our town. A strange lady, beautifully clad, has come to town. She is changing cars there, getting off a Lake Shore and Michigan Southern train to take the I.B. & W. The I.B. & W. later became the Big Four—a branch of that system.

I am a newsboy, a slip of a boy at the railroad station and there is that lady. My father comes into the railroad station, a little drunk. "Do you suppose she could be a princess?" I asked. Another man would have laughed at me but not father. "I think very likely she is," he said. We walked together up and down the railroad station platform looking at the lady. He discovered a principality for her, I remember, in a strange green land, far away over seas. There was a white castle on the side of a hill.

And so my father drank, and we ate corn meal mush, and mother sorrowed often but two of my brothers painted and a sister, who later died, wrote sometimes rather delicate little verses, that never got printed.

But what has all this to do with farmers?

Just this, I fell to thinking of my childhood, sitting in my little print shop in Marion, Virginia, and of the farmers who come in here. I was thinking of how, as a boy, I went often with my brothers to work on farms. We set out cabbage plants, acres of them, and later cut and hauled cabbage to market; we hoed, cut and shucked corn, we picked strawberries in a strawberry field, cut firewood in the forest in the winter, helped to pick and pack apples in the fall.

I am thinking only that imagination can be applied to the land as well as to my own trade of writing.

Here we have politicians talking of "Farm Relief." Well! Farmers going on in a set way all their lives. They plant corn—if all their neighbours plant corn, or cabbage, or cotton. Once they begin to plant one crop, they go on and on.

I think my own father did, for all his faults, of which I myself have more—teach his children a kind of self-reliance. "Use your imaginations. Stand on your own feet."

"Trust God and give 'em Long Melford," said Old George Borrow, a manly man who knew a lot. By "Long Melford" he meant an unexpected punch with the left.

And so I am thinking that every farmer should have on his farm a few experimental acres. He should talk these experimental acres over with his sons, with his hired men, as my father talked to me of the colour of a night-sky over Fenn's Pond in Ohio.

"We are raising corn, wheat, cotton, tobacco—what-not." Let us set these few acres aside. We will play with them, experiment with them.

"We will throw manure on this land, plow it deep."

Why should every farm not be a college, too? O, the nonsense talked about education!

Books, books, I am weary of books. I am weary of the gabble of congressmen and presidents.

My own education was got on the farm, on the night streets of a town, in factories, with women I have loved. Nearly everything I have learned—and I have not learned much yet—has come by a thrust out into an experimental field.

For example, my running these country weekly papers in a Virginia town, has been an experiment in my life. I do not know how much the people here have got from them but I have got a lot.

They have been experimental acres on the farm that is my life. I have plowed deep, put in this crop and that. I myself have never been much of a farmer, but I have always loved the land. Many of my best friends are farmers. I think the modern age has sold the farmer out. The industrialists have got—from government—a lot, labor has got something, the farmer has got talk, nothing else.

I think he will continue to get—talk.

The farmer is an individualist like the artist. His one chance, I believe, is in experimenting. As I have said, every farm should also be a college.

A few acres should be set aside each year for Experimental Land Education. It should be the land on which the imaginations of the farmer, his wife, his sons, his hired man, are let loose, as my father let loose my imagination, swimming at night at Fenn's Pond and walking near a railroad station in a town in Ohio.

Small Town Notes II

PRING'S coming does something to people in small towns.
It is a little hard to define. In some years Spring, in all the central
parts of America, breaks cold, raw and wet. We all live in a violent
climate.

It grows warm about the middle of April. The warm sun comes
out and there are a few warm rains.

As I write this the wild flowers are coming out in the woods. I
will not attempt to list them, being no naturalist.

There are white ones that nod in the wind; others cling to
stones on hillsides; others thrive in the deep wood.

Now also the fruit trees are putting forth blossoms. Farmers
are plowing and town people are going fishing.

Everyone wants to be outdoors. It is wonderful now to be
young and to be in love. What is lovely in nature, in the Spring, is
ten times more lovely if felt through another.

Now lovers who go out in automobiles do not talk much.

A young boy sits beside a girl dumbly. They hold hands and
look out across the country. I am taking it for granted they have
driven up to some high hill. The hill may be above the very town
in which they live.

Well, we are making this picture—let us go on with it. I like to
think there is also a cemetery on the hill. There are new graves
there. In a town a good many old people seem to like to die just
before the Spring comes.

201

There will be no deaths for weeks and then, suddenly, many deaths. You may well fancy it is like this. A lot of older people have just been holding onto life for a long time. Disease is eating at them. They hold on and hold on.

Then suddenly they let go. They die.

There are new graves scattered over the hill. You see little mounds of fresh earth.

To the left, around a hill from the town, a valley opens out. An apple orchard is in the valley and climbs up a hillside.

A road goes down the valley and winds and twists out of sight among distant hills. Many of the hills are wooded and now show a faint flush of green—the Spring coming up there too.

Along the valley road there are houses. Working people must live down there. The houses are small, poor little things but they look nice and comfortable from this distant spot.

On the hillsides open plowed fields—houses far away up along the valley, clinging to hillsides. How nice houses are thus clinging to hillsides.

We were speaking of young people in an automobile on such a hill, on such a Spring day. I would rather not have the sun shining. A warm mist-drizzle of rain, grey mist lying far up the valley. In such an atmosphere the colours come out more strongly. The wetness acts like varnish on the fading canvas of a painter.

I see many such couples in the Spring and Summer in my town and on the roads about town and others must see them too.

I know how they talk. People are always speaking of the younger generation, shaking their heads. "They do so and so. Isn't it terrible?"

They can't be doing that all the time.

I am very sure sometimes they are just silent, clinging to each other's hands, dumb, tender-hearted.

Because everything is so lovely sometimes and they are not.

Who can be as lovely as the Spring—or the Autumn, or the Summer, or the Winter?

Human relationships are very difficult. It is hard even to have a friend of your own sex, to get at all close to your own son, or your own daughter.

Or a wife—someone you live all the time with, in a house, eat breakfast with, sit with in the evening.

There are men, and women too, who think such a life isn't respectable. They say, "It can't be done. I have to dull something in myself to pull it off."

And the other one growing dull, too—a person you once thought lovely growing less lovely. Who wants anything to grow less lovely?

Do they think of such things, all these people you see in a town? What do people feel, young people, sitting out on hillsides as I have described them—in Spring, Summer, Autumn, Winter days?

Ralph Richardson has just been in here, in my room, talking to me. He is a young man. He clerks in a hardware store.

Sometimes people begin talking strangely. I do not know this man so well.

Yesterday it rained. Ralph says he went, in the afternoon, to deliver some goods to a farmer, four miles from town. I am writing now in early Summer. A moment ago I was writing of Spring. I presume that what I am trying to convey is a sense of the effect of nature on people.

Moods, in the Spring, in the Autumn, in the Summer, in the Winter—moods in nature, in everything, carried into people.

Ralph came home from delivering these goods, he says, in the early evening. It kept on raining—softly, quietly. He put his truck away.

He said it was an open truck and he was wet through. On the way home he had stopped on a hill.

A valley had opened out before his eyes.

Our town lies at the foot of the valley.

So he came on in, got on dry clothes, had his dinner. He turned the radio on. He read the newspaper.

His children went to bed.

He was sitting alone with his wife. They were about to go to bed. Suddenly he got ashamed.

Why?

It is a puzzling question.

He told his wife he had forgotten something at the store, wanting to get away from her.

You are to understand he has just been telling me all this. I am only writing down what he said. He has been talking to me for thirty minutes perhaps and has just gone out.

He came into this room, where I am sitting now, joked a little, had a cigarette with me and began to talk.

He said, in substance, that last night, suddenly, he was ashamed that he was not finer, in some way more dignified and nice in the eyes of his wife, and that she was not more lovely in his eyes.

He made an excuse and went down-town.

The town was nearly all closed up. There were a few men in the drug store. He went in there. Our druggist does not sell whiskey on doctor's prescriptions. The druggist could get the privilege from the government by applying.

He would make a good deal of money.

Lots of people in town would be sore if he did it. He would lose some trade.

Would he gain or would he lose? They were discussing this question in the drug store. Some of the men in there were advising the druggist to do it while others were advising him to let it alone.

The point is that Ralph Richardson listened a moment and went out feeling queer, he says, feeling lonely, feeling ashamed.

For himself and everyone else.

The whole of the business part of town was quite dark. He walked about, he says, in several streets.

He was noticing things. There was a porch of a house, about to fall down. There was a lilac bush in a yard. There was a cat creeping along a fence.

And so and so. He got into the lower end of town. There was a light in a window, upstairs in a building.

It was a lawyer's office. Ralph said he knew the man. He went up there.

The lawyer was making out papers for a divorce.

That was all of that.

The lawyer was making out papers and he talked a little about the case.

A man had been up to something. He had gone creeping into another man's house and had got caught.

The woman in the other man's house was about to have a child. Her husband asked her—"Is it my child or is it his?"

She was defiant. "It is his child and I will have other children by him if I please. I will have as many children by him as I want to have. I love him, not you."

Just that—Ralph Richardson, who told me all this, and the lawyer, a man I do not know, speaking of it.

Ralph says they got to talking. "A lot of life is pretty second class, eh?" the lawyer said.

"Yes."

"I wonder why it has to be so."

"It just is."

"I am that way myself a lot."

"So am I."

"I am always doing things of which I am ashamed."

"Me too."

"It isn't things people call bad."

"I know."

"It's just things I do, thoughts I have. They are so second-class."

"There's a lot of shoddiness about."

"A heap of it."

A sudden outburst of intimate talk, getting nowhere, Ralph said. He said he and the lawyer, the man I do not know, went out of the office and walked about.

He said the sky had got quite clear and that the stars had come out.

Ralph walked with the lawyer down to his house. It was on a street that crossed a bridge and there were dark houses everywhere along the street. Then the lawyer walked part way back, toward the centre of town, with Ralph.

They got to the bridge, Ralph said, and stood there a long while, saying nothing. He said it was nice there. There were bushes growing along a creek that went under the bridge and the creek made a pleasant sound.

Both men stood listening to the sound made by the creek, they smelled flowers growing on bushes.

They felt the night damp and the sky over their heads.

"We didn't talk anymore," Ralph said. I will have to leave it to the reader to figure out what he was trying to convey.

What he said was that he wanted to talk all night to that

man—a man he did not know very well, and that the man wanted to keep on talking to him.

About feelings, perhaps.

They couldn't.

"Good night," the man said.

"Good night," Ralph Richardson said.

He, Ralph Richardson, said he went on home. His wife was in bed asleep. There was a dim light burning in another room.

He undressed quietly, he said, without awakening his wife.

Then he went in to where she was. He tried to tell me something, how oddly aware he was.

Just of the room, the bed, his wife, things in the room.

"I was ashamed," he said.

He thought it was queer, he said, that, at times, even things in a room, chairs, tables and such things, the walls of a room, what a man knew was outside the room, in the darkness outside, were like other people in the way they made a man ashamed of himself.

Country Squires

THERE are thousands of them. In some states they are called "justices of the peace," in others "squires." Theirs are the little neighbourhood courts in which are tried the chicken stealers, the small damage suits—as when a farmer's horse gets into another's corn—the assault cases, some of the liquor cases, petty thefts of all sorts. When I was a boy we had a Squire as a neighbour. He had a tremendous voice.

The man was an early riser and in the summer was abroad at five. He stood on his front porch. Seeing a neighbour three or four blocks away, he began a conversation. His voice rang through the little town and honest citizens, awaking, cursed the Squire.

Still the man was liked. He laughed with his whole body. His fat belly shook and he waved his arms. He had a trick he could do with the muscles of his belly. He drew the belly in and let it fly out. Grasping a small boy he embraced him enthusiastically. The belly was drawn in, taking the boy with it, and then it was let fly. The breath was knocked out of the boy. He fell to the ground and the Squire stood over him, roaring with laughter. All the by-standers laughed too. Such a man could be elected Squire over and over. No one could beat him.

There was another one who was a shoemaker and had lost a leg in the Civil War. He leaned toward the socialistic theory of government and, as he pegged shoes, he quoted Karl Marx. The men of the town went to his shop on winter afternoons. He leaned forward and punched at the floor with his shoe-maker's awl. "The capitalists are bringing the country to ruin," he declared, the blue veins standing out on his forehead.

The Squires are nearly all small farmers. In Virginia, where I now live, three Squires rule over each squirarchial district. The size of the district is fixed quite arbitrarily. In our county we have three such districts and therefore nine squires, while in the next county, but slightly larger, there are seven districts and twenty-one Squires.

The Squire receives no salary but is paid one dollar for issuing a warrant and two dollars for trying a case. When the prisoner is found guilty he must pay the costs, the Squire's fee, the fee to the officers who serve the warrants, and the witness fees. Witnesses receive fifty cents for coming in and testifying and, when they must come more than five miles, a certain sum, per mile, for the cost of getting there. If the prisoner is found not guilty the cost is paid by the state.

The court of the Squire is held in the winter in a farmhouse living room and in the summer on his front porch. In most farmhouses there is a bed in the living room. The Squire's wife is working in the kitchen. You can hear the rattle of pans. When the case interests her, as for example when the fatherhood of an illegitimate child is to be determined, or when there is some other misdemeanor that comes directly into the world of woman, she comes in her kitchen apron, and stands by the door listening.

There is always a crowd present. The men and women have come from all the neighbouring farms. In the summer, children are playing on the lawn before the house and the women have fixed themselves up. They sit stiffly on chairs brought from the house, in their stiff clean calico dresses, and whisper to each other.

The Squire's court is the theatre of the countryside. Here the tragedies and comedies of the neighbourhood are played out to an appreciative audience. For the smaller cases there is rarely a lawyer present. The country people are suspicious of lawyers. They are a necessary evil at times but it is best, when possible, to go on without one.

And the Squires are also happier when there are no lawyers

present. A lawyer is always telling you how to do things. He has ideas about the procedure of a court. He brings law books with him. "In such and such a case, State of Vermont, volume so and so, page so and so..."

"Eh!"

"The devil! What have we to do with Vermont?"

In a Squire's court the man or woman being tried is personally known to the Squire. "Well, Jim—or Lizzy, what about it, eh? Do you agree to tell the truth, the whole truth and nothing but the truth?" Often several people are talking at once. Lizzy has had a fight with Martha Smith. On Sunday evening, Martha went to church and got to flirting with Lizzy's husband. Lizzy saw her talking to him in the road. Then on the next day Lizzy and Martha met in the same road. There were words and a fight started. Lizzy got a black eye and Martha had her face scratched. It was Martha who took Lizzy with a warrant. "I wasn't doing a thing. I ain't that kind of a woman," Martha says.

She begins to testify, and in the midst of her testimony makes a statement that seems to Lizzy an untruth. "You lie," screams Lizzy from her place on the Squire's front porch. Both Lizzy and Martha have to be held back by their friends or they would go at it again, right in the Squire's court. The man about whom all this fuss is being made sits sheepishly under a tree. The other men are laughing at him. He is filled with resentment. His wife should have gone on home about her business. He and the woman Martha weren't up to anything. Now the men of the neighbourhood are whispering together and laughing. His wife has got him into a hell of a mess.

The Squire may not pass on a case involving a felony, where there is a prison term hanging over the accused. He may, however, ask questions, find out if there is enough evidence to justify the man's being sent to court or to the next meeting of the grand jury. Most of the liquor cases have become felonies now. These stiff penalties they are putting on for violations of the liquor laws, are cutting down the number of cases that properly belong in the Squire's court. It cuts his income too.

In the court of Squire McHugh, who is an old man of eighty-two, the case of Jim McGrew is being heard. Jim is a thin-lipped, smiling man of forty-five, who has a slight limp. His case has attracted wide attention, and neighbours have come to court from all the cornfields around.

It is such an unusual case, that the sheriff, who took Jim and his two sons, Harold and Burt McGrew, has come over from the county seat, and the county Prosecuting Attorney has come.

It is obvious that these two men are bent on convicting Jim and his sons, who are accused of chicken stealing.

But Jim is slick, with a hard good-natured slickness difficult to get past.

There have been chickens missing from the neighbourhood for months. It isn't a question of a few chickens. Mrs. Sullivan, a widow, lost forty-two fine hens in one night, and John Williams, a prosperous farmer, lost thirty.

The hen-houses were safely locked at night and there was no noise, not a sound. On the night when Mrs. Sullivan's hens disappeared she was lying awake. She did not sleep a wink all that night. She remembers having locked the door to the hen-house. They were just gone. Not a sound from the hen-house.

In these days, when almost anyone can own a cheap car, a carload of chickens may be lifted in one neighbourhood at night and be a hundred miles away by daylight. A man who looks like a farmer, drives up to a dealer in poultry in some distant place. He sells the chickens, gets the money and leaves. The hens are shipped off to a distant market. How are you going to identify chickens after they get into the dealer's shipping crates?

The man named Jim McGrew lives in a little house on the side of a hill and has six children. They are all in court, with Jim's wife, and look like a brood of young foxes. All of them have sharp eyes, like Jim's, and you can get nothing out of them. The whole neighbourhood knows that Jim never works. He lives in one neighbourhood until it gets too hot for him and then moves to another. Wherever he goes things just disappear.

He's slick. In spite of themselves, the Squire and the neighbouring farmers, who have gathered in, admire his smartness.

They might have got him one time—there was a hen-house, filled with fine friers, back of the rich man's house—but for Jim's brood of kids. When Jim operated he could scatter kids all over a neighbourhood. People said they had a system of signals. A dog barked or there was the mew of a cat. Then Jim got out into the road and came moping along, as innocent looking as you please.

He likes to smile at the Sheriff, with that cold smile of his. "What are you doing here, Jim?"

"Well Sheriff, if you want to know the truth, I came out here to get some whiskey. A man was going to sell me some. I guess he saw you here and he lit out."

Whiskey indeed. Jim was after them friers.

The Prosecuting Attorney is after something now. He scents a liquor case. "Where does he live?" "I don't know." That smile is playing about Jim's lips.

The Prosecuting Attorney is asking him to describe the fictitious man who was to sell the liquor.

"Well," Jim drawls, "he had two gold teeth, like you got, and had grey hair, like the Squire there." He points out the more respectable men present. The fictitious whiskey seller had eyes like this one, wore a hat like that man over there, had on a suit of clothes like the man leaning against the tree.

In the Squire's court everyone talks when there is something to say. The Squire can't be too dignified. He is a man of the neighbourhood. He stops the procedure of the court to borrow a chew of tobacco from the man accused. He and the Sheriff and the others will get the man if they can. It is a game. Most law cases, even in the higher courts, are a good deal that way.

In the case of Jim McGrew, the Prosecuting Attorney had something up his sleeve. He and the Sheriff had got Jim and two of his brood of kids on a country road at midnight two or three nights before. It is true there were no chickens in the car that night but Jim had in the car several empty bags and there was a heavy wire-cutter.

And, on almost any night, for two weeks, there had been chickens missing from hen-houses in just that neighbourhood. The hen-houses had all been stapled and locked and the staples had been cut with just such a heavy wire-cutter.

They had taken Jim and his kids to jail and one of the kids had talked.

Then afterwards, when he was brought into the presence of

his father, the boy had tightened up. "Yes, I did say we stole the chickens but it was a lie," the boy declares now. He says he was bluffed into telling a lie. There had been a trick played. They had made the boy think his dad had confessed. It is all right, the Prosecuting Attorney says, smiling at Jim, who smiles back at him, "We can't get you Jim, but we can get the kid."

He explains to Jim that he can send the boy up for what he calls "perjury". The idea frightens Jim. Perjury is a big, dangerous-sounding word. Jim gets up from his seat on the grass, his back against a tree in the Squire's yard, and calls his wife to one side. The Prosecuting Attorney is smiling at the Sheriff and the old Squire is smiling. They have got Jim. Jim's wife is a heavy woman with a shrewd face. She and Jim whisper together.

"They can get the kid for telling a lie, eh. Can they send him to jail? Well, I guess they can send him to the reform farm."

"Huh," says Jim, "one of my kids going off there, eh."

He comes back and calling the Prosecuting Attorney to one side holds another whispered conversation.

The crowd is tense now. "You ain't go no case against me and you know you ain't, but I don't want one of my kids stuck. You went and bluffed the kid and made him tell a lot of lies. I'm an innocent man."

It is the Prosecuting Attorney who is smiling now.

"I'm going to get the kid."

"What is the least you will give me if I come through."

It is agreed that the Prosecuting Attorney will ask the Squire to be as light as he can on Jim and Jim confesses. It is to save his kid. They have got Jim this time but all the men in the crowd feel a certain sympathy for him. The Squire feels it too. He will let Jim off light.

And so Jim makes his confession to the Squire and to the men and women gathered in the Squire's yard. He makes it as dramatic as he can. After all, even in a chicken-stealing affair there is such a thing as art, and Jim is an artist.

He tells how it was done, how he and the kids have been working, how he got Mrs. Sullivan's chickens and John Williams' lot. There was a night when he and his kids did a stunt. They stole the chickens of the Sheriff himself.

It was a night when the Sheriff was right at home and was

sitting on his front porch. Jim looks at him and grins. He and the kids got the chickens right from under his nose. They had their car parked within a quarter mile of the house.

Jim is making the Sheriff cringe a little as he tells his tale. He takes a shot at the Prosecuting Attorney, too. "We would have got yours if you had kept any chickens", he says. Then he takes the jail sentence that has been agreed upon with his characteristic cold little smile and is marched off.

As for the people who have come to the trial, they all feel they have got a good show. They go away along the road talking it over.

"After all he stuck to his kid. If it hadn't been for him sticking to his kid they wouldn't never have got him," they say, as they go back to the fields and to their work in the corn.

At Amsterdam

I AM here at this World Congress Against Imperialist War at Amsterdam, Holland. I am writing in a great noisy hall—thousands of people from Germany, England, France and some twenty or thirty other countries are here. The room is tense. There are some noted literary figures here but the general mass are workers. They are socialists, communists and pacifists from many countries.

Speakers spring up and talk. They are peasants. They are factory workers.

How well they talk. Always the workers speak better, more directly, than the intellectuals.

As in America, all Europe is in the grip of a vast depression. Many of these workers have come here afoot. They are strong looking men. Suddenly they all break out into song. These workers have been taught by long years of suffering to stand together. They sing together. The rafters of the building shake with song and shouts.

The hall—a vast automobile exposition building—is divided into groups. After a speech from the central rostrum—on which I now sit writing—men spring up in various parts of the great hall. The speech from the central rostrum is reported in many languages.

From America there are some thirty delegates, representing farmers, ex-soldiers, sailors, textile workers, carpenters and miners. I am the only professional writer from America.

215

It is amazing how well the workers and the peasants speak. There is a kind of force, a strength that shakes the nerves. In Europe they have quit being afraid of the words socialism, communism, etc. You feel everywhere in the people the conviction that the world is in a great period of change. There is a struggle. This and that idea is thrust out suddenly, boldly. The hall shakes with shouts of approval or with hisses.

Today—Sunday—the day of the great mass meeting—the workers of Holland marching today—the streets outside the hall are filled with marching thousands.

Against this the beautiful quiet city. Never before have I been in a more beautiful city. The whole city is spotlessly clean. Down the middle of the wide streets go tree-lined canals. Nearly all of the freight brought into the city to be distributed is floated directly to the door of the store or warehouse. Everywhere you see barges floating, some propelled by long poles, some by engines.

The European is unlike the American in that almost every man speaks three or four languages and here I have been able to meet with and talk to writers from all over the world. It has all been very exciting and absorbing to me.

As to the Congress—from all these European countries you hear the same cry, "It is of no importance to sign petitions for peace or to go to the League of Nations." Every speaker cries out the same thing.

"If the workers, in the munition plants, will refuse longer to make munitions—if the transport workers will not transport munitions..."

"Strike. Strike against war," is the universal cry here. Not in one country but in all countries. The great effort is to get the workers of all countries together, to get them to quit hating each other. "Workers of the world unite!" The feeling is that all but the very rich man suffers from war. The hope here is to make this understood by more and more workers from all countries.

There is something alive here, glowingly alive. Let the capitalistic newspapers of the world play all this down. In the end it will assert itself. Here workers of the world, for once anyway, have got together.

It is a beginning. There is a song of hope in it. There is a fist raised. It is a mass of workers, from many countries, having sincere feeling for each other. Internationality. Do not let anyone tell you that the workers' world congress against war is not a success.

Delegation

YOU get caught. It isn't as though you thought you really knew anything about government. You know you don't.

There is, however, this thing going on. Suppose you happen to be a man like myself, a born wanderer. You drift from town to town. Nowadays, if you have a small car, it's easy. You keep seeing and talking to men, and often to women. There are always places to go in a town. There are often meetings being held, or you can go to a part of town where workmen congregate in the evening. They're glad to talk. You keep finding out things.

But all of your thoughts do you no good. Thoughts don't seem to help. You see men and women everywhere defeated. They don't want so much—a job to do that is at least a bit interesting, decent food, clothes and shelter, the chance to play a little. What gets you in a time like this is the terrible humility of men. Someone says to you "Come on. Let's protest," so you do. You sign things, serve on committees. You protest. You send telegrams to governors and judges.

I went with some three or four others to make a protest to the President. That was Hoover, then. It was when the ex-soldiers came down to Washington and camped there, demanding the bonus. You will remember how the government got after them with machine guns and soldiers and bayonets and tear gas and drove them like sheep down across Maryland and Pennsylvania. It seemed a shame.

Some earnest fellow got after a little bunch of us highbrows and worried us and teased us into going down to Washington to protest. I think they had telegraphed the President and asked him "Will you see them?" and that he had wired back "No." I can't be sure about this. We who do the protesting are seldom taken into the confidence of the men who run such affairs. The Communists, for example, go in deep for mystery. I am a little uncertain as to whether I ever met a real one.

Anyway, I came into New York and went to the Pennsylvania Station, and there were three others. There was a kind of manager of things. He kept running around and saying that a lot of newspapermen were coming to interview us, but none came. We got on the train and sat in the smoker. There were two men we took to be real revolutionists sitting opposite a friend of mine, who is a writer, and myself, and we spent most of the time trying to prove to them by arguments that if they would only let us alone, let us stay at home and write beautiful and stirring prose, we, in our own subtle ways, would correct the wrongs and the injustices of the world a lot faster than they ever could by chasing around and worrying presidents—or by nagging us into doing it. You can see how it is. You seldom get a sock in the jaw sitting at home and writing beautiful prose.

And then, bang, we were in Washington and at the White House offices. There were a lot of police and soldiers and any number of bright, alert-looking newspapermen. We stood there in the White House offices, in a big outer room. It was a hot day. I forgot to say that at Baltimore our delegation had been joined by a colored man. He was the editor of a Negro newspaper, a modest, nice fellow. Someone had got up a manifesto, and we had all signed.

Men kept running up to us, newspapermen, some of whom I knew. It was the President's birthday. The newspapermen told us about other delegations that had come, the Girl Scouts with a bouquet of flowers, a delegation from the Chamber of Commerce with a cake, etc. I was thinking "Suppose he does see us. He won't, but suppose he does. Would there have to be speeches made?" The truth is that I felt as I usually feel when I go into a bank to try to borrow some money. When I get like that, my back always

aches. Think of me protesting for soldiers. I'd make a bum
soldier.

I do not know how long we waited, perhaps an hour, before we
were shown into a big room. There was a youngish-looking man
sitting at a desk, and beside him sat two very fat, important-
looking older men. They didn't pay any attention to us, so we
lined up against a wall. Instinct may have led us to do that. I
wondered how the others felt. As for myself, I think I felt much as
a young man feels when he goes to speak to her father about it.

Then I noticed something. There was that youngish man, the
President's secretary, sitting at the desk, and right away, when I
looked hard at him, I got onto something. "He is just as scared, he
feels just as uncomfortable as we do," I thought. It was a grand
thought and turned out to be true. I have seldom had a thought
that gave me such comfort.

The man got up from his desk and the two fat, important-
looking men left the room. They stopped at the door and looked
back hard at us highbrow Reds, and I had another thought. "Gee,"
I thought, "who knows? They may be Secret Service men." I have
always wanted to have a Secret Service man after me.

We were alone in the room with the one man. A marvelous
thing had happened. The man facing us, this big official man, was
as upset as we were. It seemed to me he was actually scared. As he
advanced toward us, the sheets of paper held in his hand
trembled. He had gone a little white. When he began to speak, his
voice trembled.

First he made us a little speech. He told us we were in wrong. "I
am not speaking for the President," he said, "or in my official
position as the President's secretary. I speak," he said, "as a
fellow-American and a fellow-craftsman."

After that he lectured us. I can't remember all he said. It was
something about upholding someone's hands. He read the speech
from the piece of paper he held in his trembling hands, and
afterward our spokesman also made a little speech. He tried to
tell the man what we represented. He may have been wrong. I am
not sure that we represented anything much.

I don't think that is the point. We had been asked, pleaded

with, to go down there, and we went. When we got there, we felt silly, at least I did.

Then this thing happened. That man, that President's secretary, was so obviously afraid of us. It seemed wonderful to me. We went out of the office and down a street, and a newspaperman I knew, a man named Buck, from my old Chicago days, came and put his arm through mine. "Do you want some beer?" he asked, and I said "Yes." I made my friend, the writer, come with us. Afterward I read in the newspapers that we were followed by Secret Service men and that we went from the President's office to Communist headquarters. It is a mistake. We didn't know there was any such place. We went to a speakeasy and had some beer. It was a hot day.

Afterward we came out, just the two of us who had come from New York. We walked along a street. "Well, that's that," my friend said. We were walking under some nice trees. They have nice trees along the streets in Washington. "Yes," I said, "that's that, but did you notice that we scared that guy? We gave him indigestion," I said, and my friend wriggled with delight. A look of the most beatific pleasure spread over his face. "See," he said, "so you noticed it, too."

Winter Day's Walk in New York

AWINTER Sunday's walk down Sixth Avenue, from near Washington Square—a gray day—not windy—plenty of cars—not many people walking.

Talk with a friend walking with me—Alfred Stieglitz—Julius Caesar—Voltaire—is Georg Brandes' Caesar translated—does anyone know? "I don't know. I'm reading it in the German."

The South—why southern poets can't bear Whitman, etc. Someone should explain that. There is an explanation all right. It would make a good thing for *The American Spectator*, that explanation.

Nature—a walk like this—on a cold Sunday afternoon in New York is as fascinating as any walk by rivers—in the woods in winter—dead leaves on the ground under foot—cold-looking farm boys walking in the roads with their girls—nothing more desolate-looking in winter than most American farm houses.

A crowd down by the Battery—men out walking with their wives. Most men out walking on Sunday afternoon with their wives look bored. The wives look bored. They are all going into the Aquarium to see the fish. Who's a fish?

Back of the Aquarium a fire boat—shining copper and brass—she looks like a little queen sitting there—Alice in Wonderland—so clean—so shining—so small and fat.

Swell to take a trip in her—go up rivers—wash out a lot of

towns on rivers. A lot of southern towns need washing. Wonder
if there's any river goes up to Scottsboro, Alabama?

"My Alabama gal
In the moonlight,
I'se hungerin' for a sight of
My Alabama gal."

What happened to that crowd of southern writers who started
the agrarian movement in the South—"I'll Take My Stand."
Allen Tate, Stark Young and others? Wonder if they weren't
really thinking of sitting on the front porches of colonial houses
down South and looking out over southern fields while the
niggers did the work?

"Let the niggers do the work—do the work—
do the work—
Let the niggers do the work."

A broad street up the East River front—Sailor's Mission—
Spanish steamship at a dock unloading—fish wharves—fishy
smells.

Canal boats lying in slips. The light is nice. You can't beat the
New York light—New York climate. To a provincial, there is
something in the air here that exhilarates.

Feeling gay—feeling nice—swell. Wish I could dance.

Remember the kind of tramps that used to come on the stage
in burlesque shows—small, swarthy fellows with black whiskers
sticking straight out—black hair sticking straight up—high red
cheek-bones showing—husky whiskey voices? Plenty of them
down here.

Plenty of ragged drunks lying in doorways—Brooklyn Bridge
from down underneath—Hart Crane—"Julius Caesar started the
whole modern show, didn't he?"

Do certain civilizations make great personalities or do great
personalities make great civilizations? Our *American Spectator*
crew might take that one on for a talkfest. Places along the river
front, strangely like Havre. Spent a week there once fascinated by
the sailors ashore—out drunk, reeling and singing, on the
wharves with their Molls. I liked them, and Havre.

The Murphys must have been big shots in the canal boat line—
Elizabeth Murphy—Maude—Aice—Kate—Hattie. Asked a man
why canal boats were always tied up, why they never seem to be

used. "Hell, they don't do nothing. They just lie there. They ain't got nothing to do."

Like us—nothing to do—something to learn—how to do nothing. Swell—feeling good—walking, so strangely quiet. "Let's go over to Joe's and get a cocktail."

"Okay. Shall we take a taxi?"

"No, let's walk."

"Look—there's an old rope walk over there! Gee—it's hell—this being Sunday. I always wanted to see the inside of a rope walk."

City Scapes

THE Guggenheim.... The applications pour in. Since the depression, the number of applications from young scientists, students and doctors has not increased much but, among the young writers, painters, sculptors, etc., my understanding is that it is rather a flood. As for the painters, they are asked to send in samples of their work. An empty store room is rented and three or four painters, their reputations already made, are asked to come in and pass on them. I gather there is a process of slow selection. I suspect that it is something like this:—Sometime ago I took to Dreiser the work of a young writer I admired. He looked at it. "Huh," he said, "of course you would like his work. He writes like you."

I was speaking to a young writer of real ability, one who applied for the Guggenheim and didn't get it. "This is the way I did it," she said. "I thought up a project that I thought would impress them. It wasn't what I wanted to do at all. I wanted some money so I would have time to tell a very simple story. I thought I would get the money on the big sounding project and then do as I pleased." She didn't get it. If she had told them what she told me she might have. Who knows?

Waxey Gordon.... I spoke to one of the jurors who helped send Waxey, the beer baron, to his reward... a fine of eighty thousand... ten years in prison. The juror told me about it.

227

Waxey went on the stand. He didn't have to and the tip was that his attorneys put him on because, in a similar case, income tax evasion, the big banker Mitchell went on and got away with it. The banker came clear. The juror said… "when we got into the jury room we were all sorry for Waxey. We thought he was guilty all right but he had made such a pitiful showing on the stand. Then we got indignant. After the showing the big bankers made down in Washington we thought we had a right to expect something better from the big racketeers. To find out they were the same kind of weak-kneed saps as the big bankers was just too much."

In a city court room.… A thick-necked Austrian father had his daughter up, wanting to have her put on probation. The girl was perhaps nineteen and very pretty. She had a job in a small restaurant at ten dollars a week and did not often go to church. Sometimes she went out, to a dance or a party, and stayed out until after midnight. She had a young woman friend who had once been divorced. The magistrate kept trying to find out what was wrong with the girl. "I want her to obey me," the father kept saying. Once, when she came home quite late and the father kicked up a row, the girl told him to go to hell. In the court room she kept looking at her father with cold indifference and the magistrate kept trying to explain that the girl, having been born in America and raised in America, was an American woman. "I would have to put all the women and girls in America on probation if it came to a question of their obeying either fathers or husbands," the magistrate said.

The father couln't or wouldn't understand. He kept saying the same thing over and over. "She is my daughter. I want peace. I want her to obey me."

"Shut up," the magistrate said. He was tired of it. The father's thick neck got more and more red and he tramped out of the court room. The young woman, I presume, went back to her job.

The extra overcoat.… The man told me about the trouble he had with his extra overcoat. He said he had two. They were both last year's coats but pretty good yet. He had a job but his wages had been cut. Men without overcoats kept ringing his door-bell and asking for an overcoat. He kept refusing. It got on his nerves he said. He said he got more and more bitter about the matter. "Look here," he said, "didn't Hoover or someone talk about two automobiles. If a man can have two automobiles, why not two overcoats?" He had a brown coat and a black one. He liked them both. "Sometimes I liked to wear one, sometimes the other," he said. He didn't want to give either of them away.

He said he must have got a bit hysterical. He couldn't sleep. He lived in a New York suburb and men without overcoats kept ringing his door-bell when he was at home in the evening.

And then, one night, after three men had come to his door, asking for a coat and he had dismissed them all... he cursed the last one... he suddenly, in the night, when he couldn't sleep, got out of bed and went down into the cellar. He took one of the coats, the black one, and threw it into the furnace. "Wasn't I a damn fool?" he said. "That's the kind of damn fool I am."

Stewart's on the Square

THE New York proletariat also has its high life. Just now, aside from Harlem, it is pretty much centered about Sheridan Square and the big Stewart's Cafeteria, on the Square.

The waiters told me; Mr. Buff, the bouncer, told me. But, since customers serve themselves, there are no real waiters, and Mr. Buff, the bouncer, rarely bounces. He is big, suave, and competent. What a bartender he would make! Excuse it, Mr. Buff. He told me that in his youth he once drove a hack out of Washington Mews. Great generals, competent presidents of republics, and good bartenders all have something in common. They can rise above small annoyances. They know how to handle the people.

But wait! Did I speak of Stewart's, on the Square, as the centre of proletarian high life? Excuse it, proletariat. These swarms of people, male and female, coming into the big bright room...

The place never closes. It is busier at twelve midnight than at twelve noon. At three or four in the morning it is a whirling mass of humanity. Pies fall to the floor, a poached egg on toast falls. There are not enough tables, not enough chairs. The room is a great V-shaped one with the mechanical equipment of the cafeteria across the wide end of the V—steaming pots of savory meats and cooked vegetables, rows of pies and baked apples... slide your tray on the rail, get your own tools and paper napkins.

These people are not really of the proletariat. They come in

231

swarms. They are all young. They are chorus men from the big musical shows further uptown. Some are respectable clerks or floorwalkers in big business houses and department stores. These make the crush only on Friday and Saturday nights. On Saturday night they are good for all night.

They come flocking out of the Village. It would be interesting to know how many are New York born. Few enough, I suspect. They are people who want—want—want. They want, some day, to be great actors, singers, sculptors, painters. In the meantime, there they are, young. Youth can seldom wait. There is the thing and there is the shadow of the thing. If you cannot be it, at least you can walk like it. Let the hair grow long. Wear a beard. If you are a woman, be mannish. Walk with a stride. Shoot the cuffs, lassie.

After two, on a Friday or Saturday night, they keep coming thicker and thicker. The word has got out. Here you may see, at first hand, a certain side of city life. Crowds of young men and women from the outside—not real belongers, not regulars— push and shove their way in. More eggs falling, face upward, on the floor, the toast on top astride the egg; pies falling. A good deal of coffee gets spilled on white starched cuffs of ladies who wear white starched cuffs.

It is uncomfortable gaiety, a crowding and pushing. On Saturday night they make a ruling, "No check for less than twenty-five cents." I hadn't known you could go into a cafeteria, take a check at the door, and then later go out, without buying any food, on the blank check. It seems you can. On week nights a good many do. As Mr. Buff said to me, "You can't make 'em trade in your place if they don't want to trade. We're selling food."

They are not coming just for food. The average food consumption, on a Saturday night, will run to about twenty-three cents. But they keep coming. It is, as it is at Klein's, on Union Square, where women's gowns are sold, on the cafeteria plan. At Klein's, on Union Square, a woman sits in a high place in the room into which the women crowd to try on gowns. She sings out to another woman at the door of the room:

"One in. One out."

So it is at Stewart's, on the Square.

"One in. One out."

"Two in. Two out."

The checks, at twenty-five cents each, fall like the feet of pigeons alighting on iron roofs. They rain down on the marble counter. It is feverish. You think of crowds at country fairs. There also, on the big days, there are too many people. Who was it spoke of American crowds as always taking their pleasures sadly? There is a crowd mania, a blind desire to be with others, the more others the better. At the country fairs, also, there are not enough places to sit. The crowd moves all day, restlessly, determined to be amused, as at Stewart's, on the Square, they move all night.

It is a place to check on city life. In the morning, at breakfast, there is quite another crowd. Young stenographers hurry in for the morning toast and coffee, old and young men come. There is a clutching at morning newspapers, a looking at watches. At night there are no newspaper readers.

Then comes noon, with its men from nearby wholesale houses. They lean back and take it easy, sit after eating to smoke cigars and discuss the affairs of the fur trade, the stockings and cotton-goods trades.

The third life—you hear whispers from the believers that it is the ultimate, ultimate life...it has its firm believers...ah, art...ah, beauty—the third life begins slowly, in the late afternoon. Now is the time when you may go in and sit and later get out on the blank check. There are also afternoon breakfasters. As they come in, they form little groups. There is no hurry. No newspapers are read. "Let the great world roll on. It has pushed us aside. Now we push it aside." Pale young men and equally pale young women sit looking longingly at the door into the Square.

"Where is my beloved?"

There is one young man who has got himself a large snake, which he keeps as a pet in his room. He would bring it with him, let it drink milk out of a saucer at his table, but he knows Mr. Buff would not permit it. Mr. Buff is somewhat crude and does not understand the more subtle relationships of life. The young man has read Mr. George Moore's "Confessions of a Young Man." He is at work writing his own confessions.

There is a young woman who has taken the name of a famous lightweight prizefighter. She is a little out of training, a bit heavy for ring work, but says she will take on anyone, male or female, at any time. Anyone at any weight at any time.

Although it is four in the afternoon there are young men not yet wholly awake. They sit rubbing their eyes. They want shaving. But why shave? "With this world of shaved, alert men in the street outside and still coming in here to get food, I have nothing to do." Later the young man will go back to his room to prepare for the night.

Big Rudy. Maxie (he used to be seen often at the Bird's Nest). The Dill Pickle. Sameta Grande. Miss Steppy. The Little Princess. There are a dozen, fifty others. They sit sleepily over the 4 P.M. morning coffee. I had not dreamed the little world of the children of the arts was so well populated. "There are thousands of us," a young man tells me. He tries to explain how it is. "We are in all ranks of society. We are the chosen ones. The outer world is too harsh, too brutal. We choose to make our own little world."

The life of the chosen ones, at their chosen place of meeting, grows with the night. At ten the restaurant is full, at midnight crowded; at three or four in the morning, on the big nights, it is a restless, moving whirlpool.

They are not all of the chosen. Word has gone out and the curious come in flocks. Here you may see, among other things, the artists of the future, the future great. They will tell you so themselves. The taxi-driver, off duty, brings his girl down. She is a little factory girl. They sit at my table. Why, the fellow is also touched.

"Life is a problem to me and I am a problem to life," I hear him tell the girl.

"Ah go on. None of that stuff for me, Ed," she replies.

There are a few real workers, coming in the early evening. They are young painters who paint, young writers who write. They do not belong. They sit and scoff.

One of the regulars, a young man, comes to sit at my table. It is past four in the morning, and in the three hours I have been here twenty people have been at the table. How many cups of coffee? How many poached eggs on toast? "You have not been here before? You are not one of us?"

"No."

"Uh." He looks at me sadly and, shrugging his shoulders, goes away. I motion to Mr. Buff.

"Yes," he says, "one of our veteran regulars. He has been with us from the beginning."

It is time to go home. I am sleepy. Mr. Buff tells me that many of the little children of the arts have beds on the cooperative plan. They sleep in shifts. "Four hours in bed and then four hours here," he says.

"And this for art, for the ultimate ultimate?"

"I don't get you," says Mr. Buff.

I got out, pushing my way through the crowd. Many young men and women, new arrivals, are pushing in through the crowd. They are holding cups of coffee, wedges of pie, poached eggs on toast. Voices are crying.

As I go through the door, three young men, arm in arm, are pushing their way in. There are three policemen in the street near the door. The three young men, going in, have new suits. I turn and stare. Such an outburst of outside pockets, of belts, of pleats. One of the young men has on a belt with a silver belt buckle. He is wearing silver slippers. We used to get such suits from mail-order houses when I was a lad in a country town. I remember the advertisements: "Boys, with one of these suits you can knock 'em cold. One of these hot-dog suits will make you stand out from the crowd. It will mark you as a real gentleman. Wear one of these suits and they will know you are somebody."

There was one thing I missed at Stewart's, on the Square. It is another sort of ultimate ult. They have one at another Stewart place, the one at University and Eighth. It is a pancake-baking machine. It is so deliberate, so clocklike, such a silvery thing. The cakes fall out with a kind of absolute certainty, like death coming, each cake baked to just an exact pastel brown. It has amused and delighted me all through a hard winter. Two white-clad priestesses attend it.

"But the two priestesses, with such old-time frying pans as my mother used, could bake twice as many cakes," a friend said to me. He was a stupid man.

"Don't be foolish, fellow," I replied. "Don't you know that the machine age, too, must have its ultimate ult?"

Sherwood Anderson's
Motor Trip

IT'S the thing my wife laughs at—a crazy desire to go anywhere.

I start to go right off.

Five hundred lousy miles.

When I started I picked up a Macon, Georgia, boy, a student at Emery College, in Atlanta (Methodist).

"Where you going?" I asked. "I won't have you unless you can drive."

"To Westminster, Pa."

"Why?"

"To sell Bibles."

"Get in."

I'd haul anyone to Westminster, Pa., to sell Bibles but he was a good driver at that.

Hell, but the revolution is a long way off!

He had white stockings and plenty of innocence.

"You got plenty of nerve to think you can sell anything to these Pennsylvania Dutch," says I.

"Yes," says he, "but they are good pay when you do sell them."

I thought he'd succeed.

He talked quite a spell about Emery College.

"How's the English department down there?"

That kind of a lead, you know.

237

He said they had a swell man on Shakespeare.
"He's been to Avon," says he.
"The hell he has!" says I.

I got driving drunk. I picked this Emery flower in Tennessee—542 miles from York, Pa., from where I write this. It was early morning, the day in a daze of equalization.

I guess he's pretty characteristic—a pretty decent Bible selling kid.

He didn't know a damn thing that would be any encouragement to anyone I know, but he could drive a Chevrolet.

"You'd have to be some kid to sell even Bibles to these Pennsylvania Dutch."

"Yes, I know, but if you do sell them they pay."

How can you beat the good American. What I say is—let him alone.

Factory Town

HERE at least is something going forward. Steel is brought in here. It becomes something man will use.

It becomes a coffee-grinder, a plow, a knife to cut bread, an automobile.

The wheels fly, the grinding machines grind. There are a thousand fabricating machines. They fabricate steel, cotton, silk.

The silk mill is a thing of glory. Once you enter it, give yourself to it, you will never forget the experience.

I went into a cotton mill. The looms were weaving ugly cloth. The machines worked with faultless precision. In a corner of a room were four women harnessing a loom.

The various colored threads were being passed through the complex machine. This was done slowly, painfully, by hand.

There, before the workers, was the design of the cloth to be made. Someone had designed the cloth.

Let us say it was to be used for the covers of the seats of automobiles.

There was this slow painful patient harnessing of the loom to make this cloth. Once the loom was harnessed it would go on and on, repeating the design over and over. Harnessing the loom was like laying out the telephone system of a city. It was as complex as that.

Now you start the loom. The wheels turn. All the little steel fingers run back and forth. The shuttles fly. The eyes cannot follow them, so swiftly they fly.

There is this cloth being made, a thousand yards, a hundred thousand yards, a million yards.

Automobiles by the thousands with this cloth covering the seats.

Who designed it? Why is it so ugly?

Suppose an artist were to come into this mill, to design cloth. Let him accept the limitations of the machine as the poet accepts the limitations of the sonnet form.

Here is something gay that might be done, something joyous.

The automobiles, with this cloth covering the seats, will travel on a thousand roads. Lovers will ride out of towns in the automobiles, middle-aged people, clerks, small merchants, lawyers in country towns, doctors, will take their wives and families out to the woods on Sunday.

The cloth being made here, in this factory, will go with them. The design is ugly. It is commonplace. The colors are without gaiety. There is no joy in this cloth being woven here in these looms.

The looms themselves are marvels of perfection. Every year the machines grow more and more complex. They run swiftly. There is a clatter, a whirl, a dance, going on in the factories.

There is more going on in the factories of America than anyone dreams of. All of those who make our laws, who write our books, who sing our songs, stay outside the factories.

I have met labor leaders who have never been inside factories or have merely passed through. There are no factory workers in the halls of Congress. The factory workers do not write for newspapers. They do not edit magazines.

Before day, through the long winter months, these men and women get out of their beds...most of them in ugly houses...they eat hurriedly and stumble through dark streets to the gate in the factory yard.

The factories, in which so many millions of Americans work, become every year more and more like prisons. You must have permission to go in. You are escorted.

I would like to see the factories thrown open to all. Let all of us, who buy and sell, who write books, who argue cases in law courts, go in and stay in. Let us wander from machine to machine, seeing the wonder of the machines. Let us talk to the workers who are becoming every year more and more a part of the machines.

Modern industry is a Mississippi. It is a Mississippi in flood. No one understands it. It is controlled by a few men who are cunning in finance. They do not understand it. The factories have become as much a part of our lives as the forests, the fields, the rivers, but they are sealed up. We, on the outside, know little or nothing of them.

We know little or nothing of the lives of the workers. Their lives are lived in the factories. There, behind these walls, are these thousands of people. Within the factory walls they grow a little to know each other. Brief conversations are held. Glance meets glance. Loves come. Whole lives are lived inside the walls of the factories. The workers, coming out at the mill gate at night, or in the morning if they are on the night shift, are tired. They eat, sleep and return into the factories.

In every industrial center miles and miles of little ugly houses in grim streets. The factory workers are buried away in these streets. They are without social standing. Every year the factory workers fall lower and lower in the American social scale. Those who buy and sell, those who make nothing, feel themselves above the workers. They have succeeded in making the workers feel socially inferior. There is an odd humbleness in them.

The humbleness in the workers often results in an amazing kind of quality.

A man who had got rich writing books visited a mill town. Times were hard. There were many people out of work. The man went home and later sent them two barrels of apples. They were as pleased as children, not because they had received the apples but because a man, high up in the social scale, a successful man, a man whose name was on the front pages of newspapers, had noticed them, had remembered and had a kindly thought of them.

The lives of all the factory workers are precarious, and every year become more precarious. Every year the machines in the factories are improved, and with every improvement more and

more men and women are thrown out of work. No man knows
how long his job will last. There are unemployed men standing at
the factory gate. When the job is lost everything is lost. The
factory worker, who is strong and willing to work, becomes an
object of charity.

SOUP KITCHEN

Have you ever visited a soup kitchen? I saw one recently in a
Southern industrial town. Some seven hundred people were fed
on the day I was there.

They were Americans, such people as you and I. I stood
watching them. I was ashamed of my warm overcoat, my stout
shoes.

I made men ashamed standing there.

There was one man approached the soup kitchen three times.
Each time his eyes met mine. He was a man of perhaps forty. No
doubt he had a wife and family at home. By an odd chance he
looked exactly like pictures I have seen of the vice-president of
the Southern Confederacy, Mr. Alexander Stephens. The man
was ashamed that I, a strong, prosperous-looking man, should see
him thus defeated, reduced to going to a soup kitchen for food. He
stopped beside me. He lied. I had said nothing about his wanting
hot soup. "I am not here for soup," he said defiantly. "I came here
to meet a friend."

I moved away, went into a corner grocery where I bought a
package of cigarettes. I stood by the door looking out. The man
dashed into the soup kitchen—it was in the basement of a small
church—ladies of the town, their automobiles standing in the
street, were down inside there serving the soup.

Presently the man who looked like Alexander Stephens came
out. He had consumed his soup and had been given a loaf of bread
which he put under his coat. He came hurrying past the corner
grocery inside which I stood. I drew back and he did not see me
again.

Young girls came to the soup kitchen; children came; men and
women came. There was an industry in a depressed state. The
factories of the town were running on part time. Thousands of
people were out of work.

A woman saw me standing before the store and asked about the soup kitchen. "Where is it?" she asked.

"I do not want any soup," she said quickly. She lied. I saw the hungry look in her eyes. She said she wanted to talk to some of the ladies who were serving the soup. "They are friends of mine," she said proudly.

There was an old workman who came to stand with me and who began to brag. He pointed to the line of people going in and out of the soup kitchen. "I am out of work," he said, "but thank God I am not like that.

"I save every cent when I have work," he said, "and I never take a drink.

"It's so," he said. He said that too many workmen, when they had been working all week, felt they had to have a bottle of moon when Saturday night came.

"They blow in their money like that," he said, "but I don't do it.

"I save mine," he said, "every cent of it.

"And now. You see," he said, "now I am out of work but I do not have to go there. I have got me a little money saved. Not much, but a little. I can stand here. I can watch the others go in. I can get me a few slices of pork to fry and some slices of bread," he said, putting his hands into his pockets and walking proudly away.

There is something broken and distraught about factory workers, out of work, shut out of the factories. They stand idly on street corners. There is a queer air of being disconnected with life. They are like hurt creatures standing there.

Automobiles whirl past them in the streets. The life of the city goes on. They have nothing to do, nowhere to go.

In the factories the wheels keep turning. The machines are there, the complex marvelous machines. Every year they become more marvelous, more complex.

They are ready to do their part. Man made them. These men and women, standing in the streets now, so distraught, looking and feeling so baffled, so out of place, are willing and ready to serve with the machines.

Cotton Mill

OF all the American industrial developments none I have seen excites me more than the cotton mill. The cotton mill—all of them I have seen are in the South—is usually housed in a long brick building. The building is as large as a city block. To this building the cotton comes in its bales from the gins. You go in. It is a little difficult to get into a Southern cotton mill these days. Cotton-mill owners and managers have become suspicious of writers. I wish they would not be suspicious of me. I would like to stay in such mills for long, long hours. I would like to go in day after day, to sit for hours watching the mechanical wonders of these places. To me modern industry is like an ocean, it is like a river in flood. It is irresistible. There is a Mississippi of machinery here. There is something stirring to the blood here. Here, in this Southern cotton mill I have come into, is one of the finest manifestations surely of the modern American mind. There is something singing here, something dancing. Here, in making this mill, man has created something as complex and strange as the growth of a tree or a stalk of corn. I am enamoured of it all. Little fingers seem playing over my nerves. See that doffer there. He is a workman. He has tuned his young body to the dance of the machine he attends. It frightens me a little when I think of him making those strange, rapid movements all day, in tune with that machine, but I am not he. I am a man out of another age. I am getting old. Old men are of no account. I do not understand my own sons. See that workman there. He is fitting all the movements of his young body to the rapid, jerky movements of that machine.

I would like to write prose like that. If I could write a volume of such prose and the writing of it shook me to pieces, so that I died, what would I care? I would like to make prose dance with the strange, rapid, jerky movements of these machines. I would like to make it dance as the machine dances and as that young cotton-mill doffer is dancing there. I would like to make it dance with the machine.

In here, in this mill, I forget the grim streets of this Southern mill town. I forget the tired "lint-heads" pouring out at the gates of the mill yard at night. I forget the long, hot, sultry summer days in the mills, the dust and lint in the air. I am an American enamoured of the machine. In here something inside me dances with the machine.

You see here—in this cotton mill—it is a modern one—the cotton coming in. The bales are broken open. It is attacked by the pickers. They are loosening and shaking the baled cotton. They shake it out of the bales in which it has come from the gin, they roll and toss it, they pick at it, they shake it.

See, it is becoming a fluffy, rolling mass now.

It is, however, not clean; it is not shaken, loosened enough. The room is full of dust. Negroes work in here. Dust and dirt gather in great pans under the machines, the pickers. The bales have come directly from the fields to the mills. You know about the movement in the South, the great movement, the movement to take the cotton mill to the cotton fields.

The movement, when it started, sprang up all over the South. It came after the South had begun to recover a bit from the depressing effect of defeat in the Civil War and after reconstruction, after the Tragic Era.

The cotton barons of the old South had come near ruining agriculture over great spaces of the South. In the State of Georgia there are, I am told, millions of acres of unproductive land. The land, after the great cotton barons had passed on, was being cropped by tenant farmers, mostly blacks.

The people all over the South were poor. After the Civil War it was thought rather a disgrace to have money anywhere in the South. It meant you had not given all to the Cause. They have got well over that.

Besides the merchants, the professional men, and the blacks there was, from early days, a huge number of poor whites. These people had lived miserable lives. Their lot had been a sorry one in slavery days. It was worse afterward. They had fought for the old South and after Lee's surrender came home to live on the depleted land and in the hills. Every one has heard how they are of the purest Anglo-Saxon stock, what fine old Anglo-Saxon names are to be found among them, and all that. It is true enough that there are some fine human types. They are certainly not all fine. They stood absolutely still for a long time. America moved forward into the new industrial age but, until the coming of the cotton mill to the cotton fields, they did not move. As a class they were poor, uneducated and miserable. There was no money for education. The South was ruined. How can you have schools to educate people if you cannot tax the people or collect taxes? It is difficult to collect taxes from people who have nothing.

So there the South was and then the cotton mill came. A few mills had been established before the Civil War and, when intelligently managed, they had been profitable.

They were profitable in more ways than one. Besides bringing in money for their owners these early mills began at once to do something else. A few poor whites began to trickle into the mill towns. The mills began to bring into employment a class of people who, under the old Southern system—the labor in the fields being largely Negro labor—had been apparently quite useless, not taken into account. After all, only a very small percentage of the whites in the old South were slave owners. There weren't so many barons.

These early mill builders were often quite heroic men. They had to fight hard to get capital for the new and untried enterprise, they had to educate their labor to the work. Theirs was not an easy task.

The poor white labor was scattered. It lived in the hills. It lived in little, unpainted shacks out on the hot, red plains.

The people had to be gathered in, they had to be trained. Because most of the early mills were run by water power they were built on the banks of creeks and rivers, often far from the towns and cities.

It was necessary to build villages for the people. All of the early mills had their villages. A tradition was established and it is to be said for these early mill builders, the pioneers of the cotton-mill industry of the South, that from the beginning they realized the need of education for their people. It was the only way to raise the standard of workmen. The early mill-village children were worked at a tender age but this had been the old tradition of cotton mills. In New England mill children of twelve were being worked fourteen hours a day.

There was William Gregg, of Graniteville, in South Carolina. Doctor Broadus Mitchell of Johns Hopkins has written a book about Gregg. He was the master of one of the more famous pre-Civil War mills. Here he comes, down along a dusty Southern road on a spring day. He is coming from his own big house on a hill and is going to his mill, at Graniteville.

He is driving his horse Jim, both he and the horse being widely known in all that country, and sits there in his buggy, a huge figure of a man with a buggy whip in his hand. Surely, at any rate, here is not the typical figure of the old South as we, in the North, have been taught to see it. There is no long, black coat and black tie here. This man has not the orator's mouth.

It is a hard, strong-looking figure of a man with a shrewd eye. As you look at the man, see him in an old print, you at once begin thinking of sturdy determined Northern men who helped to bring on the industrial age—let's say Mr. Mark Hanna, of Ohio, or Cyrus McCormick, of Illinois.

Mr. Gregg is looking about him with a wary eye as he rides along the road. Now he sees a movement in the bushes. He climbs quickly from his buggy and dashes into a thicket.

Some boys of six or eight are hiding in the thicket, having seen him coming. They are playing hooky from the school set up by the mill. He drives them out. He is holding his buggy whip in his hand.

"Get out of here, you. To school with you. If I catch you again, not going to school, I'll take your hide off."

This William Gregg, who thus drives the children of the poor whites into his school house and later to the mill, will go on picnics with them. He will drive through his mill village in his buggy, back of his old gelding Jim, the buggy piled high with peaches and apples from his farm, throwing the peaches and apples to children running beside him in the road. He died at sixty-seven, after the Civil War, after he had re-established his mill, died of a sickness got standing all day to the waist in icy-cold water—it was in the winter—working among his workmen, repairing the broken dam that brought the power to the mill.

The Civil War came and went and the South was a destroyed South. The old cotton barons were gone now, the blacks were free. No one knew quite what to do with them and they did not know what to do with themselves. The South was broke. It was a wreck.

Then the people began a little to stir about. Life did go on. The Negroes were getting back to the land. Gradually the carpet-baggers were driven out. A new kind of Southern life began.

What began in the South then is going on now. The South had to make a complete readjustment.

There were the Negroes, brought thus suddenly into a new relationship with the whites. That problem had to be handled and it was a real problem. It isn't settled yet. In trying to settle it the South has had to go through terrible times. There have been outbursts of brutality, race riots, lynchings, queer cross-currents of religious and social prejudices of all kinds.

Out of the old South, however, something did survive. The new cotton mills survived. In some way, in some of the mills, after the Civil War, the wrecked machinery was repaired, money was found (at cruel rates of interest), new machinery was bought, dams were repaired, the wheels started turning again.

The South knew how to make cotton and at that time the boll weevil had not yet come. There was the land. The labor of the land, Negro labor, knew how to crop for cotton, how to tend it. Cotton came rolling in. The wheels in the mills turned. Profits began to trickle in.

The white South shook itself. It blinked. "Well, here's something," it cried.

The cotton mills were something for others besides the poor whites. Not every young man who wanted to rise could be a lawyer or a doctor. Already every Southern town was overloaded with young lawyers and doctors. The North had gone in for industrial development and wealth was pouring in. Men from the South, going North, looked about. The Civil War had passed, apparently almost unnoticed there. There were a few old soldiers standing about and telling war tales, politicians were waving the bloody shirt and there were parades, but new lands were being opened up, new factories being built everywhere, towns were springing up and everywhere great, brick school houses and colleges. "The mills will do it for the South too," the Southerners cried, going back South.

"Take the mills to the cotton fields."

"Take the mills to the cotton fields."

The industrial movement in the South took on something of the nature of a religious revival. There was Henry W. Grady, of *The Constitution*, at Atlanta, crying out of the new South. Even Northern schoolboys recited his rolling sentences. You may see his statue on a busy street in Atlanta now, not far from the press rooms of *The Constitution*—a short, strong, little figure of a man he was—he stands there with an arm raised, one foot advanced.

"There was a South....

"There is a South...."

The new South wasn't yet, in spite of these stirring cries, but it was in the air. Every one was in the movement, every Southern town wanted a cotton mill. American towns, North or South, have never yet had the courage to say to industries, "Come in but come in on decent terms." They have always let them come on any terms.

Capital was in some way found. The records for profits, under adverse conditions, made by the Southern mills that had survived the Civil War, brought in Northern capital. The East always has been financially friendly to the South.

There was labor, cheap white labor, plenty of it. White labor was poor, miserably poor. It could be had on almost any terms and pretty much can yet.

Mills and mill villages were built everywhere. The South is dotted with them. They are clustered about the edges of the larger cities, strangely isolated, set distinctly off from neighboring houses, they are in the very heart of big Southern American towns. Sometimes the mill village stands alone. It very near makes up a town. There are only a few houses, set outside the circle, and these are for the necessary white men, the mill superintendents, doctors and others. There is a sense in which the mill hands of the South are not white men. They are "lint-heads." The mill village is not a village. It is a hill. It matters not how level the land on which it stands, it is on a hill. The mill village is called "Mill Hill."

The cotton mill is a complex thing. Here is this cotton, brought into the mill in its bales. The machines begin to handle it. They roll and toss it. Now it has begun to move forward in the mill, a moving snowy mass.

As it moves forward the machines caress it, they stir it—iron fingers reach softly and tenderly down to it.

The cotton has come into the mill still impregnated with the dust of the fields. There are innumerable little black and brown specks in it. Tiny particles of trash from the fields, bits of the dry, brown cotton boll, cling to it, tiny ends of sticks are enmeshed in it.

The cotton gin has removed the seed but there are these particles left.

The fibre of the cotton is delicate and short.

Here is a great machine, weighing tons. See the great wheels, the iron arms moving, feel the vibrations in the air now, all the little iron fingers moving. See how delicately the fingers caress the moving mass. They shake it, they comb it, they caress it.

Every movement here is designed to cleanse the cotton, making it always whiter and cleaner, and to lay the delicate fibres of the mass, more and more, into parallel lines.

And now it is clean and has begun to emerge from the larger machines in a thin film. You have been in the fields in the early morning and have seen how the dew on the spider webs, spun from weed-top to weed-top, shines and glistens in the morning sun. See how delicate and fragile it is.

But not more delicate or film-like, not more diaphanous, than the thin sheet now emerging from yonder huge machine. You may pass your hand under the moving sheet. Look through it and you may see the lines in the palm of your hand.

Yonder great ponderous machine did that. Man made that machine. He made it to do that thing. There is something blind or dead in those of us who do not see and feel the wonder of it.

What delicacy of adjustment, what strength with delicacy. Do you wonder that the little mill girls—half children, some of them—many of them I have seen with such amazingly delicate and sensitive faces—do you wonder that they are half in love with the machines they tend, as modern boys are half in love with the automobiles they drive?

I myself have heard mill girls talk. I have sat with them in rooms in their houses in the mill villages talking. They are almost always tired. The great body of these girls and women in Southern mills work twelve hours a day, sixty hours a week. They are, by any decent modern standard of living, criminally underpaid and often criminally young for such work. No doubt there is being done through them, through this exploitation of the young white working womanhood of the South, what the cotton barons once did to so many thousands of acres of the Southern soil. They are being depleted, sapped of their strength while they are young.

They talk, always of the mills. They speak of the low wages and long hours, but that is often but a passing phase of their talk. They are quite hopeless about any remedy for that now. "There are so many of us wanting work," they say. "There are so many of us."

They speak of that but you should see the fire in their eyes when they speak of the superintendent or the mill owner who does not know how to run his mill, who does not know how to keep the machines clean and in order, who is not up to the efficiency of the machines. There is American scorn of the bad mechanic in every one I have heard talk.

But now the thin sheet, the diaphanous film-like sheet that has come from the more ponderous of the machines—quite clean now, the fibres lying in their parallel lines—comes forth and gathers itself together to be spun. It passed over and, by some inner convolutions too complex for my brain, about a flying spool.

It has emerged from the great machine in a thread as large as my finger, soft and fluffy.

Now it begins to travel, faster, faster, faster. The thread flies through the air. It darts down into other machines and emerges again. It flies on and on. It flies in the air. It is picked up by iron fingers. It is caressed by rolls covered with leather made from the tender bellies of sheep. It is elongated. It is twisted. The air in the great room is filled with the flying thread.

The room is as large as a city block.

There are flying belts everywhere.

Long rows of spools whirl and clatter.

Fingers, like the fingers of a violin virtuoso, touch it.

They pick it up.

They grasp it.

Two threads are twisted into one.

Now four, now six, now eight, now ten.

The thread breaks and a little mill girl springs forward.

Her quick fingers clutch it.

They twist it, they tie it.

On it goes.

(A conversation overheard.)

"Jim, did you see the face of that kid down there? Look at the forced intensity of the eyes. The eyes look tired, don't they?"

"Well, it is a killing pace. Faster, faster, faster. We are sure nuts on speed, Joe."

"The speed-up, eh? Sure."

"Well, cotton is still king. Long live the king."

"Do you know, Jim, that they speak of kids like that in this town as 'trash, Crackers, lint-heads,' do you know that travelling salesmen, insurance agents, soda fountain clerks, a lot of gabby guys, that couldn't do nothing with their hands, have contempt for such kids?"

"Does she do that all day, Joe?"

"Sure, Jim, she can't take a chance on losing her job, can she?"

"Take a look at these machines, Jim, listen to them. You don't think they can stop, do you, because a kid like that is a little tired, because maybe she's sick? If she can't stand the gaff let her get out of the way. There's plenty of kids."

The thread is moving. It is getting firmer and harder. It flies here and there faster and faster. Watch and, if you are made that way, you will think of gulls flying.

You know how the gulls above the red river, down at Savannah, whirl and dive and fall and rise.

The thread you see flying there will make cord to tie Christmas packages, it will make cord for fish nets, it will make thread for weaving fine cloth and rough cloth, firm soft cloth and hard cloth. It will make a thousand kinds of cloth, ten thousand kinds. The journey of the spun thread has just begun.

II

It is with an odd feeling of futility that a man interested in modern industry, sensing something of its possibilities, moved by the strength and power of its marching stride through the world contemplates the attitude taken toward it by so many of our modern American writers. To be quite in line now a man should be quite hopeless of everything American and surely America is industrial. There the factories are. They are everywhere. They have crept out through the Middle West. They are invading town after town of the South.

The factories are there and they have walls, too many walls. Nowadays more and more of them have fences built about them. Every one speaks of them in an impersonal way. It is too much taken for granted that all of this marvelous American advance in the manufacture of goods means nothing, that there is, in the American people, in the American character, nothing that may eventually turn all this to account.

We see communistic Russia striving desperately to industrialize. What does that mean?

The attitude toward the factories and industrialism is too much like the present popular attitude toward the American small town.

We all remember that, a few years ago, there was published here a certain very popular novel built about an American small town. It has been read all over the world. It has made a certain definite fixed picture of life in the American small town in innumerable minds.

It is because I am interested in labor and industry as I am in the small town that I speak of this matter. It is because a particular book brought to a kind of focus a general attitude here toward all American small towns and all life in American small towns.

So there it was. The book came into my hands on a certain summer afternoon. I got it at a book store one day several years ago (the windows were piled full of them) and went with it in my hand to a certain house. I sat down in a room in the house and began to read.

There is no doubt the book was done with a certain skill. As I read, people passed before me in its pages and when I lifted my eyes certain living people, seen through a window, passed before me along the streets of the town I was in. In the pages of the book held in my hand that day people were living their lives. I remember yet the peculiar feeling of disdain the lives of these people gave me. I had myself always been a small-town man. On the whole I like the people I have found in American small towns and have many friends among them. I like to hang about the court houses of small towns, go to ball games there, go fishing with small-town men in the spring and hunting with them in the fall. I like to go to county fairs and the Fourth of July celebration. At night, when the moon is shining, I like to get with some small-town man and take a walk with him on a country road, preferably in the hills.

But let us return to the town of the book. I haven't a copy of that book with me as I sit writing of it but I remember a man back of an ugly little house on a side street, shaking ashes through an ash sifter.

I remember hot and dusty places. The air is filled with heavy, rank smells. I remember pretentious people, mentally dishonest people.

When I think of the book town people are always, it seems to me, spitting on the floor. Rotarians are always making speeches. I smell people's unwashed feet. I do not mean to suggest that all these details are in the book, but what I am trying to suggest here is the effect the book had on one man's mind. I am trying to suggest the kind of memories and feelings for the American small town left in the mind of every man to whom I have ever spoken of this book.

We have got, through this type of American literature, this picture of the American small town. It abounds in Rotarians who are always Rotarians. They are always absurdly boastful and hopeful, never discouraged, never tender about anything or anybody, never human. I am not saying that this kind of writer has worked with this end in view. I am telling what has happened. They have made for us towns in which no grass ever grows. Grapes and apples never ripen there. There are no spring rains. They are towns to which no ball teams ever come, no circus parade. I am convinced that, to a large extent, the success of books, written in this tone, is due to just that quality in them that arouses people's contempt. There is that streak in all of us. We all adore hating something, having contempt for something. It makes us feel big and superior.

And how does this concern the field of labor?

I have seen recently a sample of what can be done in the field of Southern industry. A certain well-known and very popular writer recently issued a small book about the cotton mills. As I understand the matter the writer went to a town in the South in the employ of a certain newspaper syndicate. There was a terrible situation there. Certain people, mill hands, were fighting for better working conditions in the mill. They wanted, of course, better wages and shorter hours. A strike was called.

The strike was called at night when the night shift was on and the workers, men and women who had left the mill, gathered about the mill gate. This was in the early morning, in the gray dawn. The strikers at the mill gate tried to stop the workers of the day shift from passing through the gate. The sheriff, with his deputies, had been called.

A struggle started and five or six workers were killed. It is said they were all shot in the back as they were fleeing from the scene. It is about this incident that the story of Southern industry, as told in the booklet, is built.

It is a booklet that sets forth the wrongs of labor, and I have no quarrel with that. It attacks certain people, mill managers, a certain merchant and others. Let these people look out for themselves. All the usual stage figures, so commonly used nowadays in writing of the small town, are in this town. There are, of course, the Kiwanians and the Rotarians. There are bullies swaggering through the streets.

It is like so many of this kind of books and magazine articles. You can't quarrel with its facts, only it does not tell enough facts. This sort of thing is no doubt good reporting of certain phases of life now in all American towns and, in particular, of our industrial towns. It is good reporting of certain phases of life now in towns and cities all over the industrial world.

It is good reporting and it is to my mind very bad reporting. There are too many bullies, too many Kiwanians.

For example, in the description of the Southern town to which I refer, there is a lot of space devoted to a certain lady stockholder of the mill. We are given a quick, sketchy picture of the woman. She, it seems, is a maiden lady who sits, I presume in a great house, somewhere in a distant city, and receives dividend checks. From time to time she is presumed to issue orders. The screws are put to the little mill girls of the South at her command. It is this kind of writing that seems to be all nonsense, and that is at the bottom of the harm such ink-slinging can do.

To my mind this particular rich woman (I know nothing of her, but let us take her as a type) is simply an American woman who has money.

But who makes money more easily than some of our popular American writers? I cannot help wondering in what stocks and bonds they invest.

There is this unknown maiden lady of a distant city who has this money invested in a cotton mill. Let us say she inherited it. She may never have been in a mill town. As an individual, put into personal touch with one of the little mill girls, she might well be more moved, more personally sympathetic than the writer who uses her as a kind of terrible example.

Labor in America, and in particular in the South, has got a long struggle ahead of it. The situation is infinitely complex. As we all know the coming of the machine and the constant improvement of the machine has everywhere intensified the problem of American life. The machine—and at work it is a gorgeously beautiful thing—is every year throwing more and more men and women out of employment.

And out of all this situation what will we get from much of the

writing about the Southern labor situation? We will get new
people to hate. A few individuals, a few mill managers will be
selected. We will be made to feel that he or she is to blame.

American people need now, more than they ever did need
anything in the whole span of our complex civilization, to realize
that working people are people. They need to know that the
woman investor in a cotton mill is just a woman, caught in the
trap as we are all caught. They need to know that the little mill
girl, flying about down there, so intense, so weary sometimes,
beneath that huge beautiful machine, is a little girl. They need to
know that she is exactly like your daughter and my daughter. The
travelling salesman needs to know that, the Rotarian, the mill
owner, the intellectual.

As to a particular woman investor in the stock of a cotton mill,
selected here as a type, I know nothing of her, but a few days ago,
as an experiment, I went with her case into a mill village.

It was a Sunday afternoon. There was a little mill girl I had met
who lived in the worst mill village in the Southern city I was in, a
mill village of which the other mill owners of the city were all
ashamed, and I went to see her.

Her father was ill. He was an old workman lying on a cheap
bed in a cheap, ugly room. I sat in the chair beside his bed. The day
was cold and gray, and there was a small fire burning in a fire-
place. The old workman had hurt his back, lifting a bale of cotton
in the mill, and said he would have to stay in bed for two or three
weeks. I passed him a cigarette and we smoked.

It was just such a house and such a mill village as I had seen
described in many of the articles about mill towns. The walls of
the room were dirty. There were old newspapers pasted on the
walls to keep out the cold.

The old workman's daughter sat there, and during the
afternoon other girls, all mill girls, all lint-heads, came and went.
There were fat girls and slim girls. Some of the girls had coarse
sensual faces, while the faces of others were fine and sensitive.
They were just people.

And so I took up with them the case of our lady investor. I
described her position, gave her a fictitious name. I spoke bitterly
of her. I blamed her for the poverty of the mill village in which

they lived. They did not know who owned the mill in which they worked. I pretended my fictitious lady owned it.

We discussed her. One of the girls laughed. I remember that she had just explained that she was tired. She couldn't have been over fifteen. All of these girls worked in that particular mill twelve hours a day. "I never do get rested," she said.

She laughed about my fictitious lady and her case. "I'd sure like to have a million dollars myself," she said. "I wouldn't speak to any of you kids," she laughed at the others.

"Gee, but I would wear swell clothes," she said.

Again I brought the conversation back to my rich woman investor. "Ah, you let her alone," the girls said. They were all agreed that she should not be thus attacked.

"Ah, you let her alone," they said, "what does she know about us?"

Again I have returned to the mill. I am in a weaving room now. It is another huge room. This room is a forest of belts. The belts, hundreds of them in this one room, go up to the ceiling as straight as pine trees in a Georgia wood.

They are flying, flying, flying.

There are fifteen hundred looms in here. This mill has fifty thousand spindles. The looms are not so large. They come up to a man's waist.

They clatter and shout. They talk like a million blackbirds in a field. Here, in this room, as everywhere in modern industry, there is something vibrant in the air. The inside of such a room is like the inside of a piano, being played furiously. It is like the inside of an automobile, going at eighty miles an hour.

All modern industry is like that. We who stand aside from it know nothing. (Most of us do stand aside. We know nothing about it.) It is only these women in this room, these boys, these young girls, these dim figures that come here in the dawn, stumbling along the streets of mill villages—some of the villages quite neat, well-built villages, with paved streets and flowers in the yard—others horrible enough—these people stumbling home at night filled with a weariness unknown to us who do not stand all day by these machines, these are the ones who know.

Drive a high-powered automobile at sixty miles an hour, twelve hours a day for twelve months. That will tell you something.

How can a man stand for even an hour in the presence of modern machinery and not get into his own being at least some desire for something of the balance, the delicacy, the truth that in some queer way do lie in the machine?

I am protesting against an unbalanced view of modern industrial life. I protest against the point of view that sees nothing in the small town but Rotarians and boosters, that sees nothing in industry but devils and martyrs, that does not see people as people realizing that we are all caught in a strange new kind of life.

Is this man, this mill superintendent, showing me through this mill, a brute? Is every man and woman in America who owns stock in a mill thereby outside the human circle?

It is true perhaps that these people do not see what all this modern, gorgeous machinery is doing to people. Who does see?

There is, in a recent article I have seen regarding a Southern mill town where there was a strike, the figure of a little merchant. He is a little brute. Often the merchants of these small towns where there are mills do turn against labor when labor is in trouble, when labor is striving to better its conditions.

But in the article to which I refer the particular merchant is again taken as a type of all American small-town merchants. He swaggers up and down the lobby of a small hotel. He calls people names. He tells what he would do to labor if he had a chance.

He is but one figure. Right now, in towns all over the South— the textile industry being in the slack period, many people being out of work—are quiet, small merchants who are going broke, giving credit to down-and-out mill people they know can never pay.

Let me repeat again. American people need, more than they have ever needed anything else, to realize that working people, in factories and mills everywhere, and the industrialist too, are people.

Let us return for a moment to the American small town. A moment ago I spoke of a certain book, taken as a type, that has created a certain impression. We have to presume that any writer, writing thus of life in American small towns, getting small-town life so, got his impression from the small town from which he himself came. He must have seen his home town as an ugly place and so all towns became ugly to him. The conclusion seems inevitable.

There it is.

There is a young painter living in the city of New York. He works there at night in a stockbroker's office. When he is not too tired he tries to paint in his room during the day. Once, by chance, I saw a painting of his. I bought the painting. I own it now.

The painting was of fruit in a basket. There were apples in the basket and pears and peaches and grapes. A bottle sat on a table. I bought the painting because it seemed to me that the young man had painted apples because he felt apples. He felt the ripeness of grapes, the flesh of peaches.

He was a young painter who, having no money and wanting to paint in the daytime, worked at night. He dreamed of a day coming when he would not be tired. "Perhaps I will really paint a little then," he said. He spoke of open fields, of apples growing on trees. He spoke of red apples fallen on dry, gray grass in an orchard in the fall.

He spoke of many things and among others of a country from which he had come as a young boy, and to which he hopes some day to return. "I want to go back there," he said. "I want to paint there."

He spoke of river valleys and of creeks at the edge of his native town. It was an American town. He said willows grew along the creek. He spoke of white farmhouses seen through trees, of white farmhouses clinging to the sides of hills.

"There is something to paint there," he said. "If I ever get money enough I'll go back there and I'll stay there."

"It is a lovely town," he said, and I speak of this young man here because, by an odd chance, my young painter came from the very town from which had come the writer mentioned above who, we must conclude, by the way in which he has written of the American small town, has hated it so.

City Gangs Enslave Moonshine Mountaineers

WHAT is the wettest section in the U. S. A., the place where, during prohibition and since, the most illicit liquor has been made? The extreme wet spot, per number of people, isn't in New York or Chicago. By the undisputed evidence given at a recent trial in the United States Court at Roanoke, Virginia, the spot that fairly dripped illicit liquor, and kept right on dripping it after prohibition ended, is in the mountain country of southwestern Virginia—in Franklin County, Virginia.

Franklin is a big county and practically all mountains. It lies just south of the county seat, Rockymount, and some twenty-five miles due south of the industrial city of Roanoke and but a few miles from Lynchburg, home town of Senator Glass.

These big towns and others, growing factory towns, Staunton, birthplace of President Wilson; Winchester, place of many battles during the Civil War, home town now of Senator Harry Byrd; Lexington, home of Stonewall Jackson and the place where Robert E. Lee went to become a schoolteacher after Appomattox—a Lee was among other recently being tried in the United States Court—all of these towns lie in the famous rich valley of Virginia, the Shenandoah Valley. Lynchburg, as you go west from tidewater Virginia, is really the beginning of the mountains—Virginia's portion of the famous Southern highlands, land of moonshiners and of the feuds.

Involved in the trial at Roanoke were some of the solid men of the big mountain county. There were merchants, automobile salesmen, liquor financiers, sheriffs and deputy sheriffs, a member of the state prohibition force, a federal revenue man—makers and more makers of moon—and the charge on which these men were tried was not alone that of liquor making, but of a conspiracy to beat the government out of the tax on liquor. Carter Lee, a grandnephew of Robert E. Lee, was up there, facing a possible prison term, and the South was shocked. He came clear. The jury declared he was not guilty. He is the prosecuting attorney of the mountain county and, of all the men indicted, he and two unimportant deputy sheriffs were the only ones who did come clear.

As to the amount of liquor made in the mountain county right on in the years after prohibition ended, some notion may be had by the figures given in the testimony.

Fred O. Maier, representative of Standard Brands, Washington, D. C., testified that 70,448 pounds of a single standard brand of yeast, such as is used in distilling, was sold in the county in four years. The yeast was sold in pound packages, each containing thirty-two pieces. That sounds something like 21,000,000 brews. A lot. Franklin County, Virginia, has a population of 24,000. The city of Richmond, with 189,000 people, used 2,000 pounds of yeast during the same period. There were said to be single families in the county that used 5,000 pounds of sugar a month.

There were other startling figures introduced by the government. These, totaled by government statisticians, revealed purchases of commodities useful to illicit liquor makers as follows: Sugar, 33,839,109 pounds; corn meal, 13,307,477 pounds; rye meal, 2,408,308 pounds; malt, 1,018,420 pounds; hops, 30,366 pounds; and miscellaneous grain products, 15,276,071 pounds.

Some one had invented a five-gallon non-gurgling tin can. That was an idea. Most of the liquor made in this Virginia mountain county had to be run out to some distant city, and one of the pests to the rumrunner is the gurgling sound arising from containers on rough roads. The non-gurgling cans apparently worked.

And they sold. Into this one mountain county during a four-year period there were shipped 205 carloads of 516,176 pounds. One witness testified that a carload runs about 3,000 cans, which means that the county consumed more than 600,000 of the five-gallon cans.

That would account for some 3,501,115 gallons of moon liquor pouring down out of this one mountain county, being rushed at night in fast cars into the coal-mining regions of West Virginia, to the big Virginia towns along the valley, to Roanoke, Lynchburg, Norfolk, and on into Eastern cities. The business, once organized, kept growing. They were at it up to the moment when some thirty-four of the more prominent citizens of the county were brought into the United States Court.

In this mountain country in the very heart of America, the government in its recent wholesale raid didn't pay much attention to the little moonshiner ("blockader" is the local name for the illicit liquor maker). He exists everywhere but he doesn't count. On the witness stand at the big trial some of the big makers spoke of these little picayune makers, and always contemptuous-ly. "These little cobwebs," they said, meaning the poor little hillside farmer, the poor mountain white, who creeps off up some mountain stream, under the deep twisted laurel, with a homemade still, to run himself off "a leetle run" for his own use, or perhaps to sell a gallon now and then.

In Franklin County the little fellows were out. The officers, it seemed, had to make a show now and then, a few stills captured and cut up. So they got the cobwebs. Any number of the little fellows testified at the trial. "I tried making a little run but I got caught."

Sometimes one of the big fellows, or a county or state officer, came to call on such a little cobweb.

"Howdy, Jim."

"Howdy, Jake."

"You been making a little now and then, eh, Jim?"

"You know I have, Jake. But I ain't had no luck."

"You got your still cut up, eh?"

"I sure did, Jake."

A smile from Jake. "Suppose, Jim, you go see Jeff. You know

who I mean. You talk to Jeff." (Jeff would be one of the big shots.) "I think, Jim, you might have you a little better luck than you been having."

It was the contention of the government in the conspiracy trial that the little fellows, the old-fashioned rifle-toting mountain moonshiners of romance, had been quite put out of business in this section.

The county had been divided off into sections, a big blockader and a state officer for each section. Some of the really big operators didn't make any liquor at all. They let out the job to other mountain men. "Jim, I'll be up your way next Wednesday night at about ten. Where'll be a good place to leave the stuff?"

Witnesses at the big trial, testifying:

"So I was working for Jeff [or "Henry" or "Peg"]. I was hauling. So I hauled the yeast out, the sugar out, the meal out."

"Where'd you leave it, Ed?"

"I left it just where I was told, sometimes by a bunch of trees or laurels just off the road—maybe ten, fifteen, twenty hundred-pound bags of sugar, so much meal, so many cans, so much yeast."

"You just dumped it down there in the dark? And there was no one there to receive it?"

"There may have been some one there. I dunno. It was black night. I didn't see no one."

"And what did you get for this, Ed? Bear in mind, Ed, you were running the risk of going to prison every trip you took."

"Yes, I know. I got maybe a dollar, maybe a dollar and a half."

There was plenty of testimony of that sort. Men running stills, back in the mountain laurel, for the big fellows, working for the big fellows—some of them testified, turning out moon at ten cents a gallon.

There should have been money in that for the big fellows! There was.

There were plenty of romantic figures at the trial. The government had two attorneys and the county men had some ten or twelve. In a United States Court the judge can question witnesses. He can make comments.

One of the lawyers pleading to the jury for a mountain man: "Men, send him back where he came from. Send him back to his mountain home."

The judge: "You mean, send him back to keep making the same kind of mean whisky he was making."

There was Willy Carter Sharpe on the witness stand. She is a rather handsome slender black-haired woman of thirty. It came out, when she was questioned, that she had been a mountain child from a neighboring county, and as a child had gone down into a Southern industrial town to work in a cotton mill. Then a spell in an overall factory and a job in a five-and-ten-cent store. She met and married the son of a big shot.

"I began selling liquor around town, drumming up trade."

She had, however, a passion for automobiles and developed into a fast and efficient driver. A Virginia businessman at the trial, full of admiration, whispered of her accomplishments: "I saw her go right through the main street of our town and there was a federal car after her. They were banging away, trying to shoot down her tires, and she was driving at seventy-five miles an hour.

"She got away," said the businessman. He liked her, as did every one in the courtroom. She told her story frankly, as did many other witnesses. It was evident that something new had sprung up in the mountains—big business, mass production, introduced by a few shrewd determined men, the plan being to make the little fellows work at a dangerous occupation—prisons staring at them—for little more than a day's wage.

There were mountain boys and men working nights at the stills—big stills some of them, 1,000- or 2,000-gallon capacity. Men hauling the meal, sugar, yeast, and containers back up into the hills at night.

"What did you get?"

"Oh, I got a dollar a trip."

The lawyers for the defense didn't even cross-examine Willy Carter Sharpe. She told a story of mountain men become big-time promoters, convoys of cars on the roads at night, herself in a fast car acting as pilot, government men, not fixed, coming in from Washington, the chase at night, cars scattering, dashing through the night streets of towns, the big business carried right on after prohibition ended.

Men in the crowd in the courtroom whispering: "This is the biggest it's ever been in the mountains. "This'll clean things up."

One of the men accused—he had pleaded guilty and faced prison: "I'm glad it's over. It had got too big. We don't want our county to be like that."

After she had been on the witness stand and had told her story, Willy Carter Sharpe talked freely. "It was the excitement got me," she said, and spoke of other rum-runners employed by the big shots. "They were mostly kids who liked the excitement." There were women, some of them of respectable families, who came to her—this after she had been in jail, had been in the newspapers. "They wanted to go along with me on a run at night. They wanted the kick of it," she said. She refused to tell who they were. "Some of them had in their veins what you call the best blood of Virginia," she said.

The trial was extraordinary. Even some of the big shots— mountain men who had gone into the outlaw liquor business in the new big way—came down out of the hills to testify for the government. The jury was made up pretty much of mountain men from neighboring counties. The mountain men came down, some of them, to convict themselves. They seemed to want it stopped. They seemed to want to go back to the old ways.

The big way was too cruel. It brought out too many ugly things in men.

The Time and the Towns

I T is a queer time in the American small town. As I write this, the country is in a period of industrial depression. There was, summer before last, a prolonged drought throughout the great agricultural sections of America, the South and the Middle West. In spite of this there was overproduction of food. The farmers' crops were not bringing good prices. In great sections of the country, cattle had to be sold off at a sacrifice because of the drying up of pastures.

In the towns the merchants have felt the pinch of the coming of the chain store. These great organizations are apparently moving forward in the effort to capture the retail business of the country. The chain store is usually under the management of a man from outside the town. They sell at reduced prices and for cash only. A good many small merchants have been thrown out of business and many of them will land in the class of workers.

There are too many workers now. No men in the world have been more ingenious than the Americans in developing automatic machinery. For a long time the automobile was the passion of almost every American youth and now the same feeling has been transferred to the airplance. Every male child apparently dreams of becoming another Lindbergh.

The machine dominates American life. On the farms now two-thirds the number of men employed a generation ago produce more food stuff and in the factories everywhere, new and more

truly automatic machines appear. In a town near the one in which
I live a large cigar factory was suddenly closed. The company
owned two factories in two towns. A new machine was
discovered that would enable the company to produce, in one of
the factories, as many cigars as were formerly produced in two.
One of the factories was closed almost overnight and five hundred
employees, mostly women, were without work. There will be no
more work for them at that trade. The trade is gone.

This sort of thing is happening everywhere. Here is a machine
with which one man, or woman, can do the work of ten, or
twenty, or thirty. The machine is introduced into one factory and
immediately all factories in the same field must have it. Such
machines multiply indefinitely. For a long time the resultant
unemployment was not felt much. It passed unnoticed. Only a
short time ago there was still new land opening up. Surplus labor
could be taken up in developing the new territories.

Then the modern credit system was worked out. Any man,
having any kind of job, could buy on time an automobile, an
electric refrigerator, a radio. Men and women in some of our
small towns, having a weekly wage of fifteen or sixteen dollars,
went into debt for radios and even for automobiles. Second-hand
automobiles were sold on time as were new ones. The poor
people should not be blamed for this. The towns were filled with
high pressure salesmen. The manufacturer of radios said, "How
silly of them to buy automobiles," while the automobile man said,
"They have all gone crazy on the subject of radios." "Spend,
spend," became the cry. In the flush times, during the World War
and for a few years afterwards, nearly every factory increased
capacity. It was one way of cutting income tax for companies
making often as high as a hundred per cent on investment.

The expansion of the credit system, to include almost every
kind of man or woman, having any kind of a job, kept the
factories going. The average man got a new outlook on life. The
leaders he looked up to, the great industrialists, the editors of
newspapers, all preached the new doctrine of spend, spend,
spend.

America was to have a new kind of life, a life never before
known in this world. There was to be a car standing at the door of
the most humble house. The house also was to be run almost

automatically, like factories. There were to be electric washing
machines everywhere, electric churns on the farm, cotton picked
by machines, corn planting and harvesting, plowing, all done by
machinery, houses heated automatically, food automatically
cooked. Already, in all material things, America had pushed out
ahead of the rest of the world. Could it be kept up? To say "no," to
express doubt, was to be accused. "Why, you are a knocker, a
crepe-hanger," every one said. The best way to get yourself
disliked and even hated was to express doubt. I presume it is the
same way in Russia. If you express doubt of communism, out you
go.

It has happened that, for the last few years, I have stayed
constantly in the towns. I am of the artist class, a writer, but
recently there has been in me little or no impulse to create in the
imaginative world. The actual world, the new world of the
factory, has become to me more absorbingly interesting, more
fantastic than the world of the imagination.

I have gone a great deal to factories in the towns and
sometimes have been permitted to enter. There has been in many
cases some question about my presence there. Was I trying to stir
up workers? No.

I had come on account of the machines.

They are fascinating. Why, who can write of the towns now,
without writing of factories. Every town that hasn't one is
scheming to get one. Every town dreams of becoming a city. In
America yet, every impulse is toward bigness. Few want to
remain small, to take life as it is. The movement toward the city
from the towns has also included a movement toward the towns
from the country. The Southern mill towns, many of them very
ugly places, are filled with former small town farmers of the hills
and the red Georgia and South Carolina plains. The movies call,
the lighted streets of the towns call. The life in the hills and on
the hot plains brought food and some freedom, but there was no
money for cheap imitations of New York clothes. In the towns
there would be some money coming in and money would buy
clothes, made quickly and cheaply by machines; it would buy
radios and second-hand automobiles.

The machine. The machine. Give us the machine. The
movement has included a going away from nature, from the fields

and woods. Food is eaten out of tin cans, having been put rapidly and efficiently into cans by the machine.

You go to the factory in the town. There is a contrast here. Very often the factory is located in the most disorderly and unsightly little town, but, at any rate, these factory builders are not disorderly men. There is pride in them. They may well be the captains of the new day. You cannot help feeling much of the ugliness of the town's physical life, the cheaply constructed houses, often many vacant lots—a thing rarely seen in a European town—the lots made ugly by an accumulation of rusty tin vegetable cans and old newspapers—the tired puzzled look in the eyes of the people.

Then the factory. In the best of them, the most modern, the newer ones, what order. There will be a green lawn by the front door with beds of flowers.

Inside you are caught up, fascinated by a new, an inspiring order.

The machines in there stand in great, airy, lighted rooms. Much depends upon what particular industry the factory belongs to. In some factories in the towns I have seen thousands of almost completely automatic machines in one room. There were a few people going about, usually neatly and well dressed. In factories where there is no smoke and dust, workmen and women are compelled to keep clean. In one factory all clothes, left carelessly about at night, were thrown into a furnace and burned.

The machines work with a kind of absolute precision and order in the great lighted rooms. What a queer contrast to the life of the town outside factory walls. The machines move at terrific speed. Light plays over the moving machines.

Lights play over them and through them and a river of goods pours out.

I have felt the poetry of all this. I have felt the terror of it. After having written no verse for several years and after visiting the factories of the towns I have again the hunger. In some moods I want to be the poet of industry, of the machine. For the machine, as the American has developed it, I feel only admiration and love.

It works so freely, so swiftly, so beautifully. There is a play of light and colors in a great clean space. I want painters in here with me. There is something very marvelous here. New forms are breaking into being, they are constantly changing, moving with precision in light.

And goods. More goods. Rivers of goods.

As I have visited the towns I have talked, when the opportunity offered, to the owners and managers of factories. "In your factory also every year sees the replacement of more men and women workers by automatic machines? In spite of this you produce more goods than formerly?"

"Yes."

"But are you not also destroying the consumers of goods? How can they buy goods if they have no work?"

"I don't know."

"Have you any plan to meet the situation?"

"No." (A little angrily.) "I do what I can."

Every year the factories themselves invade new towns and the towns not yet invaded by the factories are still invaded by the machine. The factories themselves every year move deeper and deeper into the former agrarian sections. On every hand the machine controls our lives. Now the players do not come to the towns. They are in Los Angeles. We see but the shadows of players. We listen to the shadows of voices. Even the politicians do not come to us now. They stay in the city and talk to us on the radio.

There is a queer half world in which we live. There are the fields near the towns and the houses and streets of the towns. There is this actuality, the town itself.

Then there is this other life, our imaginations fed with new food, the inside of that factory there, the lives of these people in the talkies, the voices coming to us so persistently on the radio. We feel ourselves in some strange new world, half in it, half out. We are half born men. Perhaps the new world of which men have dreamed so long already exists. Dare we step into it. We stand outside, trembling a little, uncertain, perplexed.

It is the only sane way in which a man may speak of the life in the towns now. There are the ministers of the churches, the merchants, the workers—we are all in the same boat. It is absurd to take Mr. Sinclair Lewis' version of the ministers as a reality or to take his "Main Street" as a picture of the towns. People feel we are passing into new times. We, in the towns, are frightened a little, we look at each other with perplexed eyes. Anything may happen in the towns.

If there is to be a new world we want it to be an American world. Many of us are looking forward to a new time of restlessness. There is much hidden just under the surface. There may well come soon now, in the American towns, a time of protest, of wide discussion, of seeking. There may be a new literature, a new romantic movement, new religious impulses. If the machine has really made for us a new world we may at any time now begin the movement of trying to go into the new world. God grant it may be a better one.

The Writer at His Craft. (Circa 1940)

Why I Write

The New Note

THE new note in the craft of writing is in danger, as are all new and beautiful things born into the world, of being talked to death in the cradle. Already a cult of the new has sprung up, and doddering old fellows, yellow with their sins, run here and there crying out that they are true prophets of the new, just as, following last year's exhibit, every age-sick American painter began hastily to inject into his own work something clutched out of the seething mass of new forms and new effects scrawled upon the canvases by the living young cubists and futurists. Confused by the voices, they raised also their voices, multiplying the din. Forgetting the soul of the workman, they grasped at lines and solids, getting nothing.

In the trade of writing the so-called new note is as old as the world. Simply stated, it is a cry for the reinjection of truth and honesty into the craft; it is an appeal from the standards set up by money-making magazine and book publishers in Europe and America to the older, sweeter standards of the craft itself; it is the voice of the new man, come into a new world, proclaiming his right to speak out of the body and soul of youth, rather than through the bodies and souls of the master craftsmen who are gone.

In all the world there is no such thing as an old sunrise, an old wind upon the cheeks, or an old kiss from the lips of your beloved; and in the craft of writing there can be so such thing as age in the souls of the young poets and novelists who demand for themselves the right to stand up and be counted among the soldiers of the new.

...Be ready to accept hardship for the sake of your craft in America—that is craft love.

...Given this note of craft love all the rest must follow, as the spirit of self-revelation, which is also a part of the new note, will follow any true present-day love of craft.

...Why do we so prize the work of Whitman, Tolstoy, Dostoevsky, Twain, and Fielding? Is it not because as we read we are constantly saying to ourselves, "This book is true. A man of flesh and blood like myself has lived the substance of it. In the love of his craft he has done the most difficult of all things: revealed the workings of his own soul and mind?"

To get near to the social advance for which all moderns hunger, is it not necessary to have first of all understanding? How can I love my neighbor if I do not understand him? And it is just in the wider diffusion of this understanding that the work of a great writer helps the advance of mankind. I would like to have you think much of this in your attitude toward all present-day writers. It is so easy for them to bluff us from our position, and I know from my own experience how baffling it is constantly to be coming upon good, well-done work that is false.

In this connection I am tempted to give you the substance of a formula I have just worked out. It lies here before me, and if you will accept it in the comradely spirit in which it is offered I shall be glad. It is the most delicate and the most unbelievably difficult task to catch, understand, and record your own mood. The thing must be done simply and without pretense or windiness, for the moment these creep in your record is no longer a record, but a mere mass of words meaning nothing. The value of such a record is not in the facts caught and recorded but in the fact of your having been able truthfully to make the record—something within yourself will tell you when you have done it truthfully. I myself believe that when a man can thus stand aside from himself, recording simply and truthfully the inner workings of his own mind, he will be prepared to record truthfully the workings of other minds. In every man or woman dwell dozens of men and women, and the highly imaginative individual will lead fifty lives. Surely this can be said if it can be said that the unimaginative individual has led one life.

The practice of constantly and persistently making such a record as this will prove invaluable to the person who wishes to become a true critic of writing in the new spirit. Whenever he finds himself baffled in drawing a character or in judging one drawn by another, let him turn thus in upon himself, trusting with child-like simplicity and honesty the truth that lives in his own mind.

If this practice is followed diligently, a kind of partnership will in time spring up between the hand and the brain of the writer. He will find himself becoming in truth a cattle herder, a drug clerk, a murderer, for the benefit of the hand that is writing of these, or the brain that is judging the work of another who has written of these.

... I would like to scold every one who writes, or who has to do with writing, into adopting this practice, which has been such a help and such a delight to me.

New Orleans, the Double Dealer and
the Modern Movement in America

FOR the last five years there has been coming to life in America a new type of magazine that must seem to the average man and woman, standing a little aside from the impulses that are creating it, rather without definite aims. And I am particularly interested in this matter just now because I happen to be living for a time in New Orleans, because I love something basically cultural in the life here, because there is published in this city the *Double Dealer*, one of the periodicals of the sort I have in mind, and because I have repeatedly, since I have been here, heard the question asked—"What does the *Double Dealer* stand for? What are such publications up to, anyway?"

Very definitely I think they are up to something and I am glad enough to have the privilege of saying, in the pages of one of this newer sort of magazines itself, what I think is in the air of America that is calling them into existence.

People who have not given the matter much thought will hardly realize, I believe, just what has happened in the publication field in America within the last generation.

There has been, for a long time now, and with America and Germany as the most outstanding leaders of the movement, a tremendous standardization of life going on in every country of the western world. By the western world I mean all of the Occident as opposed to the Oriental world.

As an example of what I am trying to get at, let me start by re-

281

stating a fact, well known to every American past forty, the obvious fact that within our own day there has come a great change in the mechanics of the everyday life of every American man, woman and child.

There have been these two things—the speeding up and the standardization of life and thought, the one impulse no doubt the result of the other.

In my own father's day, for example, there was not a man of our Ohio town, counting himself at all a person of ordinary intelligence, who did not know the name of the editor of every New York, Chicago, Cincinnati or New Orleans newspaper. Not only the names but the personalities and dominant characteristics of these editors were known to everyone within the radius of the territories in which they circulated, and often far outside. The entire daily press of the country was dominated by men of strong individuality who were continually making a direct and powerful appeal out of their own complex minds to readers all over the country.

One has, you see, but to compare the city newspaper of today with that of a generation ago to get a quite startling realization of what has happened. In the newspaper world now are there any such towering figures as our fathers knew? If there are, who are they?

When it comes to that, does the average citizen of any American city today know or care who is editor of the newspaper he reads in the morning? One doesn't think of personalities in connection with newspapers any more. The passing from active service of Colonel Henry Watterson, of the Louisville *Courier-Journal*, saw pass also the last of the old type of unique individuals impressing their personalities on people in general through the ownership or editorship of newspapers. Chicago, a city of, the gods know how many hundred thousands, nameless human beings drifting daily through crowded noise haunted streets, in and out of the doors of apartment and office buildings, department stores and factories, has two morning newspapers, printed in English.

Paris, a city half the size of Chicago, has some thirty French daily newspapers.

And Paris, you will remember, is inhabited by one people

while Chicago has within its limits a conglomeration of peoples from all over the world, newly come together, and trying to make of themselves one people—a new people—the Americans of the future.

There is something very amazing indicated by all this.

In one city the attempt is being made to channel the minds of all men into one iron groove while in the other the idiosyncracies of individuals and groups are given breathing space and many channels of expression. The impulse has its significance, hasn't it, in the somewhat strange notion, that has for a long time been becoming more and more prevalent among us, a notion that to conform to type is man's highest mission?

A rather strange doctrine, that, to be so universally accepted in "the land of the free and the home of the brave?"

It was I believe a doctrine held in high esteem in Germany in the days of the Hohenzollerns. There they succeeded in making this doctrine the national ideal. They made every man a soldier, disciplined every citizen with an "iron hand," crushed the individuality out of everyone and succeeded finally in creating the terrible military machine, that made the rest of the world tremble in anticipation of the time when it would be set going against them, but that, by an ironic turn of fate, the French, perhaps the most individualistic people in the world, did manage to turn aside at the Marne.

However, I have no desire to become grandiloquent in discussing this matter.

What I am trying to set forth is merely the fact that standardization of all life and all thought has gone much further in America than most of us realize, and to point out that what might be called the Modern Movement is really no more than an effort to re-open the channels of individual expression.

What I have said about the newspaper field is equally true of the general magazine field, and it is pretty much true nowadays of the whole book-publishing business.

In the beginning the publication of magazines and books in America was almost entirely a cultural undertaking, with thoughts of profit taken into consideration only as a secondary element. Nowadays organizations such as Hearst's, the Butterick's, the Curtis', the American Magazine crowd, Munsey's and others, own, edit and publish sometimes as many as a dozen magazines each. These magazines are run through the shop in bunches, as the modern factory turns out cheap furniture. I beg of you, if you are under the illusion that there is left any individuality among them, go to the nearest news stand and run your eye over the covers of a dozen popular magazines.

On the cover of each magazine is to be seen the same Broadway New York conception of womanly beauty. She has tilted her head a little more or less to this or that side. Now she is swinging a golf stick, now driving an automobile. Oh, ho, it is winter. She is now setting forth for the frozen lake clad in expensive furs and with a pair of skates on her shoulder.

There is one thing for which I have always been devoutly thankful. I have never seen this magazine cover female in the flesh, and I hope I never shall. I try to be a gentleman and would dislike being caught in the act of throwing a brick at the head of a lady.

As for the contents of these magazines, some of them, *The Saturday Evening Post, Pictorial Review,* and one or two others, that carry a great many pages of advertising and are very profitable business ventures, have been able to develop a type of writer who is really quite amazingly clever.

When you bear in mind that all of these magazines are run primarily for the purpose of the advertising pages, and that the first thing always to be borne in mind by the editors is the building up and holding of tremendous circulations, it will be easily understood why America had to develop a special type of writer to meet the demand.

A sort of continual and terrible perversion of life goes on here. After all there are human men and women in America. Where among us live these creatures of the popular magazine short story, the best-selling novel or the moving picture? One reads the stories published in these magazines and they are very skilfully done. There is a strange exterior semblance of life in the people who parade before us and do for our edification these brave, clever or humorous stunts.

The trick when analyzed is very simple. The appearance of life is given by exterior means entirely. The doctor's office, the city street, the vacant lot beside the factory, are described with an amazing finality and fulsomeness of detail. Into these places people are cast, wearing the ordinary clothes such as one is accustomed to see wrapped about the bodies of his friends and neighbors.

There is a kind of legerdemain that with practice may be acquired. Having tricked your reader by these purely mechanical details into having faith in the people you are writing about, you simply make these people do and say things no human being has ever really been known to do or say.

In the pages of these magazines no one ever acts as people do in life or thinks as people do in life, and of course, the writers of the stories care nothing for human life. To begin caring for human beings, thinking of them, and trying to understand them a little, would so quickly destroy their technic and their income and jerk them down off their pasteboard thrones.

The point is that such writers are one and all no doubt men who might have been at least half artists under decent conditions. But they have been twisted out of their natural function as artists because, for nearly a generation, there has been in America no periodical press through which they could channel an honest reaction to the life about them.

A magazine having a circulation of a million is in a rather ticklish position when it comes to handling any such matters as honest reactions to life. There are so many things the editors of all such magazines have to be careful about. All such basic human attributes as sex hungers, greed and the sometimes twisted and strangely perverted desires for beauty in human beings have to be let alone. The basic stuff of human life that all real artists, working in the medium of prose, have handled all through the history of writing has to be thrown aside. The writer is perpetually called upon to seem to be doing something while doing nothing at all. There is the perpetual tragedy of unfulfilment.

Every intelligent man knows that, since Eve tempted Adam with the apple, no such thing as a pure man or woman has ever existed in the world, but these poor devils are compelled to believe, against all the dictates of their common sense, that purity is a kind of universal human attribute and departure from it a freakish performance. In order that none of the million subscribers be lost or any good advertiser offended they are forced to spend their lives firing off blank cartridges, shooting pith-balls at pig bladder.

I remember that my father, a man given to outbursts of picturesque cursing used to sometimes startle us children by some such pronouncement as this (some neighbor had perhaps won his disfavor): "Damn his hide. I hope he has to live all the rest of his days in a pie factory with a muzzle on," he cried, shaking his fist at the neighbor's house.

The man in the street, engaged in the important matter of watching the baseball score, or wondering how he can beat the income tax or the races, will also be wondering what all this has to do with human life in America.

It has a good deal to do with it I should say.

When one thinks of America as it was, but a few generations ago, a vast wilderness across which railroads had to be laid, whose forests had to be cut away and whose cities were yet to be built, one can understand that there was a time in America when to be perpetually on the go, to be a hustler and a "go-getter," was a kind of moral duty.

Then perhaps there was no time to be wasted in this foolishness of trying to understand each other, of trying to really call up before ourselves, through the work of our artists, something of the inner quality of our lives. To be a "go-getter" was then perhaps a moral duty. A tree might have fallen on the head of the pioneer, who for a moment lost himself in the effort to understand his neighbor. Alertness was the mood of the times.

It may be now that a time has come to ask ourselves questions.

Are our lives worth living?

Is it living, at all, to spend all of our best years in helping to build cities larger, increase the number and size of our factories, build up individual fortunes, make more dirt and noise and indulge in an ever-increasingly louder talk of progress?

Or is there a quieter, more leisurely and altogether more charming way of life we might begin to live, here in America, instead of having to run off to Europe to find it?

Whether the time has come to ask the question or not, it is being asked. That is the most important question the young

Modern is asking. A sharp and ever more and more searching criticism of all the old American shibboleths is going on. Books are being written and printed today that simply could not have found a publisher five or ten years ago and a new and vastly more intelligent audience has already been developed for these books. In the future—sometime perhaps—we will have less loud talk of freedom and a more determined individual effort to find freedom.

When it comes to the Arts it is probably true that there is more vitality to the Modern Art Movement, as expressed in America in sculpture, painting and writing, than in any of the older cultural centers of Europe.

The simple fact of the matter is that, if America will but begin to turn more of its natural vitality into the Arts, and if we begin to think more of quality than of quantity and more of living than of accumulating, and also if we can bear, without too much flinching, a determined criticism, I myself believe—and I am far from alone in this belief—that the center of culture for the whole western world can be shifted to America. In short America may become the center for a new channeling of life through the Arts, for a new renaissance.

In this article I have used the word "culture" several times, perhaps too often. It is a rather dangerous word to use to an American audience and frightens some of us horribly. As a people we have always been most fearfully afraid of being called cultural. The idea has got mixed up in our heads with the study of geometry, the translation of Homer in schools, and such things. Not fancying these things we have become almighty proud of our lowbrowishness. Which is all right, too, but there is no necessity of being too proud of our lack of subtlety in definitions.

When I came from New York to New Orleans, a few weeks ago, there was an oyster shucking contest going on in Lafayette Square, in the heart of the city. It was for the oyster opening championship of the world. Mike Algero, a handsome Italian, won it. I took that in and then went for a long walk on the docks, extending for miles along the Mississippi river front, looking at negro laborers at work. They are the only laborers I have ever seen in America who know how to laugh, sing and play in the act of doing hard physical labor. And the man who thinks that, man for man, they do not achieve more work in a day than a white laborer of the North is simply mistaken.

That was a day for me.

By that time and by the time I had taken a ride through the "Vieux Carré," the old French Creole town, and had gone, in the evening, to see a bang-up negro prize fight out under the stars in an open air arena—

Well you see, I went back to my room and wrote a letter to a friend declaring New Orleans the most cultural city I had yet found in America.

"Blessed be this people. They know how to play. They are truly a people of culture."

That was the substance of what I wrote to my friend.

Really, you see, we Americans have always been such a serious, long-faced people. Some one must have told us long ago that we had to make ourselves world-saviours or something like that. And it got under our skin. Every long-jawed, loose-mouthed politician in the country began to talk about our saving the human race. We got unnecessarily chesty. The grand manner got to be the vogue. It sticks to us.

What is the matter with us anyway? What are we bluffing ourselves about?

Does not a real culture in any people consist first of all in the acceptance of life, life of the flesh, mind and spirit? That, and a realization of the inter-dependence of all these things in making a full and a flowering life.

What I think is that the Modern Spirit in America really means something like a return to common sense. I am sure that even such serious representatives of the Anglo-Saxon race as H. G. Wells or Oswald Garrison Villard aren't after all so much fussed about the destinies of the English and American peoples. I am sure any man is at bottom more concerned with what he is to have for dinner, how he is to spend his evening, explain himself to his friends, or perhaps even with the anticipation of the woman he hopes to hold in his arms, than he is with the destiny of any nation.

"Where can a man get six bottles of good wine? I have some friends coming to my house to dinner."

"I am a working man and my wife is going to have another kid. What kind of tobacco is that you are smoking? The bird I got this stuff from stuck me with something that bites my tongue like the devil."

I proclaim myself an American and one of the Moderns. At the present moment I am living in New Orleans, I have a room in the "Vieux Carré" with long French windows, through which one can step out upon a gallery, as wide as the sidewalk below. It is charming to walk there, above the street and to look down at others hustling off to work. I do not love work too much. Often I want to loaf and I want others to loaf with me, talk with me of themselves and their lives.

It happens that I have a passion for writing stories about people and there is a kind of shrewdness in me too. If I can understand people a little better perhaps they in turn will understand me. I like life and haven't too much of it to live. Perhaps if I take things in a more leisurely way I shall find more friends and lovers.

I sit in my room writing until the world of my imagination fades. Then I go out to walk on my gallery or take my stick and go walk in the streets.

There are two girls walking in Saint Peter street. A man has stopped at a street crossing to light a pipe. A quiet, suggestive life stirs my imagination.

There is an old city here, on the lip of America, as it were, and all about it has been built a new and more modern city. In the old city a people once lived who loved to play, who made love in the moonlight, who walked under trees, gambled with death in the dueling field.

These people are pretty much gone now, but their old city is still left. Men here call it the "Vieux Carré."

And that I think charming too. They might have called it uptown or downtown.

And to me it is altogether charming that almost all of the old city still stands. From my window, as I sit writing, I see the tangled mass of the roofs of the old buildings. There are old galleries with beautiful hand-wrought railings, on which the people of the houses can walk above the street, or over which the

housewife can lean in the morning to call to the vegetable man
pushing his cart along the roadway below.

What colors in the old walls and doors of these buildings.
Yellows fade into soft greens. There is a continual shifting
interplay of many colors as the sunlight washes over them.

I go to walk. It is the dusk of evening and men are coming
home from work. There are mysterious passageways leading back
into old patios.

"My beloved put in his hand by the hole in the door,
And my bowels were moved for him.
I rose up to open to my beloved;
And my hand dropped with myrrh,
And my fingers with liquid myrrh,
Upon the handle of the bolt.
I opened to my beloved;
But my beloved had withdrawn himself and was gone."

I am in New Orleans and I am trying to proclaim something I
have found here and that I think America wants and needs.

There is something left in this people here that makes them
like one another, that leads to constant outbursts of the spirit of
play, that keeps them from being too confoundedly serious about
death and the ballot and reform and other less important things
in life.

The newer New Orleans has no doubt been caught up by the
passions of our other American cities. Outside the "Vieux Carré"
there is no doubt a good deal of the usual pushing and shoving so
characteristic of American civilization. The newer New Orleans
begs factories to come here from other cities. I remember to have
seen page advertisements, pleading with factory owners of the
North to bring their dirt and their noise down here, in the pages
of the *Saturday Evening Post*, if I remember correctly.

However I am sure these people do not really mean it. There
are too many elements here pulling in another direction, and an
older and I believe more cultural and sensible direction.

At any rate there is the fact of the "Vieux Carré"—the physical
fact. The beautiful old town still exists. Just why it isn't the winter
home of every sensitive artist in America, who can raise money

enough to get here, I do not know. Because its charms aren't known, I suppose. The criers-out of the beauty of the place may have been excursion boomers.

And so I proclaim New Orleans from my own angle, from the angle of the Modern. Perhaps the city will not thank me, but anyway it is a truly beautiful city. Perhaps if I can bring more artists here they will turn out a ragtag enough crew. Lafcadio Hearn wasn't such a desirable citizen while he lived, in the "Vieux Carré."

However I address these fellows. I want to tell them of long quiet walks to be taken on the levee in back-of-town, where old ships, retired from service, thrust their masts up into the evening sky. On the streets here the crowds have a more leisurely stride, the negro life issues a perpetual challenge to the artists, sailors from many lands come up from the water's edge and idle on the street corners, in the evening soft voices, speaking strange tongues, come drifting up to you out of the street.

I have undertaken to write an article on the Modern Spirit and because I am in New Orleans and have been so completely charmed by life in the "Vieux Carré" I may have seemed to get off the track.

I haven't really. I stick to my pronouncement that culture means first of all the enjoyment of life, leisure and a sense of leisure. It means time for a play of the imagination over the facts of life, it means time and vitality to be serious about really serious things and a background of joy in life in which to refresh the tired spirits.

In a civilization where the fact becomes dominant, submerging the imaginative life, you will have what is dominant in the cities of Pittsburg and Chicago today.

When the fact is made secondary to the desire to live, to love, and to understand life, it may be that we will have in more American cities a charm of place such as one finds in the older parts of New Orleans now.

There has been a good deal of talk about the solid wall of preferred prejudices and the sentimentalities of the South and there may be a good deal of truth in the charge of Southern intellectual backwardness.

Perhaps the South has only been waiting for the Modern Spirit to assert itself to come into its own. It is, I believe, coming into its own a little through such efforts as the publication of *The Double Dealer*, a magazine devoted to the Arts, in New Orleans.

And, as I am supposed to be proclaiming the Modern Spirit I repeat again that it means nothing to me if it does not mean putting the joy of living above the much less subtle and I think altogether more stupid joy of growth and achievement.

Educating an Author

THIS is a subject on which I have long wanted to write. With what eagerness I set about my task. Writing of authorship will of course enable me to write of authors, and I think authors are such wonderful beings. I am one myself. People who do not know authors personally, never realize what charming, highly cultured people they are. Years ago, when I was myself not an author, I used to go into restaurants where authors sat. There they were—perhaps four or five of them—sitting at a table. Almost without exception their heads were beautifully shaped. I always thought they had such expressive hands. Of course, I could not hear their conversation although occasionally, even in those days, I did venture to walk past such a table. I pretended to be looking for my hat. Sometimes I caught a word or two. What golden words!

Before I myself became an author, I used to go about thinking that my desire to see my name on the printed page was peculiar to myself. I never dreamed anyone else had it. In those days I had many thoughts and impulses I was very sure were peculiar to myself.

For example, let us suppose that I am walking in the street. There is a tall and very beautiful building, by a bridge. I may have passed the bridge dozens of times before, but on the particular occasion of which I am now thinking, something led me to look closely at it. Perhaps the sun was just going down in a mass of gray smoke behind the building. Until that moment I had always thought of it as being white. Suddenly it became rosy red, it became blue, it became purple.

I had discovered that the building was beautiful and was very sure that of all the thousands of people who passed it daily, I was the only one who ever had made the discovery. I looked about me resentfully. It was evening and people were going home to dine. Men were driving trucks. They were hurrying to catch street-cars. What stupid men, I thought.

You will understand that all this occurred before I became an author and began to associate with other authors. Sometimes, nowadays, when I am in France, San Francisco, New Orleans or England, people ask me if we have such a thing as an American culture. "To be sure we have," I cry joyously. "Look at the number of authors we have."

Often nowadays it seems to me that everyone in America is at the business of becoming an author. My son of nineteen, who is in another city, has just written me a letter. He tells me that he has written a play. What a warm feeling I have inside myself. "Another author," I say to myself. "Slowly but surely America is coming into its own. Culture is growing here like mushrooms."

I have another son of seventeen. He goes into a room and closes a door. I go trembling along the hallway. *"Et tu, Brute,"* I say to myself. "It is as I hoped. He is at a desk. His brows are wrinkled. He is composing something."

My dog, when he smells a book or a bottle of ink, wags his tail with joy. How often nowadays I think of the beautiful lines of Julia Moore, Michigan's sweetest singer:

*"It is my joy to compose and put words into rhyme
And the success of my first book is this little notebook of mine."*

I remember once going to a dinner given by authors for authors. It was in the city of Chicago. Mr. John Drinkwater, Mr. Sinclair Lewis and myself were the guests of honor.

Voilà—as we say in French—here we were. In the room, besides the three immortals, were some two or three hundred others—all authors.

It is so wherever I go. I have recently come to Europe—to Paris to be exact. I came on a ship. I do not come to Europe often, as I do not often have the price of the passage. However that has nothing to do with the matter. That is not what I intended to tell you. Before I sailed, I met another author on the street. He also was bound for Europe. Will I be betraying a secret if I tell you that authors in general, while they love other authors in the mass, as one loves his native country, do not often love other authors *as individuals?*

But you see how it is. They are often together. It is because of culture. Everyone wants culture and where else is one to get it? You see, I do not mean to suggest that we authors do not have, in our hearts, a deep sympathy and even tenderness for each other. If you are an author there is something within you that impels you to be talking always in a very cultural way, that is to say, about books, painting and sculpture, and of authorship. You see I am doing it now. I cannot help it.

And while I am on the subject, there is something else I might say. We authors are all very sensitive and the sensitive are cursed with a thing called self-consciousness. "I am a writer. Am I also an artist?" we are always saying to ourselves.

It is a dreadful question and it is always popping up. What we authors do is to reassure each other. Sometimes I am afraid that corruption is creeping in among us. We do love flattery. I tell you this by way of confession. Ordinary people, you see, will not give us flattery enough, but we authors understand, each of us, the need of the other for flattery. Ordinary people, I suppose, have their own business to which they must attend. They have to go to a store; they have to catch a train. When they see one of us on the street they do not have time to notice the shape of our heads and the delicate lines of our faces. I do not blame ordinary people for this. I am just stating it as a fact.

The unfortunate part of it is that we authors have too much flattering to do. It is all very nice and comfortable when the other fellow is piling it on for me, but when it comes my turn—what a bore!

However, as I started to say, when I was in New York and

about to take a ship, I met another author on the street. He was about to take another ship. Naturally we both expressed great regret that we were not going on the same boat. "My dear fellow, you must get your passage changed. We must by all means be together." "No, *you* do it. You go on *my* ship."

A moment of self-sacrifice did come-to one of us at the last. I think it was the other fellow. He said something that I am sure he did not mean. Now that I think of it I am quite sure that he was only being literary.

"Oh, Hell, man; I want to be the only author on my ship. You go to the devil."

On the boat I did take, there were six other authors. How many he found on his ship I do not know. I hope he found at least fifty. On my ship no one paid any attention to me. I never had such an uncultural time.

One good thing about constantly meeting other authors is that your mind is kept continually on the alert. If you do not say nice things to your fellow author when you meet him, how are you to expect him to say nice things to you? It is a test of the mind. It keeps you on the alert. You have to be always thinking up new things to say. My dear, my dear, I grow so tired of it sometimes.

Ships loaded with authors. Authors walking everywhere in the street. There is that train you see over there in the distance. Look; it is just passing between those two hills. Formerly, trains running from town to town in America were loaded with travelling men going from place to place to sell goods. Now the trains are loaded with authors going from place to place to give lectures.

The travelling men, some of whom I formerly knew, were terribly uncultural, but they were gay dogs. I used to be one myself. In those days when I started on a journey, I went at once into the smoking car and found another of my kind.

We began to tell stories. "Have you heard the one about the mule and the miner?"

"My father used to tell me that one, but here is one that is brand new."

The travelling men with whom I associated during the darker period of my life threw their stories about with reckless abandon, but we authors do not do that. We have to save our stories. My God! Do we not live by them?

Writers, when together, usually speak to each other on the subjects of "form" and "style". It is a much higher type of conversation.

But I was about to say something of the dinner given in Chicago for the three notable writers—that is to say, for Mr. Sinclair Lewis, Mr. John Drinkwater—who is English—and myself.

You will perhaps also notice that in speaking of these three notable writers, I have put myself last. I have done that hoping that if either of these two men have occasion at some time in the future to speak in public of other writers they will put my name in and will put it first. What I wish to convey to you, the reader, is that I am a very subtle man. Everything I do and say has a purpose.

To return again to the dinner. (It may really have been a fifty-cent luncheon.) There we were—we three notable ones—sitting at a table at the head of the room and naturally, under the circumstances, looking as important as we could. I have to confess that Mr. Drinkwater—being English—succeeded better than Mr. Lewis and myself. Whatever else you may say of present day Englishmen, who are authors, this you must say: "They do succeed in looking more like authors than we Americans can. It is something we must learn."

There we were, I say, and there in the room were the three or four hundred other authors. Having adjusted myself as best I could, that is to say, having made myself sit in a chair and compose my face and head as I thought the face and head of an author should be composed, taking Mr. Drinkwater and not Mr. Lewis as my model, I looked about me.

There before me in the room sat the five or six hundred other authors. I had at that time lived in Chicago for a long time but had not known how much we had advanced.

In a far corner of the room sat two little old ladies. At first I could hardly believe what my eyes were telling me. They were by way of being aunts of mine—two very respectable and charming little old women.

Well, now I do not propose to take their authorship on my head, and after all they were my aunts *by marriage*. At first I did not believe they were authors. "How delightful," I thought. "They have in some way managed to get in here in order to pay respect to me."

The thought quite warmed my heart. To be sure, had they wanted to pay me honour they could have met me at any time by simply inviting me to dinner. One of them at least was a very good cook.

They had, however, come into this public place to do me public honour, I thought it very sweet of them and as soon as the luncheon, the necessary speeches and so forth were at an end, I went to them, pressing my way through the throng, that is to say, through the six or seven hundred other authors in the room.

There they were, being very modest, it is true, quite pressed against the wall by the mass of authors, in fact, but each held a book in her hand, and each was the author of the book.

It is all quite true. The impulse toward authorship has in America become something national. It is all very encouraging to one who has at heart the cultural advancement of his native land.

But I am presumed to be speaking here of the education of authors. What everyone in America wants to be, I am presumed to be telling them how to be. Ye Gods, Mr. Editor, would it not be better for me to attempt telling these people how to *escape* being an author.

No. Well, I see your point. You are after circulation. If I could really tell people how to do it and do it quickly, your circulation, you think, would go up by leaps and bounds.

Very well, then, I will tell them. If any of your readers really wish to be authors and want to know how to succeed, I will tell them how to do it.

In the first place, and as I am addressing an American audience there is one thing I must tell you which will shock you a little. If you really want to succeed as an author in America, you should be born at Englishman. Very likely you were born poor. It may even be that your own people did not have many opportunities to associate with cultural people. It may even be that you are a clerk in a shoe store.

How are you to know about that great world of which you must necessarily write—if you are to succeed as an author?—That is to say, of the great world of Fashion!

It may seem to you a very hopeless prospect, but I am come to tell you there is hope for you.

There you are, confined all day in the shoe store, and at night I dare say you are compelled to associate with other shoe clerks and people of that class.

Of course you find them of a very low class. Hardly any of them have any vocabulary to speak of at all. And you must have a simply huge vocabulary if you are to succeed as a writer. In particular you must have ready at hand to drop here and there in your prose, a lot of very hard words.

Well, my dear man, I have promised to tell you how to succeed as an author in spite of these handicaps, and I will do it. You can read, of course, and that is what you must do. As soon as possible you must cut yourself off, as much as you can, from the life immediately about you and sink yourself into the life of books. It would be a good thing for you if you could read, all you can get hold of, of the books of Mr....

There, I was about to give you the name of a very successful American author who has a beautiful vocabulary, but I will not do it. So few of my fellow authors ever boost me. Why should I do it for them?

And anyway, what I wanted to say was that, being a shoe clerk and being cut off as you are from real life, you must go to books. Very few clerks are fortunate enough to work in stores where aristocrats or millionaires come to buy their shoes and these are the people you must in the end know most about.

Oh, the conversation of English aristocrats and American millionaires! It is wonderful to hear.

And what lives these people live. We ought to be very grateful to our popular authors who have given us such exact and glowing pictures of these men and women into whose presence we cannot go, and who, in doing so, have besprinkled their books with such marvelous words.

Well, there you are, you see. I have really told you all I know of authorship. I have told you how to do it. If you are to succeed as an author in America all you have to do is to read the books of successful authors. It is really very simple. When you hear that a book is a best seller, run and get it. You will rarely be disappointed. Out of every book you will get something that will help you on your way.

I might, to be sure, be very old-fashioned and tell you to write, as simply and clearly as you can, of the life immediately about you. But that would be a betrayal. In the first place, who cares for such writing? And in the second place who cares for such lives?

Take your own life, for example. Is it not a terrible thing? There, I knew it was. And so is mine.

The lives of these other people, that is to say, of the people of the great world, the lives of millionaires and movie stars, to say nothing of the aristocracy of England, with which our best books are filled, are of course far beyond our own poor lives. You and I cannot live such lives. It is simply impossible.

We can, however, acquire some little education as we go along. We can increase and enlarge our vocabulary. It may be that if you will do as I suggest—and I think I may promise you success if you do—and do it seriously and for a long time, you will, no doubt, learn many words you cannot pronounce. But when you have succeeded and can associate more with other authors you will hear some of them pronounce these words and can see how it is done. It is like going to a grand dinner where, if you are at all clever, you will watch and see how other people use their forks.

And you will also find that other authors who have been before you in the great world, in the world that I might speak of as the field of the cloth of gold, will be glad to tell you any little things you do not know.

They will do almost anything for you, if you will only remember, first of all, when you come into their presence, to speak in glowing terms of their work.

America on a Cultural Jag

THE great fault with American writing just now is, I am pretty sure, that we American writers are being taken too seriously. We are faced with a queer situation. America seems to be on a cultural jag. We are suddenly, and as a people, terribly intent on getting culture and getting it now. If you are any kind of a writer in America now it isn't difficult to get fame. The great difficulty is not to get it.

Look at the situation, will you? There are several books of the best short stories of the year; prizes for great novels are given by publishing houses constantly; there are books of great short stories of the world—we stop at nothing—and how many literary magazines are there?—how many literary pages in newspapers?

All of the men employed in literary discussion cannot possibly spend all of their time talking of each other, and the popular writers give them so little fresh material. To be popular, as everyone knows, is always to write the same story over and over, year after year, from the time when you begin writing until you die.

Perhaps after all it isn't that we are taking writing too seriously. Few enough men in any age know anything about writing. What we are demanding is figures, personages; we want great writers, great men.

But a man cannot be even a decent writer and be a great man. To be great, a man must surely separate himself entirely from the life about him; he must draw himself away, be like a king or a Napoleon, something special in life.

The great difficulty with all of this concentration on writing is the thing it does to the writer. Nowadays, a man cannot possibly escape. There is no hole left into which he can crawl. It may all have come about because of syndication and standardization. I don't know. But, my God, look at us!

You take my own case for example. Well, here I am. I am an American man. I haven't been to school much and I started out in life as a workingman.

I presume from the beginning I had a leaning toward books and the written word. I like to write. Sometimes I think I do it fairly well and sometimes I know I do it badly.

Being a writer, I am of necessity deeply interested in people. For the most part, I have never sought the centers where literary men congregate. I have never lived in Greenwich Village— knowingly, at least—and have never spent more than a day at a time in the city of Boston.

Of course I have written books, quite a lot of them. There they are standing on the shelf. There are too many of them. I have never written a book or a story that satisfied me, except for a brief passing moment. When they get cold, I can never bear to open them again.

For example, I think of a story I once wrote and published. "It was pretty good," I tell myeself. I go and get down the book in which it was printed. It never satisfies me.

It may be that in writing I am seeking a kind of perfection, a blending of the matter with some inner thing, I hardly dare speak of, and that such a blend can never be perfectly made.

And what of that, too? Why all the furor? I have never pretended to be a great writer. I do not think I am one and I am pretty sure that, if I were mighty, few men would know it.

What has always puzzled me is the assurance of the men who write about writing. I gather from what some of them say that there is such a thing as a standard of perfection, and that these men have it at their fingers' end. Why they do not give it to the world, so that we may all know it, I do not know. How very selfish they are!

As for the particular criticism of the particular thing—up to this time I have never answered any critic of my own world and I am pretty sure I never will. If they want to know it, I can go further than they can. I have never had a legitimate criticism of my own work that had not already gone through my own mind.

Of course I do not take into account such ideas as sex obsession, dirty-mindedness, gloom, etc. I am not gloomy and have never had a sex obsession. The man who has that doesn't write. He goes out and satisfies his obsession. I am told by men so inclined that it isn't so difficult.

But to get back to what I really wanted to say. I think, after a time, when a man has had a certain amount of what is called publicity, the one great yearning of his soul is to be let alone.

It can't be done. Once they get after you in America, you are a gone goose. Your private life is searched into; your face is constantly being printed somewhere, and the worst of it all is that everyone is quite convinced that is what you want.

Well, what are you to do? Are you to get ugly, flee, knock someone down? What a corking newspaper story that would be!

Let us say you are, like myself, a writer of tales. Surely everyone knows that to write tales of people in any understanding way, you cannot separate yourself from people. And such a man as myself does not want to separate himself. As a matter of fact, I have always been absorbed in life.

But what chance have I with people who have been told that I am some impossible thing like a famous writer? What chance have I if I am any kind of a newspaper figure?

To a certain extent I am one. How am I to wipe out this blot?

I have been thinking of this matter for a long time. It is becoming rather an obsession with me. The condition has grown worse, I imagine, in America because of the growth of standardization in newspaper making and the coming of the movies and the radio.

Are we coming to a time when all life will be public life? It may be. It is surely pretty hard on anyone who has a tendency toward any one of the arts. So-called great men are too easily destroyed. The interest aroused by most publicity is not in a man's work, but in himself.

We are all too much praised and too much blamed.

But that is not the thing that interests me. I am chiefly

interested in remaining a writer and avoiding, if I can, the necessity of being any kind of a public man.

And how may that be done? It is true I might write under a *nom de plume*, but there is something shameful about that. And it does no good. Samuel Clemens, after he became Mark Twain, remained Mark Twain.

What I am thinking of is a suggestion. It has been in my mind for a long time. I am wondering if it would not be possible, as a sort of antidote to all of this easy public attention, that so raises the devil with a man's life, to have a general movement started for doing away with all signing of the written word.

For example, why not have at least one magazine in America in which no man signs anything?

We writers have to make a living in some way, so pay us on the merit of what we do. Let the editor or the editors of the magazine decide. Let him buy the works of men and not their names. The thing has been done before in the world's history. I believe there were no names signed to the lovely work done on the cathedral of Chartres. Surely there were workmen there as important as any the modern American world can produce.

The Future of Japanese and American Writing

THE last ten years have seen a rather intense awakening in one form at least of American writing. It began, in America, with a new criticism of American life. I fancy that we American writers began to feel sharply a certain truth in the attitude of writers and artists toward us of other countries and our American lives. We were for one thing, all pressured to be rich and a good many of us are rich.

There had sprung up suddenly, in America, a tremendous periodical press. This press was primarily interested in industrial growth. Advertising took a great boom. Of course no magazine can interest people or keep them reading on advertising alone. Our great American popular magazines were compelled to offer inducements to those of our writers who were clever enough to create exciting stories that would hold the readers to the pages of the magazine while at the same time giving no offense to those who could not bear any criticism of our growing industrialism and the accompanying standardization of all life and thought.

We have had, in America, for a long time now, a condition among writers perhaps never known before in any country in the world. I mean that pure cleverness gets tremendously paid here. The great trouble is that to succeed as a writer in America it is almost necessary to distort life out of all semblance of truth.

The result of all this is of course that we have a great many clever men over here. In America there was, at the beginning, no old tradition. The whole country was new. People were pouring in from all the countries of the old European world. The people who came were not usually of the intellectual or artistic classes. When the artist class began to spring up it was, at first, almost altogether concerned with the expression of the nation's eagerness for success and power. Cleverness in distorting all presentations of the tone of life into the glorification of power and success, while at the same time making it seem true to our lives, became the pathway to success, money and recognition.

All of this however is changed or is rapidly changing. Our younger men are more and more turning their backs on quick success and money making and there is a real effort being made to get into our writing the real tone of American life.

And now as to Japanese writing and in particular modern Japanese writing. It is amazing how very little of it we have in translation. Again and again I have met younger Japanese and have talked with them. From them I have yet the feeling that the same problems that confront the younger writers here you also know.

I get the impression of Japan faced with the same problems we have. The growing population of your country, the lack of space in which to spread out, the difficulty of acquiring new territory. What I suspect is that, like ourselves, you will more and more embrace industrial life. This, of course, will bring the same new elements into Japanese life as it has brought here.

It is surely absurd for the modern artist to waste himself in fighting this change. It is revolutionary. I myself am not an old man but I have seen startling changes for example in American life.

As a boy I lived in a middlewestern American village. The automobile was unknown, there were few telephones and the telegraph was rarely used. In the light of modern developments all of our towns were extremely isolated.

As the country was so vast and the distance between towns so great our isolation was greater than that of the Japanese village. We were an agricultural people, factories were rare. Men were born, lived and died in one small community.

I do not think you need be told how this has changed. The almost universal use of the telephone and the automobile, the radio, the flying machine, has pretty much swept away all sense of distance between places. In America everyone travels now, everyone goes everywhere.

This almost universal movement, so characteristic of our lives, has led to other changes, for example, to standardization. There is in America just now a tremendous movement toward standardization of all life and all thought.

We all dress alike, read the same kinds of newspapers and magazines, talk alike, live in towns that all look alike and we all pretty much think alike.

All of this has come about through the growth of the power of the machine, of industrialization.

You will see very easily how this has happened. If you are to manufacture cigarettes, newspapers, clothing, magazines, any commodity on the large scale you have to create, in the public mind, a desire for one kind of cigaret, hat, clothing, magazine etc. The natural result is that everything has to be cut down to that expression of public taste that will satisfy the greater number of people.

We are living in an industrial democracy and the arts, alas, are not democratic. The struggle of the artist is always to escape emerging into the universal type. If you, in Japan, become as highly industrialized and standardized as we are, and I suspect you will, your artists will have the same struggle.

I think that you, in Japan, will be surprised when I tell you that many of our writers, poets and painters who have attracted the most attention abroad are not all popular here. Many of them have to struggle hard to live. Our popular men, the men who are getting rich in the arts, are all mediocre men. They are the men who pick up the standardized mode of thought and express it in their work.

They create, when read abroad, an entirely wrong impression of American life. For example, they are responsible for the general impression abroad that we Americans are all rich. The typical popular story over here is that of the young man, born poor, who goes into business and becomes rich. We are a democracy but we rather like it if, after he has grown rich, he marries a woman of title. This story is repeated constantly and with so many variations in all of our widely read magazines that one gets the impression that in America it is a common experience.

Of course quite the reverse is true. As a growing industrial country the greater number of us are in the same position as the average man in any country. It is true that our working man makes more than the working men of most other countries but then, all of the necessities of life cost proportionally more here.

In the past, in America, most of our serious writing has taken the form of a protest against all these changes in the tone of our lives but this has begun to spend itself. Our writers now have pretty much come to accept the fact that the change is here and that no protest will change a thing. I am sure that among the better and more important men the whole struggle is to save what may be saved of individuality. Under industrialism and the accompanying tendency to standardization the struggle among artists will be the same in Japan as it is with us. We have to accept the machine.

The hope is that because of this condition and in the concerned struggle of all the artist class in all countries to save themselves from being merged into the almost universal greyness, so characteristic of life under industrialism, they may be drawn closer to each other.

We cannot well deny that there is a certain advantage as well as disadvantage in all of this change. In the early days here, when life expressed itself most characteristically in America in the isolated village given over to agriculture, the ignorance concerning the outside world was profound. We, in America, are as yet pretty ignorant when it comes to Japanese life and literature. I mean the real life and the real tone of life among your people expressed in writing but we have already had translations of the literature of many other countries that gives us some sense of life in these countries and my hope is that we may soon have more translations of your literature and more intimate and wholesome understanding of Japanese life.

As every artist in any country knows the reality of life remains the same in all countries, we are all in the same boat. There is the same sun, the same wind, mountains, fields, seas. Men love each other and they love women. Children are born. Hates spring up. Until now most of the energy of the moderns has been poured out into the perfection of the machine and in the struggle to save some old precious thing. An end of that impulse toward speed and the machine will have to come. Change seems to be the law of life. A great many artists in all countries seem to think that with the coming of the machine, all art is dying, but art has survived a great many things.

The mystery of existence remains. Beauty was never very easy to find. Out of all this spreading out of life, the quick passage from place to place, quick communication between all countries, there may come in the end an international intimacy too. It is I dare say a question of energy and the expenditure of energy. When we grow weary of expending all of our energies on the machine and the perfection of the machine we may begin to expend more of it upon the infinitely more difficult problem of mutual understanding.

Then the young Japanese and the young American may begin to arrive at understanding and mutual regard.

Nearer the Grass Roots

THE impulses that led me to become the editor and publisher of two small-town weeklies in a Virginia country town are somewhat complex. In the first place, I think almost every man in the country has the belief, buried away in him somewhere, that he would make a successful editor.

Formerly, when I lived in Chicago and New York, I knew a good many newspapermen. They all dreamed of getting away from the hectic rush of city newspaper work and owning a small-town weekly. Every writer has in him a love of the ink-pots, and all of the old trade words of the printer's craft are dear to him. There is, you see, a strong call in all the vast brotherhood of the ink-slingers in just the direction I am now going.

In my own case, I had the impulse, as suggested above, but I did not become a publisher for that reason. I am doing it primarily to make a living. I would like to go back of that a little.

Just making a living is hardly the problem. Almost any one can do that in America now.

It is important, though, how you make a living. The way you make your living has so much to do with what you get out of life. Even in America, making a living takes a good many hours. I am, as people interested in the tendencies of writing in America may know, the kind of writer whose work is a good deal more discussed than read. Perhaps a good many people who know my books do not know that. Well, it's true. My books have never sold

311

well. I began writing when I was well past thirty and after the adventures that commonly come to any man who has been laborer, soldier, wanderer, and factory employee. At the time I began writing I had got, temporarily at least, out of the ranks of laborers and had become a copy man in an advertising agency in Chicago. At that job I was fairly successful, and I went on with it until about three years ago.

I was employed in a large advertising agency, and my employers were very patient. Sometimes I went on for months without the impulse toward writing coming to me at all; and during those times was, I presume, a fairly good copy man. Then the impulse did come. To be sure, it caught me many times unprepared. There might have been a rush of advertising copy in the agency just then. I had to stall. Many of my short stories were written at my desk in an advertising agency and while I was presumed to be writing advertising copy. A story of mine that has been often reproduced, called "I'm a Fool," was written while I was supposed to be writing automobile copy.

The agency employing me used to send me out to various towns, where I was to spend my time writing advertisements for manufacturers. I did write the advertisements, of course, but never took as much time doing it as I pretended to be taking. The spare time gained by thus cheating was often spent writing short stories or novels in some country-hotel room or on the bank of some stream near a small manufacturing town. My people were pretty patient with me.

My employers were naturally aware of what was going on. Sometimes I used to quit work altogether for months and wander away somewhere to devote myself to my fiction writing. The president of the agency once called me into his mahogany-furnished office and said: "Sherwood, I will stand for you, but I hope it isn't catching. I never would stand for another one like you." I think it is true that almost every newspaper man and advertising man in the country has in him something of the writer. He is inclined to be sympathetic with such fellows as myself—and don't we take advantage of it! We are the unscrupulous ones. My employers were always kind. When I came back from a long period of vagabondage, they always gave me my job back. I have reason to know that they did it many times when they might have employed some other fellow more useful to them, at a much smaller wage. It was, I take it, their tribute to the brotherhood. To justify themselves to themselves, they pretended I was a fine copy writer.

I had always intended to hang onto some kind of a job outside of my writing. In spite of the fact that I got early recognition, my books did not sell. At last they did begin to sell a little, both in America and abroad. There was less and less need of my hanging on to my job as an advertising copy writer.

I gave it up. I did what every writer dreams of doing—became a man of leisure. One of my books, a novel, had sold very well indeed, and I had money with which to buy me a house and a small farm.

I thought of myself as settling down on the farm and leading the simple life. I would consort with nature, read, and loaf. Already I had published some ten or twelve books.

Whatever happens, I thought, the books I have already published, with what writing I will naturally do, will provide me a living as long as I am content to live in this simple fashion.

During my first year in the country I was quite happy. For one thing I was building a house. This kept me busy. It was during the second year that I began to pay heavily for my indiscretion. For an American, who had gone through the American grind, what I was trying to do is perhaps impossible.

We all talk of wanting leisure. I doubt if any of us want it. No writer can write more than two or three hours a day. Often he cannot write at all. What was I to do with the long hours? I wandered over the fields; went fishing; tramped around from house to house, visiting my neighbors. Often I longed for my advertising agency.

My country neighbors all had work to do. They were farmers. Theirs was a busy life. I was the only idler in the neighborhood. They began to speak of me as "the millionaire." Americans think of any man who can get through life without working as either a crook or a millionaire. If my country neighbors ever suspected me of being a crook they did not say so to my face.

Some of them read books and had seen my name in the newspapers and in the literary magazines. All Americans think any one must be a millionaire who frequently gets his name in the newspapers.

The two or three years I put in trying to be a man of leisure, a sort of gentleman writer on the European plan, let us say, were the most miserable I have ever spent. In desperation I went over and spent some months wandering in Europe. Nothing interested me much. I was associating altogether too much with one Sherwood Anderson. I never grew so tired of a man in my life.

I had come down into Virginia to settle, liking the country here and the people. In Virginia there is a touch of the South without too much of it. It suited me. I had no quarrel with my surroundings or my friends. My quarrel was with myself.

I had got into a position I did not want to be in. How was I to get out of it?

There were two newspapers published in a neighboring county seat town in the middle of a fat agricultural region, one Democratic and the other Republican. One day, on an impulse, I went to the town and purchased the papers. I have been running them now for a month, and it has been the most normal and happy month I have had since I threw up my job in the advertising agency in Chicago.

As to my policy in running these papers, I think I can say definitely that I have no policy beyond amusing myself, making them pay, keeping busy, and turning out live little newspapers. Of course, I expect to do other writing. Now that I am busy again I shall find time for that.

In reality, the small-town weekly is not a newspaper in the city newspaper sense. We do not handle any National news, pay no attention to sensational murders or divorce cases—unless they happen in our own town—and there is no rush. Such a thing as fear of a "beat" is unknown. The papers are filled almost altogether with news regarding the comings and goings of the people of this community. Death seems to be an important factor in our lives. Long obituary notices are written and sent in to my papers.

And then there are the churches and the lodges. They also fill

much space. The churches are the social centers of our towns.
Since the saloons have gone they are about the only social centers
we have. Except perhaps the local newspaper office.

Most of the editorial work and reporting on the papers I have
taken over I am doing myself. I have, however, found a young
Virginia mountain man who promises to develop into something
special. He has been up and down the world a good deal and has a
sense of humor. He is writing for me under the name of "Buck
Fever," and he has been a help. I am giving you here a sample of
his method. It is making a hit in our town. He called this thing
"The Lonesome Water Meter."

"The Virginia Table Company has a water meter. It is the only
one in town. A sad thing has happened to it. At first, when it was
newly brought to town, it worked fine. Now it has begun to
behave badly. For a long time now it has not been able to digest its
water.

"The matter was brought up at a meeting of the town council.
Mr. Gordon, being nearer the lonesome meter than any one else,
spoke very feelingly of its condition. He said he almost hated to
go home at night, leaving the poor water meter there alone in the
big, dark building.

"It would be all right, he thought, if there were other water
meters in town so that it could have an occasional evening of
companionship. On several evenings, he said, he took the water
meter home with him and invited in some of his friends.

"There was song and wassail. Some of the guests danced, but
the poor water meter would not dance. It sat in a corner and
moped.

"The council decided, and we think wisely, to make some
arrangement with Mr. Lincoln so he could pay his water bill
without the meter. It is to be sent back to live among its own kind.
We are quite sure every one will be happier when the poor thing
is gone." This kind of writing is giving our papers a humorous
turn that seems to be tremendously liked by our subscribers; and,
while it may be somewhat disastrous to my dignity as an author, I
am not letting that bother me too much.

The Buck Fever items have also started other people writing.

The contributions—many of them surprisingly good—increase amazingly. I have an idea that all such contributions take their tone largely from the tone of the paper.

The two papers are of two political faiths, one Republican and the other Democratic; and I am handling this problem by letting the local Republican leader handle and write all the political matter for the Republican paper, while the columns of the Democratic paper I am opening to the political leaders of that party.

As you know, Virginia is a strongly Democratic State. National politics do not cut much figure. However, in Southwest Virginia, where my town of Marion is located, the parties are pretty evenly divided and the county political fights are hot. I have not been through one yet. It may be when I have I shall have another story to tell.

I do expect, however, to escape this part of my responsibility of editorship largely because I am not myself a politically minded man. And then, I have always been a lucky man.

And there is Buck.

I have no desire to reform any one and have nailed no program of reform to my editorial masthead. I believe, however, there may be an opportunity for as good writing in weekly newspapers of this kind as in the magazines or in books. We are never hurried. Our weekly newspapers do not have a deadline. If we do not get ready to go to press on Thursday, we go to press on Friday or Saturday. It is all one to us, and, as far as I know, all one to our readers.

As you see, I have got myself into this local weekly publishing business, first, because I want to make a living at something outside of my writing; and, second, because I want to keep busy.

It seems to me, after being at it for but a month, that it is the most fun of anything I have ever done in my life. I do not see why more writers do not get at it. Surely, this business of grinding out stories for the magazines or trying to write books that will bring in an income sufficient to live upon is dreary enough. It seems to me that it leads inevitably to hack writing. Already, in the three years that I have been here in these Virginia hills and before I came to these papers, I had begun to feel the curse of the hack writer alighting on me.

Having written a novel, I began to think at once that I would have to get busy and write another for the next year's market. I would starve if I didn't. All of my work began to be hurried. If I had kept that up, I would soon have begun to hate the only craft I knew. It is a sad thing for a man when he no longer has stomach for the work by which he must live. And when I say live, I do not mean just bread and butter. I mean something a good deal more vital than that.

And while I am on this subject of writing, I want to say that, in any event, some of the best writing we are getting nowadays is being done by the newspaper men. There are any number of newspaper writers, making no pretense of being writers at all, who are infinitely better at their trade than half of the men who make any amount of fuss and who have managed, by making a fuss, to build up the illusion that they are writing when they aren't at all.

I think any old newspaper man or any writer who has found himself in the position of the hack will have little difficulty in understanding my impulses in becoming the publisher and editor of these country weeklies. There isn't a great deal of money in it, but, if rightly handled, there is a living and an occupation that keeps a man busy without being hurried.

And, in addition, there is the tremendous advantage of being in close and constant touch with every phase of life in an American community every day of the year.

What could any writer ask more enticing than that?

On Being Published

THERE must have been a few other things. I dare say I always scribble. I was a copy man in an advertising agency in Chicago.

One day Mr. Cyrus Curtis came in. He had been attracted to something I wrote. He wanted to see the man who wrote it. It must have been something about business, I can't remember.

However, his being attracted to it helped me. Mr. Curtis was already a big man in that advertising world. I got a raise out of that.

In some of my books I have told about a certain factory I later owned in Ohio. The tale is in "A Story Teller's Story." The truth is the factory was about ready to go to pieces. I was doing too much writing. I didn't attend to business, didn't want to. Things were ready for a break.

The break, when it came, went deep. All the life I had built up was ruined. I had been trying to be a "regular fellow." I belonged to clubs, went about with salesmen, business men, etc.

I was leading a double life. I went home to my house and into a room upstairs. Often I didn't come down to dinner. I wrote all night. I was strong. My body stood it all right.

About my nerves I don't know. I wrote hundreds of words in that room and threw the sheets away. My wife must have thought me crazy.

I am sure I did not have any great passion to be a writer. I haven't now.

319

I did seek something.

Perhaps I felt my own life, rather at the core, during that time.

I remember the scene from the window of that room. There were two gardens I could see into. One man went in for flowers, the other for vegetables. I couldn't decide which was the most beautiful.

Right now it seems to me I can see every flower, every vegetable, in those two gardens. I can see the gardens at the various stages of the seasons. I must have been writing like that madly, in that room for at least two years.

Both the gardeners, who were my neighbors, were orderly men. I had a passion for order in myself. I wanted some sort of rhythm, a swing to life—my life and other lives.

I never got it in fact.

I have approached it sometimes, on the printed page.

As for being published the first time. It was a story called "The Rabbit Pen" and was published in Harpers. I am pretty sure it was not a very fine story. I have never read it since. I never included it in any book of stories, never wanted to.

Why? I don't know why.

Being published made no great impression. At that time I was in a hospital at Cleveland.

Well, I had walked away from my factory, from that room, that town, all my life there. Perhaps my brain had cracked a little. I was an uneducated man. Many people had told me I could not write.

My notions seemed immoral to all the people I knew. I knew no artists.

There had been this intense struggle, within myself. Perhaps if I had stayed there in that place and had attended to business I would have got rich.

I did not want that either nor did I want specially to be published. What of all that? There was already too much rot published.

I was in a hospital to be examined for mental disorder. They did examine me there. I had left that factory and that town and had wandered about the country for days.

I was trying to find some order, some sense, in my own life and in other lives. They picked me up and took me to the hospital.

They were very kind to me there. Everyone was very kind. I must have written that story in that room looking into the gardens. I don't remember writing it. I must have sent it to that magazine.

Someone brought the letter, accepting the story, or the magazine with it in, to my bed in the hospital.

Perhaps they felt it a proof of my mental unsoundness that I was not elated. I wasn't. As a matter of fact it would be better for the art of prose writing if all stories were published unsigned.

I knew I had not got at what I wanted a little to get at in that story.

It was published. Well, the thing I was after, am still after, was just as far away as it had been before.

How I Came to Communism

THERE is a sense in which I believe that the little stories in *Winesburg Ohio* are as revolutionary as anything I shall ever be able to write.

You do not need to go far back into the history of writing to come to the place where the life of a common man or woman, the worker, was not thought interesting. Such lives were not thought of as material for the story teller at all. In the old fiction, old poetry, old plays the workers and peasants were invariably introduced as comic figures. Go to your Shakespeare and you will see what I mean. It is so in all the older fiction. The notion that the worker, in the factory, in the sweat-shop, in the mine, might be as sensitive and as easily hurt as the well-to-do man or woman, and that the strange thing in life we call beauty might be as alive in such a one—man or woman—as in the rich and successful, is still new.

If our present capitalist system did in fact produce, even for the few, the kind of glowing lives some of our romancers pretend I would myself hesitate about deserting capitalism. It doesn't.

I am only trying to say this in explanation. I myself wrote, when I was a very young man, a long book I called *Why I Believe in Socialism*. Afterward I tore it up. It was very badly written. Among my earlier books I wrote the novel *Marching Men*, an attempt to get at the every day lives of coal miners in a middle western coal mining town.

323

I believe and am bound to believe that those of you who are revolutionists will get the most help out of such men as myself not by trying to utilize such talents as we have directly as writers of propaganda but in leaving us as free as possible to strike, by our stories out of American life, into the deeper facts.

I mean that the lives of those who now succeed in getting money and power in our present individualistic capitalistic society are neither happy nor successful lives. That illusion also needs to be destroyed.

When it comes to the others, the workers, the real producers, the down trodden people, there stories need to be told.

I think I have always wanted to tell that story and still want to tell it. It is my one great passion. If *Winesburg Ohio* tries to tell the story of the defeated figures of an old American individualistic small town life, then my new book *Beyond Desire* is but carrying these same people forward into the new American life and into the whirl and roar of modern machines. I do not believe my own impulses have changed.

They Come Bearing Gifts

THE two most notable young writers who have come on in America since the war, it seems to me, are William Faulkner and Ernest Hemingway. I knew both men rather intimately just after the war and before either had published. Both were terribly injured in the war. One is a Northern man, the other Southern. Hemingway was with the Italian army and Faulkner with the English. Hemingway fought on the ground and Faulkner in the air.

If you want to know what happened to Hemingway and how magnificently he recovered read "The Sun Also Rises" and then read "A Farewell To Arms."

Then, if you do not get his story, I will never tell it.

Hemingway is a large man and Faulkner is small. With both men I had a quarrel.

The quarrel with Hemingway was by correspondence, during "The Sun Also Rises" period. It didn't amount to much.

I remember him most vividly as coming to my apartment one evening in Chicago. He had just got married and had got a job, as Paris correspondent, I believe, for a group of Canadian newspapers. He was leaving for Europe the next morning and had packed into a huge army knapsack all the provisions left over at his place.

That was a nice idea, bringing thus to a fellow scribbler the food he had to abandon. The big knapsack was filled with canned goods. I remember his coming up the stairs, a magnificent broad-shouldered figure of a man, shouting as he came. Why, there must have been a hundred pounds of perfectly good rations in that knapsack.

With Faulkner the quarrel was even more absurd. He is a Southerner of the Southerners and unlike Hemingway has stuck to his own place. We were in New Orleans and were sitting on the cathedral steps. It was night. A quarrel arose.

We were discussing the cross between Negroes and whites and Faulkner declared it couldn't work past the first crossing. "The result of such a cross is like a mule. It can't breed its own kind," he said, and when I laughed he grew angry and accused me of being a damn Yank, absolutely ignorant and stupid concerning all Southern things.

It may be we had both been drinking. We separated, each walking off alone and each turning to swear at the other.

Hemingway has already got his fame. He has written a beautiful novel and has made some of the few real contributions to the art of short-story writing in our times.

And Faulkner has written a beautiful and sympathetic piece of work in the novel, "The Sound and the Fury."

Here is a story of Southerners as far away from the South that most people think of—the South of romance that doesn't exist, thank God—as J. J. Lankes' lovely Virginia woodcuts are far away from the Virginia of "The Valley," the place to which come the rich from New York, trying to make themselves think they are Virginians.

II

But what I am thinking about as I sit here, writing on this Summer morning in my notebook, is of the relations of a writer to his fellows. I have just opened my mail.

There are, as everyone knows, all kinds of writers, good, bad and horrible.

They keep coming at you. Young men and young women write letters to a man like myself, an older writer. Well, I dare say my own position among American writers is somewhat established.

There is of course, a good deal of confusion about all this

matter of the writer's relations with the reader and other writers. My name pops up now and then in the literary reviews. People mention me at dinner.

They do all sorts of things to me. "He has a powerful but a corrupt mind," someone says.

"Why, I don't see anything very powerful about his mind."

Once a lady wrote me. I could not remember her but I had once been seated beside her at a dinner-table. Then she read a story of mine. It shocked her. She wrote to say that, having read the story she hadn't recovered from the fact of having sat beside me, even after two years. "I still feel unclean," she said.

That, it appeared, was because of my sex obsession.

A good many people think I am rich. They write and ask me for money. They are mistaken. I haven't any money, although I do manage to swim. That is because I am sometimes mentioned in newspapers. "How can you get mentioned in newspapers without getting rich?" they think. You cannot blame them for that. Only this morning I read in a newspaper of some young men in Chicago who had stayed up in the air, in an airplane I think it was, twenty-one days.

At last they came down. They were surrounded by a howling mob, thrusting money at them.

God knows I have come down out of the air often enough. I have stayed up there more than twenty-one days. I have stayed up for months, refueling from time to time. But no one ever thrust any money at me.

But I was speaking of letters, pouring in on an older author. I presume other men have this happen to them.

There are the first edition fellows and the people who want books inscribed. I am not a first edition man myself. I do not believe I own one first edition copy of one of my own books.

The books come to be autographed. A few people write asking, "May I send such and such a book? I want you to inscribe it for me."

There are people who have queer slants on friendships, too. They want you to make it seem that you and they are intimate friends. "Write as though you had given me the book," they say. That isn't so bad. A man can, with a clear conscience, keep such a book and throw the letter away. It is nice to have an extra book of your own in the house to hand to a real friend. Books cost authors a good deal of money.

There are a good many people of tact who write something like this: "I adore your story, 'I'm a Fool,' but I detest your novel, 'Many Marriages.' How could you ever have written such a filthy book? You must have a rotten mind. I admire you tremendously. Please send me an autographed photo and your signature."

They have got up a nice new trick now. School teachers do it. They tell their pupils to write to authors. There must be a form for this.

The letters come written in a childish hand. Here is a sample:

Dear Sir: We are studying American writers in our class now. We are all writing our favorite author. Please tell me all about your life. I am a little girl, twelve years old.

Rebecca Snyder

This as you see leaves you in a nice hole. You have to be rude to a child to get at the teacher. At certain times of the year I have got as many as three or four such letters in a day. "Well, I see school is open," I say to myself. Sometimes when I am flush I have a secretary and she fends them off, but I am not often flush. Heaven knows what she says to them. When I can afford a secretary I always try to get one with a strong character. I look at the lines of her face. I like fixed rigid lines.

They catch you, though. Young men come to see you. Two came one day last week. They said they had hitch-hiked to my farm from New York. They looked hot and dusty.

The farm woman who manages my small farm (she does wonders with it) does not understand. Sometimes I just say, "Go to Hell," and go into my room and shut the door. "They can sit there until they rot," I say to myself. In the country we are, as a rule, glad enough to see people. This is a Virginia hill country. When a neighboring farmer comes, even for ten minutes, perhaps to borrow a corn plow, his having been broken, we say "Don't go," we say "Stay to dinner," we say, "Stay and spend the night."

"No," he says, "I got to be getting along. Come go on over with me," he says. "Come go on up to my house."

The farm woman cannot understand. It seems so rude to her when I slam the door thus and walk away. Perhaps the young authors have come from a long distance. "I thought you liked people," she says.

"Well, I do and I won't have my liking spoiled." She doesn't, however, understand. She isn't an older American author.

The two young men said they were going on a pilgrimage. They were going to find the present location of and call on Mr. Dreiser, Mr. Eugene O'Neill, Mr. Hemingway, Mr. Carl Sandburg and others.

I was in a rather bitter mood on the day the young men came. "Why, you sweet things," I said, "won't the men you are about to honor so be delighted! You are taking them presents, eh. Where's mine?" I asked.

They were like the farm woman. They were puzzled too. They went away puzzled.

There is a judge writes from the Far West. He wants me to write out one of my poems on a piece of parchment. He sends me the sheet of parchment. He is getting many such sheets and will bind them into a book.

Well, perhaps he is an old man. I do as he asks. Sometimes an author may be up before him for murder. Perhaps he will let him off. A man writes from New Jersey. He doesn't want much. He sends a stamp. He says:

I wonder if you will be so kind as to advise me as to how to proceed in order to obtain of the newspapers, in the United States (as well as in continually keeping active) public opinion in certain phases of government, political economy and astronomy—three subjects which contains among them about everything practical, philosophical and scientific (Religion is included among the philosophical items).

He says a new generation is always growing up.

He is right about that. All he wants to know is how to so manage it that the newspapers of the U. S. A. will fill their pages daily with discussions of philosophic subjects. He doesn't want

them to bother so much with the news. I presume he wants me to
write to them and tell them to quit it.

III

But I was going to speak of a lady. Her letter came one day
recently, in the afternoon, and I opened it as I was going down to
dinner. We had a Georgia lawyer, with his wife, staying in the
house.

There were other guests. A lawyer and a newspaper man had
driven over to the farm from a nearby town. There was a painter
friend staying in the house. I went down the stairs reading the
letter.

It was, I thought, an amazing letter.

There was a $25 check in it. It was from a woman. She was a
Ph.D.

I had asked those two young men—who hitch-hiked here from
New York—"Where is my present?"

Well, $25 is a present all right. To an author it is a nice present.
Here is her letter:

Seattle, Washington,
921 LeGard street.

My dear Mr. Anderson: I am taking an unfair advantage of you,
not giving you a chance to refuse to be bothered.

Teaching in a school for girls and boys, I have at hand a
wealth of material which I ought to be able to present
acceptably. Realizing my need of technical help, I took a
correspondence course in short-story writing at one of our best
universities. Imagine my chagrin to find that my things are
even less successful with than without this needed training.
Before that time the *Nation,* the *Survey,* and *Hygeia*
generously accepted my stuff, while now even the popular
magazines throw it out.

What does an editor mean when he states that he wants only
the contributions of well-known writers? How is one to
become well-known if every fellow turns him down?

For instance, won't you tell me briefly, brutally, what is
wrong with the accompanying sketches? I realize of course

that my things are crude and unpolished, but so are the people whom I know best, and try to tell about.

I can never hope to do such things as you, nor can I hope to ever hold a candle to A. E. Coppard, with his delightful cherry-tree story and all the rest. But surely some of you men at the top must remember a day when you were less successful, and sorely needed such help as I am asking.

Not in compensation, but as a symbol of appreciation may I enclose a small check? I wish it were more. Perhaps some day I can do better.

Gratefully yours,
Luella Williams Grace, Ph.D.

Well, there was a stinger all right. You know how it is at dinner. Someone has to make the conversation. I took the letter out of my pocket and read it aloud.

It's a bit queer, just the same. These people! I suppress the lady's name. What is to be done? You are brutal for a time and then you grow ashamed.

There are so many people wanting to write. I suppose they have got something corked up in them.

The Georgia lawyer asked about the check. "What is its number?" he asked. "Is it numbered?"

It was number 311.

"You see, she has written a good many checks. She has had a bank account a long time. I'd say it was good," he said.

The Georgia lawyer's wife didn't say anything. She is a very beautiful woman. It was generally agreed I should keep the check.

The lawyer from the nearby town talked about that. "I'd make her sign a contract," he said.

"Whereas."

The point was that she was to agree not to write to me any more.

There was some danger she might come to see me. Still, she was a long way off.

The newspaper man had a practical turn. "In any event keep the $25," he said. "You might be able to serve a little better wine than you are serving now. It's a little too sour," he said.

The painter in the house said nothing. Yes, he did. "Good God!" he said.

I went upstairs. I knew what the sketches would be like. They were like that.

The guests in the house were all to stay for the night. It takes a lot of money to keep up a house. Even when you raise your own chickens, when you have a cow, when you raise pigs.

.   Editors are always turning you down. They never send you as much money as you think you ought to have. They never send you as much as you need.

IV

I wrote to her. I did it the next morning before breakfast. After all, she was rather on my mind, that woman.

Or was it the $25? I took down to breakfast what I had written. We were breakfasting out of doors, under some trees. It was a nice morning.

Here is what I wrote:

Ripshin Farm,
Troutdale, Va.

My dear Luella Williams Grace, Ph.D.: It was a queer sensation your letter gave me. There was, in particular, the money, $25. No one had ever done just that to me. Money is a queer thing, isn't it? It is such filthy stuff. I have the artist's hunger to get hold of it. To such men as myself it means perhaps new shirts, bottles of wine, food, etc.

I balanced the check in my hand. "Shall I keep it or not keep it?" You have been teaching school. Perhaps you earned the money by hard work.

"But why has she been such a fool as to send it to me?" A pretty hard question, that one. The very fact that you have sent it to me, an artist, proves, my dear, beyond the last shadow of a doubt that you are not an artist. Alas, you do not know what an artist is.

Easy enough to tell you about the sketches. When the publishers tell you that they want only stuff signed by well-known names they are talking bunk. Most of these fellows, even the editors of the popular magazines, are pretty shrewd. They did not want to bother to tell you that your stuff was just plain bad.

It's bad because it's writey, dear woman. I dare say that, before you took that short-story course, you had an honest straight feeling about things you saw about you and so perhaps you put them down straight.

So you thought you would learn to write. Well, they have pretty well fixed you.

My dear, every sentence you write is writey. It fairly stinks of writing. "The filmy fog wavering, fluttering, settling over the cove was an old story, and passed unseen like the intricate pattern of lace picked out by the fast baring beeches and gums against the paling western sky." O, my dear! You were thinking of words, weren't you? You thought, I'm afraid—well, you thought, "Now watch me, watch me throw some words at that fog."

So you threw the words and the fog disappeared. There wasn't a sign of it left. There were only the words.

Words not laid against each other, not fitted together, meaningless words. But I won't scold you. I'll try to tell you something if I can. I'm going to keep your twenty-five and buy some shirts. Think of me as wearing them next Winter.

Now as to something about writing. Try first of all, if you must write, if it gets something out of you that you feel rather stops you up, try first of all to forget all magazines, all editors, all that business. If you just want to get your name in the magazines, or make money, you will get there faster by getting into a scandal or something of that sort, or, if it's a question of money, you'll make more money writing advertisements.

This sounds harsh. It's true enough. Begin again to try to be as you were before you fooled with the short-story people. They never could teach anything but tricks.

Try, my dear woman, to feel rain on you. Let the sun shine on you. If you are a real woman, love some man, if you can find one worth loving.

Try to let life flow through you a little. Above all, forget words for a long, long time. Keep silent a lot. Don't even say too many words. Remember that words are very tender little things and that these goddam people have tricked you into an almost unforgivable rudeness with them.

Keep this in mind also: the magazines are full of trick stories. The popular writers have no real feeling for words, any more than they have for the people they write about, but they are foxy. They know how to seem to be tender with words just as there must be thousands of women who know how to seem to love. Skillful whores can do that and the popular writers are, some of them, very skillful whores.

It is much nicer to be a nice woman and something tells me you are that. If you weren't I wouldn't take your twenty-five. If you weren't I wouldn't have thought about you last night after I went to bed; if you weren't I wouldn't be writing to you now. I would have sent your money back and would have forgotten the incident at once.

I don't, as a matter of fact, hold you responsible. You have been caught by the same cheap shoddiness that is in almost all departments of life now. You have been made to think you want success, fame, recognition when what you want is love of life, to come into you, to go out of you.

Get this back, dear; fight for it.

When you get it back perhaps the little words will be tender and real in you again, like children wanting to come out of you. You may write then, but if you don't it won't much matter to you. You'll have something worth more to you than all the fame and recognition in the world.

Fame is no good, my dear. Take it from me. I know.

Sincerely,
Sherwood Anderson.

So that was that.

"It will make her sore," the Georgia lawyer said.

His wife said I was an old dear and the newspaper man accused me of making love to her.

"You are always doing it," he said. "I don't think it's very nice of you. You work them up."

The lawyer from the neighboring town said nothing.

He's a coming man, that lawyer. He's in politics.

"Good God!" the painter said.

Anyway, I had the $25. I put it in the bank. It helped. The bank account was low. One thing I know is that I don't know much.

The name of my farm is Ripshin Farm. Ripshin creek runs through it. I get a letter addressed to me at Pigskin Farm:

My dear Sherwood Anderson: Had you returned my hard-earned check I should not be replying to your good lambasting letter of the thirtieth. Naturally, I had worked and scrimped for that money. Otherwise I would not have counted its value so penuriously, its value in the constructive criticism I needed at your hands. Then to have the stuff ignored, ridiculed, called words, mere words!

Just for that may your shirts be unbecoming, a bad bargain, and tight in the collar, with a button perennially lost! Truly you men would be amusing if your guesses were not sharpened to the point of cruelty. Couldn't you read between the lines, son, that I'm no young flapper with literary aspiration, but an old woman, old enough to be your mother, whatever your age, a Ph.D.? I have known the love of a good man and given mine to him. The only comfort and inspiration of my senile years are his four children.

Meantime, since his death I have spent years upon years living, working, playing with plain people in this Far West country. I have been out on the Western prairies, out in the rugged places of the Rocky mountains. I have lived on rough fare, helped to marry their youth, birth their babies, bury their dead. And now I am Mother Luella to a host of people, mainly to people who live close to the earth.

Can't you see, son, didn't I even get this across, that I'm bursting with stuff about these folks, stuff that makes Eleanor Risley's prattle, and Miss Furman's propaganda look and sound like twaddle? Of course, I am wordy. Columbia said I must loosen up, let my characters tell their own stories. And there must be a beginning, a middle, and ending, even a diagram of the plot before beginning. Oh, it was awful! Like telling a ten-months-old to toddle with his feet kept straight or he will walk bow-legged. As if he cared.

Well, I tried to learn the rules of the game, and you see the result. Here are you boys really doing things. You strike out walking, swimming, flying, without any rules. It is disheartening to an old sister. But I am not giving up.

Again you men are inconsistent. Plead with me to be gentle, tender with words. Then hurl them around as if they were brick bats or bullets. I'm still dodging.

All this is by way of saying that I am not taking your perfectly good twenty-five dollar advice. I am not waiting for the love of a good man. None in these parts! No, I'm going to write. I've got to get it out of my system, and you youngsters, well, if you want peace, you must help me.

Get your shirts, first, good ones. Then some cigars. Pack into your brief-case some stuff I'll be sending in a few days, and take the train for the first little unknown town and convince yourself that I am not seeking notoriety, nor any great amount of money—just enough to keep the pot boiling. I'll go down in my stocking for a more adequate check from

                                             Yours gratefully,
                                              Mother Luella.

Well, at any rate I had made her write something. She had written that letter. I thought it pretty good.

She wasn't word slinging, anyway, when she wrote that. It was clear and plain enough.

In the two sketches she had sent me there wasn't a plain sentence. There was hardly a sentence you could read. They were all jammed up with words.

I suppose also I liked it, her calling me one of the boys—after I had been publishing books for some twenty years. I sent back her $25.

But she didn't stop. She sent me a $100 check. And this:

Dear Son: I warned you of this avalanche, so you've probably followed Byrd to the South Pole. You will not be tempted by the check. One can only wear so many shirts, drink so much wine, and eat so much food even with a bursting larder. But you will—I feel sure, be moved to help me with this last imposition—I swear it! A prominent magazine refused it with thanks, but I have worked too hard on the stuff to give up so easily.

I am sending it with Mary Ross's marginal criticism, which I have not had time to go over carefully. Please add your own before I begin to rehash the whole thing, if it is worth it. Miss Ross says nothing about my stinking style, but gives many practical, constructive suggestions which are most helpful.

More than on anybody else, however, I am depending upon you for the final word. If you can convince me the thing is no good, over it goes. But I am hoping for better luck.

Don't say criticism is not your job. Mowing the lawn is not your job either, but when Saturday comes and the wife says the word—my guess is that the lawn gets mown or mowed whatever happens.

Meantime, believe me with appreciation

Gratefully yours,
Luella Williams Grace, Ph.D.

It was a big package. It was a novel.

As I have said, there is a painter staying and working on my place. It happens that he and I have another friend, a painter, a first-class man we think, who is at present broke.

I knew what the novel would be like. But a hundred dollars is a hundred dollars.

I went down into a field and talked it over with the painter.

"It would sure help Ed, that hundred," I said.

"Good God!" he said.

"After all, it will only take a few hours. And $100 is a hundred dollars."

I wrote to her.

"After all," I said, "if I agree will you agree? Not to write me any more letters? I know it won't be any good. I won't be helping you a bit."

I drove down to the post-office and mailed the letter.

The novel lying there on my desk was like a heavy hand laid on me.

I tried to do something else. I couldn't. "Well, it's up to me," I said to myself.

I knew she would agree. I was pretty sure she would not stick to her agreement. After all, she was both a woman and an aspiring author. Other letters would come. I worked all morning. The painter lunched with me that day. We lunched in silence.

"You'll have to give it up," he said at last. He laughed uneasily.
"How far did you get?" he said.
"Why, half way through."
"Good God!" he said.
There must have been a forsaken look in my eyes.
"Don't do it," he said, jumping up from the table. "Send her back the hundred," he shouted. "Good God!" he said.
"You have to remember she is probably a nice person. She is probably all right."
"Oh, I dare say Ed will make it all right."

Dear Luella Williams Grace, Ph.D.:
I wrote you this morning that I would work on the MS. for the $100 under certain conditions. I mailed the letter at the farm. I had in mind that I would try to help you if I could and would send the $100 to a painter friend, a man of rare talent who is broke.

After writing you I started work on the book and got through the first section. Then I decided to do what I am now doing, return the $100.

This because I can not possibly help you. The whole section seemed to me hopelessly dull and commonplace. This is but one man's reaction. I'm very sorry. I would have liked to help you and would very much like to have the hundred for the young painter, my friend.

I can't take your money just to tell you this and if I went on I couldn't tell you anything else.

I'm sorry.

                                                            Sherwood Anderson.

V

So there it is. I spoke of Ernest Hemingway and William Faulkner. I knew both of these men well before either of them had ever published a word.

I walked about with them a lot. I quarreled with them.

Of course, we spoke of writing.

"There is George Moore," one said. "He says that Synge—he says that Synge stole all his stuff from him, from Moore."

"He does, eh; he says that?"

"Yes, you see they are both Irish."

"He could not bear it, eh? That Synge, being also Irish, being better than Moore?"

"Well, you know how it is."

I knew both Faulkner and Hemingway for a long time and before either of them had ever published a word.

I was an older man, an older writer.

They must have been working all of the time. I know they were.

Neither of them ever brought me to read a word they had written. I never saw anything they had written until it was published.

It is another morning and I am in my house. I am writing in my notebook. My mail has come. It contains perhaps a half dozen letters from young writers. "Am I a correspondence school?" I ask myself.

But there is something I did not tell.

It is about the two young men who hitch-hiked here from New York. They went away.

It was toward evening when one of them came back. I was in the yard. After all, there was something very nice in him, something attractive.

He came in. He stood before me.

"I want to thank you," he said.

He said he and his friend had been sitting in the woods.

He said they were not going to see Mr. Dreiser, Mr. O'Neill, Mr. Hemingway.

I remember that he stood looking at me, something rather nice in his eyes.

"You were right about the presents," he said.

"Yes," I said.

"It's all right," I said. "You have brought me mine," I said and he went away.

He said his friend was waiting for him around a turn in the road.

When Are Authors Insulted?

D EAR EDITOR:

In your capacity as literary critic you are seldom called upon to consider social and political questions. They lie beyond your province and you are content to leave them alone if they leave you alone in turn. But at crucial moments in a country's history, decisive incidents occur whose issues no critic can ignore unless he is willing to stand silently by while the powers that be treat his profession with contempt and some of its finest representatives with scorn.

Such an incident took place in Washington last Wednesday, August 10. A delegation of American writers, headed by Sherwood Anderson, and including Waldo Frank, James Rorty, William Jones and Elliot E. Cohen, called at the White House to protest to President Hoover against his use of Federal troops in evicting the Bonus Army. The President refused to see them with the excuse that he was too busy. Yet he had time that same day to receive politicians, Boy Scouts, and children bringing birthday greetings!

The President sent in his stead Theodore Joslin, his assistant secretary. Instead of allowing Sherwood Anderson to read his protest, Mr. Joslin proceeded to scold the writers and lecture them like schoolboys. "It is your duty," he said, "to spread the truth"—and then gave the writers "the truth"—a completely distorted account of what had happened during the evacuation of the Bonus Army.

The Writers' Committee was turned away without a chance to read their statement which was later given to the press. On the following morning an Associated Press dispatch appeared in the newspapers, stating that "city police, who kept an eye on the writers, later reported to the White House that the delegation, upon leaving there, went to a Communist headquarters."

This was a deliberate and wholesale fabrication. Mr. Anderson with Elliot E. Cohen and Waldo Frank, went to lunch at the Press Club, James Rorty went directly from the White House to the train, and William Jones left to keep an appointment with a friend. The Washington police and the White House officials had evidently not heard Mr. Joslin's advice that: "It is our duty to tell the truth."

We did however—and so we tell this story to you. As literary critic and editor, you must believe that our writers are the awakeners and creators of the conscience of the nation. You must believe in the dignity and high office of the writing profession.

We appeal to you as public defenders of that dignity in asking you the following questions:

1) Do you not think that President Hoover's refusal to see a delegation of American writers while he receives delegations of children is an insult to the authors of America?

2) Do you not think that the whole incident demonstrated the inferior position writers as a class hold in America today?

3) Do you not think that this is in large measure due to the indifference of authors and critics to the burning social questions of the day and their conviction that they, as writers, are not concerned with such problems?

4) Do you not think that these questions are worthy and important enough to the cause of American literature to merit discussion from you and your readers?

Sincerely,
Sherwood Anderson
Waldo Frank
James Rorty
William Jones
Elliot E. Cohen

Why Men Write

AGOOD many do it for money. It seems such an easy way. It
isn't so easy. I have never yet known one of our commerical
writers who was very happy. There are too many concessions to
be made. The business men who employ us are very stupid about
it. They are arrogant. They make the most absurd demands and
suggestions. After all, the commerical writer is usually a man of
talent. God knows he is humble enough. Let's say there is
something to be put over, the public to be befuddled on this or
that issue. The best plan would be to call one of us in. We are very
vain. "Look here John...you know I am a crook. I am about to
attempt to put over a very crooked deal. I want to make it appear
that I am a benefactor. I know you can do it. Get busy, John.
Befuddle them good."

I speak of this because, for a good many years, I was an
advertising man, an advertising writer. I worked in an
advertising agency. I dare say it was an average enough
institution. Let's say there was a man, in Chicago or New York,
manufacturing a shaving soap. God knows what was in the
mixture. It was soap, I dare say, ground into a powder, a certain
amount of ordinary water in it to keep it soft. As for myself, when
I want a shave I go into the bathroom and pick up just any piece of
soap. I rub my face with this, stir the stuff up with a shaving brush
and shave. I have saved a good deal of money in this way and look
how handsome I am. To be sure the soap, put thus into a tube,

advertised, had to sell, let's say for thirty-five cents. Without all of this word-slinging, spacebuying... some of us advertising writers got pretty swell salaries... without all this it might have been sold at a profit, for say ten cents.

And after all, to do this thing, to do it cleverly, make them believe, why it's something.

If they had only been able to let us alone. They couldn't. There had to be these meetings, "conferences," they were called. I always thought it interesting that such conferences usually began by some fellow, a business man, declaring solemnly that honesty is the best policy. The hell it is.

The business men were always telling us what to say and how to say it. An advertisement writer had always to be submitted to one of these guys. Well!

I remember what bothered me. I think I did always want to keep an honest mind. "All right, be crooked," I used to say to myself. "Lie. Write their bunk for them but, for God sake, keep in mind always what you are doing." I dare say I didn't always succeed.

You ask me to write a piece for STORY, on the art of writing, the art of story-telling in print, novel-writing, play-writing. "Your writing has influenced many younger writers. It will live." The hell you say: I wonder if I care.

Not so much, I fancy. After all it is a much more absorbing problem to just live, gather about you a few friends, perhaps love your friends, men friends, or a woman... I mean really love her... be aware. There is a lot to see in life, to feel, smell, taste. It is such a solemn and perhaps even asinine business, this being what is called great, doing immortal work, influencing the younger generation, etc., etc., etc. Why I think that writing, or painting, or making music, if it can be approached at all from a healthy point of view, is merely a tool a man can sometimes use to get at this business of living. It does concern, rather vitally I think, a man's outlook on life. It is all wrapped up in this other thing... a man's relationships... his handling of relationships, his striving, if you will, for the good life. Relationships, I should say, with the world of nature too, development of the eyes, ears, nose, fingers. It is even, I think, concerned with the way in which you touch things with your fingers.

This world of nature...so terribly important...food, houses in which a man lives, fields he walks in, flowers growing, automobiles, towns, cities, forests. There have been men who knew something. A fellow would like to be in on the know. We have had some grand fellows in our craft, swell guys.

And I think we all do want to go along, get our feet firmly planted on "IT" if we can. And by "IT," I mean something. As to whether or not I can say what I mean, in words, I don't know. I think it is possible that I may be able to get at it by talking for a moment of self. How we all love to talk of self. It is a universal passion.

For example, I remember a certain time in my own life. Let's say I was a man of thirty-one, or two. I had begun to catch on a little to the racket of life. I had come up out of the rucks of labor. I say, "up." Whether it was up or down doesn't matter for the purpose of my story. I had become a business man. I had been an advertising writer and I became a manufacturer. There was a certain advantage in that. I advertised. I could bully other advertising writers, make them dance to my tune. I had found out I had something. It was a kind of slickness, plausibility. I remember a remark once made to me by a friend. I had been out on a bender. He said... "I'll say you're some guy. You go off. You raise hell. Then you come back to us. You are eaten up with remorse. You get us together. You say, 'Look here fellows, we've all got to cut it out. We've got to reform'."

When I was a young lad I had a sister. She was an only sister. There were several brothers. She was smart, a good girl. We were poor and she did the housework in our house. She worked like a horse.

I began on her. I worked on her. I hardly know why I did it. I wanted to dominate her mind. We were rather an intellectual lot and used to sit in the evening talking. I'd lay for her. Let's say she would make the statement that Thomas Jefferson was a great man. Aha. Was he, though? I'd begin on her, work patiently. It didn't matter to me that it took two or three weeks. She had made the bare statement that Thomas Jefferson was a great man and I wanted to make her declare, not knowing that I had influenced her mind, that he was a bum.

Later this same thing was carried along with other people.

"Say, what satisfaction do you get out of this ... to show yourself strong to yourself, a little more subtle than most of the others about you, thus proving your manhood to yourself, eh?" You take a walk afterward alone in the moonlight. "Look, see what a swell guy I am."

You take this into business. Of course you can sell things. Never mind whether or not people want, or need, what you are selling. Do you want a picture of the world of business? What about this one? And always, far down underneath all of this, always of course something else. There are such things, impulses, as real manhood, or even love. There is always, after all, the dark gray, blue, green, red, white fact of life itself. How much smart men miss, being smart. I don't know what, in my own case, finally checked me, made me begin to feel uncomfortable. It may have been the fact that I was, for a time, successful. For a time I was what is called a go-getter, did rather dominate most other men, made money, was getting what I had thought I wanted.

I don't know what stopped me, if I did stop, but I think that writing had something to do with it. I became uncomfortable. Now and then I caught, in the eyes of other men ... having put something over on them ... a kind of contempt. I know that I began to walk about alone. Now I do think it is very hard, perhaps impossible, for any man to get a fair, clear look at himself. It can't be done. I fancy that I began, at first unconsciously, to put other men, imagined figures of men, in the same position I was in. You see I was in this situation. I was going about saying to myself, "What the hell? What's the matter with me?" I must presume that all of the time I was conscious, let's say dimly, of a big, a fascinating world outside of my circle.

Let's say I was just an ordinary, decent enough man. There might be a hotel clerk, in the hotel where I was living for the time, a street car conductor, an old man, broken by life, who sold shoestrings in the street where I had my factory office.

I dare say that most of us let ourselves out of this sort of thing, the nasty uncomfortable feeling that does come, by developing a feeling of superiority. "Look at me. I'm something. Really I'm a pretty swell guy."

But there is this dirty feeling that comes. "What the hell? What's the matter with me?" To tell the truth I don't believe that,

as rather a smart young advertising man, later manufacturer...company promoter for a time...I was any more slick,
plausible, any more of an ordinary mill-run, son-of-a-bitch than a
lot of other men I knew at that time.

But, you see—you get my point—I didn't like my relationships
with the others, women I was trying to get to know, the hotel
clerk already mentioned, the street car conductor, the old man
selling the shoestrings.

I used to take a lot of long walks alone. I began that. There was
a time during which I drank a good deal, got drunk almost every
night. Drink helps sometimes. I got a notion in my head. I said to
myself, "Look here," I said, "if you can't really approach people in
the real world, in the world of nature, there may be another
world," and I must say that the thought jerked a door open for me.
I do not believe that I have ever thought of myself as a fine writer,
that I have ever cared for writing in that way. The Poes and the
Charles Lambs of the world do not interest me very much. "Look
here," I said to myself, "I'll take some fellow, a little like myself,
something of the same circumstances, same experiences in life.
I'll put him down on paper, his life, his relations with others, the
story of the things that happen to him, how he feels—all this on
sheets of paper." I must say it helped.

And now I wonder if I am making this clear. I am trying to
explain the impulse toward writing. I mean real writing. I really
don't think that any other kind of writing is of much importance,
at least not to me. It seemed to me, when I began to do it, that I
could, by writing, push myself, as self, far off. I could get myself, as
self, in the unimportant position I deserved. I became, for the
nonce, to myself, just a passing thing, just one of a long, long
procession of men...any one other figure in the procession
certainly as important as myself...a kind of new gladness inside.
I even think there was a kind of nice inner honesty sometimes. I
found it pretty swell.

And so naturally I think of writing as a kind of giving out, a
going out. What is of interest to me is the fact of how very
unimportant my factory, my achievements, my position in
society, became to me. I've a notion that it would have been just as
unimportant if I had been, say, a Henry Ford.

There is you see, inevitably I think, a kind of new world

opening out before your eyes. This at least for moments...often
...oh blessed times...for days and even weeks. Nothing,
nothing, nothing. I think it explains the world of the artist in any
art. I am a little afraid that a good many people will not
understand what I am talking about.

They could though.

I fancy I am speaking of the art of the story-teller, the painter,
sculptor, song-maker, what have you, as a way of health. It should
be the very, very health. If not that, why bother with it? Surely no
man of sense wants merely to become a part of what is called "the
literati."

The Story Teller's Job

I T seems to me that the story-teller is one thing, and the thinker, the political economist, the reformer another. I myself cannot help hoping that, in bringing out my new novel, I have returned to an old love. I hope now that the return will be permanent. I intend that it shall. As an old draftsman once said to me, when I was a lad, it is best for a man to keep to his own trade.

It is true that, just now, the machinery of government and of what I presume I may call "our civilization" does seem to creak horribly but I am pretty sure that I, at least, do not know how to make it quit creaking.

But we fellows, we scribblers, do get caught. There comes, let's say, such a breakup as that of the winter of '32-'33. Your writer is always going about, looking and looking. He sees things, such as we all saw during that dreadful winter. On all sides there is misery and destitution. Oh, the faces of the beaten people seen in streets! Men are grubbing in garbage cans for food. Your writer knows that there is vast richness in a country like ours. He becomes indignant, furious, signs petitions, goes on committees, puts his name to manifestoes, goes to Washington with others to sit on the steps of the White House, trying to harass the President, even makes political speeches.

God help him!

For him it is all wrong. The business of the story-teller is with life, in his own time, life as he feels it, smells it, tastes it. Not for him surely the making of the revolution. At his best he is too much lost in the life about him, having really no absolute convictions as to the road to man's happiness, the good life. He is to remain curious, absorbed, wanting only the story, to tell it truly, with some grace, if that is possible; for the truth is that, if he can remain truly concerned with the life about him, and particularly in others, the social implications which come in, as they should, come almost unconsciously. It is the storyteller's setting out, in his own person, to try personally to correct the social evils of his times that is the real violation of his obligation.

Why I Write

ITʼS a little inhuman, this attempting to write about writing. "Say, what are you up to now?" you ask yourself. O. K. Itʼs a mixed-up world, not to say a mess. A man might write hundreds of thousands of words, volumes ... a manʼs relations with other writers, publishers, literary agents, critics, his attitude toward his own work, etc. Recently a story of mine appeared in a volume called "Caravan." They publish things you like but canʼt sell. My story was about an advertising writer. I used to be one and I was having fun writing the story. The magazines didnʼt want it because they donʼt like making fun of advertising. We all understand that.

The point is that when the book came to me, I opened it hurriedly, turned to my own story, read it. "Pretty good," I told myself. There were all these other writers represented in the book. I really intended to read their things. You see how it is. We are all like that.

Last year I began writing a book and it was to be a big book, the plain, straight story of my own experiences as a writer, how I happened to begin, my early experiences, my getting to know other writers, painters, the literary and artistic world as it was, men seen, what they meant to me, what men hurt me, what men helped me. All of this to be very frank. I have known so many men, have traveled so much up and down. I intended to go after the critics, have my say about criticism.

I wrote ... 10,000 ... 20,000 ... 30,000 ... words. One day I stopped writing and took a walk. There was something, like another person, down inside me somewhere, laughing at me. In all my writing I had never made what any man could call a hero, but at last I was doing it. I was making myself the hero of my book. That is what the laughing was about. Day after day I went back to the job, but couldn't carry on. The thing down inside kept laughing. I had to chuck the book.

We begin in all sorts of ways. It seems to me a man is or he isn't. I pick up a copy of THE WRITER and there is Mr. Sinclair Lewis saying how he would like to run a hotel or be a scientist. It's no good. He couldn't do it. If he ever gets his little wayside inn he'll find himself writing on the table in the kitchen when he should have his mind on the French fries.

On the whole, it's fun. A man's pride is often hurt by the critics, but, on the whole, criticism here is pretty honest. We all perhaps get all that is coming to us.

I myself came into writing rather by the back door. It just happened so. I must have been past thirty when I began scribbling. I had been more or less the adventurer in life, a worker, in factories and on farms.

Then a wanderer, I got into business, owned a factory. It was an old problem. My work didn't satisfy.

I was trying constantly to find out what was wrong and then an idea came. It is hard, perhaps impossible, to do a sensible thing about self. I began to invent imaginary figures, tried putting them into positions in life I had been in. I was close to them, yet separated. It was a kind of game, a relief. It led into writing. I don't remember just how long I went on with this game, perhaps five years. My business went to pot. I didn't care much.

It is all very interesting, very absorbing. Writing is not work to me. I love it. Sometimes it seems to me that I only live while at work. I love the smell of ink, the rattle of my typewriter. I believe in my own work. When something I write is adversely criticised, I am hurt. I get angry, swear, am rather childish. When some critic does not like one of my stories or novels, I begin building up the notion that he has it in for me personally. Usually I take it out on my wife, who has learned how to handle me. "Never mind. You are good," she says. That makes me feel better.

With others, and this includes those who do not go in much for my work, I am usually, outwardly a smiling, placid-seeming man. Once I was at a party, with other writers... and I dare say a few critics... when the poet Maxwell Bodenheim came in. There was a critic I wanted to choke. I was this smiling placid man outside while I was raging within. Bodenheim came and spoke to me. "Well, well," he said, "here you are. You are your usual bovine self."

It is all, I dare say, amusing but at times it is puzzling. When a writer publishes a new book it would be a smart thing for him to go off to Alaska. My wife shows me only criticisms of my books that are favorable. Sometimes I fancy she has a good time reading the ones that are unfavorable, but I may be wrong. If she gets a kind of joy in seeing me knocked off, she keeps it pretty well hidden. We get along first rate.

And we are trying for something. There is a kind of order, even dignity, in living we all pretty much want. There is the attempt to give life form and meaning.

Something else too. Everyone wants the same thing. Call it understanding. I take my own work, as a writer, seriously, can't see how a man can have any fun out of life in any other way. I am interested, absorbed in people. If I were a painter instead of a writer, I would spend my life painting people's portraits. Often I wish I had started on that road. The smell of paint excites me just as does the smell of ink or the rattle of a typewriter. Before I began to write and when I lived in Chicago, there were certain days when just walking in the streets exhausted me. On such days just a glance at a passing face was like reading the whole life history of some man or woman. It was too much. I couldn't stand it. When I went home and to bed at night, the faces kept closing before my eyes. "Tell my story. Tell it honestly," lips were shouting at me. It was a kind of madness. The only remedy I could find was to go get drunk.

And it may be that writing was just that, a kind of drunkenness. If so, it has also its mornings after. There is something very difficult for the writer to learn. He has written a new book, got it printed. There it is. Now the figures of the book, which have for so long lived only in his own fancy, may begin living in the minds of others. He has to find out anew, each time, that just because he has published another book, written another story, clocks do not stop running. It would be very wonderful if they did.

Belief in Man

IS it that long—twenty-five years? How old we grow! Can it be twenty-five years ago that, out in Chicago, we began to hear of plans, the magazine to be started, names of men we respected, looked up to as leaders, to be editors? Floyd Dell, who had gone to New York, may have written a letter to a friend and it was passed about. Floyd had been something of a literary father to me. It was at his house I first saw "literary" men. I must already have been scribbling away for five or six years. He wrote me presently, asking me to send some of my Winesburg tales and, Lord knows, I was glad to send them. I was having a rough time trying to get them published. There was a prison warden up at Sing Sing who had dared to treat prisoners as human beings. The politicians were after him and, to get him, were whispering about that he was a homo. Floyd wanted a story of mine, called "Hands."

Later I went to New York on a visit, had breakfast one morning with Jack Reed, and later, one winter night, walked with him for hours. What living talk! How human he was, how alive to others! I met and talked with Art Young, that big laughing man, had drinks with him and others of the old *Masses* crowd, and how strongly they remain yet in my mind as part, a very pregnant, vital part of something we all felt going on, just at that time.

It may have been a time rather like the present. There was a stirring, something felt, as one might say, coming up from below—as though the farms of our big fat Middle West wanted to speak, as though the growing factories of the towns wanted to speak. I wonder often if there is too much inclination to romanticize all this. We felt, I'm sure, that in writing there had been enough of the dominance of New England. There was, for the time, a lot of emphasis on sex. It was perhaps inevitable. Most of us got, for a time, the name of being "sex-obsessed." It was, I'm sure, only an effort to get sex back into a healthy place in our effort to express American life.

And it was a stirring period. The World War brought it sharply to an end. Something did happen. A new grimness came into faces seen on streets and, oh Lord, the hypocrisy!

When the old *Masses* got under way, the Provincetown crowd was getting a start on McDougal Street and, out in Chicago, Margaret Anderson was starting her *Little Review*. Someone took me to see her. "She is going to start a magazine. She will publish stuff they're afraid of," I was told. Life is full of these delicious moments. When I first saw Margaret Anderson she had a job editing a Protestant-church magazine. There was something highbrow getting under way too. *The Dial*, with Gilbert Seldes as managing editor, got going. Edgar Lee Masters was writing *Spoon River Anthology*, Carl Sandburg his *Chicago Poems*. Down at Springfield, Ill., Vachel Lindsay was making his half-mad, often beautiful cry to the gods. For a time the thing was all over the shop. Minor poets went to an Iowa town to read their verses. Seven or eight hundred people came. For a time books of verses sold like popular novels.

Without a doubt there was, until the World War came to deaden it, make it sick, something in the very air you breathed. Let's call it, "belief in life." O.K. Well, it seems to me that the impulse that led to the beginning of the *Masses* was a part of it. It was a strong, good, alive part of it. At the time it touched all parts of the country, reaching down even to New Orleans, where a little group of men and women had also started a magazine. They called it the *Double Dealer*.

What I remember of it all now is a kind of new boldness. Such a lot of things being said that everyone wanted said. Looking back to that time, it seems to me that perhaps the whole thing was best expressed, a kind of laughing boldness best expressed, in the person of Jack Reed. It may be that this whole effort to remember clearly the mood of a past time is just nerts.

Anyway, there it was, as it stays in my mind, as though to say, "why all the fuss, fakiness, bunk—this believing in what we Americans have been taught to believe in—success, fame, some one individual among us crawling up, always over the shoulders of others?..."

Why not fun in life?

Why not fun even in being a bit serious about life?

This, as I find myself trying to remember it, for the time in the very air. It may have been, at last, the beginning of realization that all of the talk our popular magazines had been so full of so long was just bunk, that because a man had managed to become, say, a millionaire, he was important. We had been getting that dope almost with our mother's milk....

Succeed. Be something big.

It had meant, ninety-nine times out of a hundred, getting a lot of money—no matter how you got it—having a big house, a lot of servants—going Park Avenue on your fellows. The *Masses* cutting across it, laughing at it, giving it the "what t' 'ell?"

When it happened, when it began, I was an advertising writer and, oh, the bunk I had swallowed. It had just happened that advertising writing was the way I had found, at least in a small way, to beat the game. You get some money to live on without putting out much of self, hope to have a bit of life left. God knows I never put out much. My general impression is still that most business men are saps.

The real thrill was to find these others, men apparently caring a little, making the idea back of what you call "comradeship" have some meaning.

And this, it seems to me, expressed in many ways, when the *Masses* was getting started, the *Masses* doing it with a kind of grand boldness, with a flourish.

And then the World War sapping it, draining it off into a kind of universal ugliness. It is a little hard to express all I have felt about it, but this I can say: that the *Masses*—old or new—will always retain for me some flavor of it.

Of what?

I think, just belief of man in man. If you are going anywhere that must be at the bottom of what you are trying to do.

Personal Protest

I WAS intensely interested in a recent article on "Proletarian Literature" in the Canadian Forum and am tempted to try my hand at some sort of expression, not surely under that head, or as an answer to the article, but rather to try a little to have my own say regarding the position of the writer in our time. It is all beastly confusing.

There is, for example, the matter of luxury. Who enjoys and, in fact, passionately loves luxury more than the artist man? The hunger for it is in his blood. The artist man is always trying to develop his senses. He wants to taste more, feel more, see more, hear more. Most of such men love fine fabrics. They love to array themselves. They respond to beautiful houses, to beautifully clad women. I have always thought that the born story teller is also partly the born actor. He is always going out of himself being, for the time, another. Now he is a poor woman, the wife, let us say, of a coal miner, kneeling at the bedside of her dead child or husband. Now he is a baseball player, a star man in one of the big leagues. He for a time leads the life of such a ball player.

Or he is a millionaire and owns a string of race horses, a scheming merchant, a little hill farmer driving a bony team across hills at night trying to elude the sheriff, attempting to get a keg of moon liquor to a certain gas filling station where he knows he can sell it. As he drives his poor horses along a little dirt road he is planning how he is going to spend the money he hopes to

359

get. He will buy some calico for his wife for a dress, a pair of shoes for the baby, a box of snuff for himself.

To tell the truth I think the proletariat does wrong to depend upon us writers. I think that any organization of men, having as its function the correction of the ills of society, does wrong to trust the artist man.

There is, you see, no stability to him. He won't stay put, won't follow the line. Often, for example, I myself have said to myself that if it were possible for me, by turning over my hand, to reconstruct the whole social situation there was nothing on earth would induce me to do it.

Why?

I'll tell you why. It is because terror would sweep over me. I would begin shaking with fright. "Who am I to do this horrid thing? How do I know how it will turn out?"

It is, as I understand it, the purpose of the artist man to remain always fluid. He wants only to observe, to feel, to record. To be sure there come times, say as it was in the United States in thirty and thirty-one, when a man goes about in city streets or visits the Hoovertowns at the edges of industrial cities, when he sees men in city streets pawing over garbage cans to get something to eat, when he catches fire.

He begins going on delegations, signs appeals, lends his name to committees.

There follows all sorts of confusion. A man finds himself being a kind of stuffed shirt. His name is up, here and there, as signer of protests he has not read, proclamations he doesn't understand.

And he hasn't read and doesn't understand because he is off somewhere in his imaginative world. Again he is being not himself, but this or that imagined figure, that is to go into one of his tales. He is trying to bring the imagined figure, born thus in his imaginative world, into some touch with the world of reality.

He forgets. He signs proclamations and protests without reading. He goes on delegations and is called "comrade" by men he has never seen before. He is confused and often, I must confess, deeply hurt.

It is this feeling of being used. It seems that the "comrades" are also often quite foxy. For example, a few years ago, I saw, by accident, in the New Republic, a long letter over my name protesting some injustice. It was evidently an injustice being done by some man or group of men I had never seen in a town I had never visited. I had never seen the letter that appeared in print. Some other man wrote it, signing my name without bothering to ask my permission.

And this is only one of such incidents. There have been others. There seems to be, among many of our radicals, a belief. "The end justifies the means," they seem to believe, but you see I do not believe that. I believe that means make the end.

Now when it comes to what is called "Proletarian Literature" I think it is purely a matter of background. Almost any writer, having sensibilities, does know that life is, on the whole, much more rich among the poor than among the successful. There is a generosity among the workers that the rich cannot know. You do not grow rich by being generous or by going out generously to your fellow men.

This granted. I myself happen to come out of the working class. I have, for the most part, all during my writing life, written of the lives of the poor and this, not out of any set purpose, but because I have found such lives more interesting.

I think our most common and greatest mistake in all of this is the attempt to prove something that cannot be proven. Tergeniev was a rich man, an aristocrat, and yet who has written more tenderly and closely of the lives of the poor than Tergeniev in his "Annals of a Sportsman". What tenderness here, what vivid and beautiful pictures of obscure lives.

And so also I can conceive of myself who came out of the working class, writing with keen sympathy of the difficulties and confusions of some rich man's life.

You cannot put your finger on it. It can't be done. You cannot say this is the road and that is not the road.

This, I think, you can say, that the life of the imagination, figures in that life, truly conceived, are as important to man as real lives. To sell people out in the imaginative life is as cheap and second rate a thing to do as to sell them out in real life and it seems to me that this is the point always being overlooked. A man has written a proletarian novel or play. It succeeds and within the week he is on his way to Hollywood. There he will sell everything out. "Ah," he says to himself, "I am doing it for money but I will give the money, or anyway a part of it, to the cause." The selling out of men's imaginative lives it seems does not matter.

But to me it is obvious that this is the very heart of the whole matter. Let men begin to have real respect for their own imaginative lives and for the imaginative lives of others and you will have in the end what will best serve all men. This is the real challenge to the artist man. It is the challenge most often forgotten by our artist men and women that come out of all classes.

The Situation in American Writing

1. Are you conscious, in your own writing, of the existence of a "usable past"? Is this mostly American? What figures would you designate as elements in it? Would you say, for example, that Henry James's work is more relevant to the present and future of American writing than Walt Whitman's?

2. Do you think of yourself as writing for a definite audience? If so, how would you describe this audience? Would you say that the audience for serious American writing has grown or contracted in the last ten years?

3. Do you place much value on the criticism your work has received? Would you agree that the corruption of the literary supplements by advertising—in the case of the newspapers—and political pressures—in the case of the liberal weeklies—has made serious literary criticism an isolated cult?

4. Have you found it possible to make a living by writing the sort of thing you want to, and without the aid of such crutches as teaching and editorial work? Do you think there is any place in our present economic system for literature as a profession?

5. Do you find, in retrospect, that your writing reveals any allegiance to any group, class, organization, region, religion, or

363

system of thought, or do you conceive of it as mainly the expression of yourself as an individual?

6. How would you describe the political tendency of American writing as a whole since 1930? How do you feel about it yourself? Are you sympathetic to the current tendency towards what may be called "literary nationalism"—a renewed emphasis, largely uncritical, on the specifically "American" elements in our culture?

7. Have you considered the question of your attitude towards the possible entry of the United States into the next world war? What do the think the responsibilities of writers in general are when and if war comes?

1. I am afraid I do not know what you mean by "usable past." It seems to me that for the story teller everything is usable. I am afraid that my difficulty in trying to answer these questions is that I spend little time thinking of either the past or the future. It is my passionate desire to live in the NOW. Mine is not a very critical mind. No, I do not believe that Henry James's work is more relevant to American writing than Walt Whitman's. There is more of the earth in Whitman's. No matter what fool things man does the earth remains.

2. This is also difficult for me to answer. I do not believe that I ever think of an audience as a definite thing. I often sing to myself in bathrooms. I tell myself stories, but just the same no man could go on working in any of the arts without a response.

You ask whether the audience for serious American writing has grown or contracted in the last ten years and frankly I do not know.

3. Yes, I do place value on criticism my own work has received. I have been helped by criticism. I know well enough that good criticism is rare but hasn't it always been rare. Of course the literary supplements have been corrupted by advertising. For nearly fifteen years I had to spend my own time as an advertising

writer because I felt myself not strong enough physically to stand day labor and couldn't make a living by my story telling. I sincerely believe that all advertising is corrupt.

4. It seems to me that the answer to this depends upon what you mean by making a living. I have had to do all sorts of things to keep going but believe also that men working seriously in any of the arts have always had a hard time making a living. Now that I have been writing for twenty or twenty-five years enough does usually trickle in to keep me going. It has, however, been a long hard pull.

5. I am sure that all my writing has always been simply an expression of my own feelings as an individual. I have a notion that any writing done for the purpose of propaganda is basically corrupt.

6. Like most writers I am really not a great reader. I did most of my reading before I began writing. Now I am chiefly interested in the lives of people immediately about me. If you are an American how can you help emphasizing what you feel and see in the particular portion of America immediately about you. My mind cannot go beyond that. From time to time I have made efforts to think nationally and internationally but it has always seemed bunk to me.

7. I suppose I am an isolationist. I do not believe in any war. I think that in any war both sides lose. In a time of war any man working in the arts is sunk. His lamps are out. A new and strange ugliness comes into everyone about him. It is for him a time of death.

So You Want to be a Writer?

I N any group of young writers you will inevitably find those
who want to write and those who merely want to be writers. They
want, it seems, what they think of as a kind of distinction that
they believe comes with being a writer. It's an odd thing. I daresay
a kind of distinction, always I fear a bit synthetic, does come to a
few, but really there are so many writers nowadays. You meet
them everywhere. You can't escape them.

Let us say you are a writer. You write and write and finally you
get a book published and then another and another. You get your
picture in the book section of *The New York Times* and in *The
Saturday Review of Literature*.

So you go about. You meet people. You are probably thinking
to yourself that everyone knows who you are. You forget that to
be what is called famous as a writer only about one out of every
100,000 people need have ever even heard your name. The
chances are that you have been associating a lot with others a
good deal like yourself.

You have been seeking such people out and they have sought
you out. You go about with so-called intellectuals. When your last
book was published, your publisher, thinking it would boost your
sales, has sent an advance copy of your book to a lot of other
writers. He has said, "We are sending you by this mail an advance
copy of Mr. Musgrave's new novel. We think it a great book. If
you agree with us, please write." Or it may be a new novel by Miss

367

Ethel Longshoreman. It seems women are nowadays writing our novels more and more. I guess they do it instead of getting married. It may be because of unemployment among the men. I don't know. Anyway it's a fact.

When it is put up to you, you do it. You think, "If I don't puff his or her book she or he won't puff mine." Very likely, however, you don't read the book. You get your mother-in-law to read it. Anyway that's my system.

The point is that you get to thinking everyone must know you. You have been about with other writers and they have said that your book is "just fine." They have said you have "a wonderful style" or something like that and you have paid them back by saying something nice about their last book and you have got rather to expecting it—I mean, you know, being something special, attracting attention wherever you go.

Then you get a jolt. Just when you want to be known, no one knows a thing about you. You have gone somewhere and have been introduced as an author. I knew a man, manufacturer in Ohio. I was always meeting him in New York. He always had a blonde with him and always introduced her as a cousin. "Cousin Alice, meet my friend Sherwood Anderson, the author."

She always thought I was Maxwell Anderson or Robert Sherwood. She put me in the theater. She wasn't the kind that reads books.

"I just loved your last play."

Once I promised one of the man's cousins a part in one of my plays.

"I have just written a new play. You are just the type for it," I said.

His cousin became excited. I gave her Maxwell Anderson's address.

"You come to see me this afternoon."

It happens that I have never met Maxwell Anderson. I wonder if he is a strong man.

You are introduced as an author and at once someone is on the spot. You are introduced, let's say, to a doctor. He doesn't go about with a certain queer expectant light in his eyes, thinking that people who don't know all about him aren't cultured. He doesn't think that just because you haven't been to his office to get some medicine for your indigestion you are an ignoramus. He may even, up to the moment when he is introduced to you, have led an honorable, upright life. Like George Washington, he has never told a lie, but he tells one now. He thinks that, being an author, you are expecting it. He is like his wife who, when you once were invited to his house to dinner, rushed down town and bought one of your books and put it on a table right in the middle of the living room, where no one could miss seeing it.

He says, "Oh yes. I have so enjoyed your books."

In a case like this, a man caught like this, in the company of an author he has never read, may try to get out of it by pretending he is a little deaf and hasn't heard when told you are an author, but he can't get away with that. It may be that you would let him get away with it, would be glad to, but someone is sure to pop up.

Let us say your name is Smith.

"How do you do, Mr. Smith. Glad to meet you," he says, and tries to make a get-away, but he is stopped.

"But this is Mr. Smith, the author," someone insists.

He gets a kind of hunted look on his face. There is a pleading look in his eyes. Please, if any of you who read this happen to become writers, when a thing like this happens to you, be kind. Don't press the man. Don't compel him to say, as he must say if you crowd him, that something happened just as he was becoming absolutely absorbed in your last book when his wife took it away from him and every time he tried to get it back she cried.

It is a good idea in such a case to help the man out. Don't force him to tell too many lies. Let's say you have written a novel about a banker. Of course, I know none of you, if you ever become writers, will be that foolish. No one ever writes novels about bankers. Writers can't even borrow money from bankers. You all know, or should know, that nowadays it isn't worth while writing novels about any class other than the proletariat. If you write novels about people of any other class the communists will get you. They'll call you a bourgeois, and then where are you?

So you are face to face with the man who has not read your novel about the banker and who has made the mistake of pretending that he has. You should bear this in mind. The man who has made the bluff about reading your book, when he has only some five minutes earlier heard of you for the first time, really made the bluff out of kindness of heart. You ought to try in turn to be kind to him. Help the man out. Give him a lead. Say something like this, say, "I think the banker in my novel was a most unusual man, don't you?" That will let him know that the book is about a banker.

Then go a little further. Mention the name of the town in which the banker had his bank. That will be a help. And then, if your banker ran away with the wife of the cashier of the bank, mention that. Try to drag it in. You will find it worth while. Authors should occasionally do these little deeds of kindness. Oh, the glad look that will come into such a man or woman's eyes.

I remember once being at a party with Mr. Ring Lardner. It was down in the city of New Orleans. Ring had come down there with Grantland Rice and Grantland was afraid the people of New Orleans might not know Ring was there. So Rice had done a lot of free publicity for Ring. He had called up the Mayor, the president of the Chamber of Commerce, the Kiwanis Club, the Rotary Club, the Lions Club. There was a big party at some rich person's house, and Ring took me along. He said, "Come on, Sherwood, let's give them two authors. Let's see if they know which is which."

So we did go and they knew we were authors. Grantland had told them. He got there ahead of us. He pointed us out. "There they are. There they come," he said.

He did everything but tell them what books we had written. He slipped up on that. That was what raised the devil with them. A kind of dark shadow came over the assembly. People went about with troubled eyes. They gathered in little groups whispering to each other but finally, out of one of the groups, a woman emerged. She was, I remember, very determined-looking. She had that kind of jaw, that kind of eyes. She was a rather big woman, strong and muscular, who, had she been a man, might well have been a professional wrestler.

She came up to us. She had this do or die look on her face. She tackled me first. Someone had given her my name.

"Oh, Mr. Anderson," she said, "I'm so glad you are here. I have been so longing to meet you." She said that she felt she already knew me through my books. She got that off, and there was a pause.

"Oh, that last book of yours," she said. She thought it was very, very beautiful and suddenly I had a vicious impulse.

"And what book do you mean? Name it. I dare you to," I wanted to say but I didn't say it. I kept still, and there was another pause. It was the kind of pause that, if it had been pregnant, should have brought forth triplets. There was this terrible waiting time and then Ring, out of the fullness of his heart, helped her out.

"You mean of course 'The Great Gatsby'," he said, and there was a look of joy and gratitude on that woman's face that I'll never forget. It was the kind of good deed on Ring's part that inspired other good deeds. It inspired me and I told the woman that Ring was the author of "Sister Carrie" and of course she ran about and told all the others. It made everything all right. It made an evening that had started to be a complete flop a great success.

A few years ago I was living in a certain town down in Virginia and I bought and ran for a time a country newspaper in the town. I don't know just why I did it. I guess I didn't want the people of the town to think of me as a writer. I figured that if they thought of me as a writer they would be afraid of me as they had a right to be. So I thought I'd get around them by being a newspaper publisher. And people have a right to be afraid. We writers, in certain of our moods, will use anyone we can. We say to ourselves that we are after truth.

Once I did an unfair mean thing to a certain man in Ohio. He was my friend and I rather sold him out. He was angry. My name began to get up in the world and he threatened me. He said he was going to write telling just what kind of man I was.

"Please do," I said. "Rough it up. Send the whole story to me. I've half forgotten." I pointed out that I could do the job better than he could. I meant it too. I was a story teller and I knew I could beat him telling the story.

There are certain men who are what I call "feeders." The story teller loves such men. They go about telling little things that have happened to them. They cannot write the stories but they can tell them. Put pens into their hands and away fly the stories.

A man who worked for me on my farm was such a story teller. What tales he told! There is a certain naïveté in such men. They look out upon life with clear eyes. They tell you the most

wonderful tales of things they feel, things they have done, things
that have been done to them. They tell everything very clearly.
The man worked for me one summer and I cleaned up on him. I
got several fine stories, heard them from his lips, while we
worked together, or rather while he worked and I sat watching
him, rushed at once into the house, put down the stories just as he
had told them. Then I was a fool. At the end of the summer I told
him what I had been doing and he grew afraid of me.

Or he thought I was getting too much for nothing. I should
have kept my mouth shut. I lost a good feeder. Now the stories he
might tell to many people through me are lost.

So there we are, we writers. We go about among people. We
are presumed to be reading people as a man reads the pages of a
book but most of the time we are doing nothing.

People keep coming up to a writer. "What are you at work on
now?" they ask. He isn't working on anything. He has a tooth
that needs filling and it hurts. He is wondering where he will get
the money to buy a new car. He isn't at work on anything but he
knows what is expected of him. It is expected that he will be at
work on some big serious task. If he is wise he gives them what
they expect. I do.

"I am at work on a history of the American Civil War," I say. It
sounds dignified and scholarly. A look of awe and respect comes
into the people's eyes.

"What a man!" they are thinking. It is wonderful. At times I
almost convince myself that I am at some such great task.

We become self-conscious. That is what we have to fight
against and it is sometimes a hard and bitter struggle. If we get up
a little in the world people write about us. They put our pictures
in newspapers and magazines. What we do about that is to send
one taken when we were thirty, when our hair was thick yet,
when our teeth were sound, when we had a fresh, cheerful look on
our face.

Occasionally someone tells us that we are great.

It is so difficult not to believe and if you do convince yourself
that it is all bunk you are miserable about that too.

So you want to be a writer?

Isn't it wonderful?

Man and His Imagination

EVERYONE knows how closely our imaginations touch our lives. It is the imagination that drives us on, that can destroy us, that sometimes makes a man do heroic deeds, that produces all of our art and our poetry, that has produced all of the inventions that make modern life so strangely different from life a few generations ago. The imagination produced our railroads, our automobiles, the telephone and telegraph, the radio. For ages man imagined himself a bird, flying through the air, before his hands made the machine in which he now takes off through the clouds—alas, too often only to drop bombs on those below. It is entirely possible that the imagination of some one man, able by the force of his personality to impose his will on others, may enable him to destroy what we call our civilization. The imagination of man is the attribute perhaps least of all understood.

But I am not going to try here to set myself up as a thinker. I have never put a very high valuation on myself as a thinker. I am, however, a man in love with the art of writing, and if I am anything of any importance at all to my fellows it is as a story teller and a story teller must always be concerned, first of all, with human life.

The lives of other humans are, as you all know, the source materials of the story teller and the story teller can sometimes be

373

very cruel. He wants, for the purpose of his crafts, to develop to the highest possible pitch his own senses, to constantly see more, hear more, feel more. He is continually watching others, noting the way in which people walk, the way they hold their heads, the shape and meaning of their hands, the clothes they wear and how they wear them. These things all have their significance to the story teller. At his best and when most aware, every movement of the body of another, the sound of his laughter, the way his mouth is held in repose and when speaking, the timbre of his voice, all of these things are full of meaning to him.

It can be a very punishing ability, this of the story teller's. It can be that and it can also be tremendously helpful and it can be helpful because it can create understanding. In his *War and Peace* Tolstoy has something to say of the difficulties that confront any story teller, and here I have decided to center my comments on the story teller's art because we are all of us story tellers. We are all doing it all the time.

In his *War and Peace* Tolstoy is telling of a young man named Rostov, a young officer of huzzars who has gone to visit certain old companions, known before the war had begun in which he and his friends are engaged. He has been in an action and the friends he has gone to visit are in a regiment that has not yet seen action.

Says Tolstoy...

"Rostov was a truthful young man, who would not for anything have told an untruth on purpose. He began to tell, with the full intentions of telling things as they had really happened, but imperceptibly, involuntarily, and unavoidable to himself he passed to the untruth. If he had told the truth to his listeners, who, like himself, had a great many times heard stories of attacks, and who had formed a definite idea about what an attack was, and who, consequently, expected just such a story, they either would not have believed him, or, what is still worse, they would have believed that it was his fault if nothing happened to him of the kind that generally happens to all the narrators of attacks.

"He could not have told them simply that all rode at a trot, that he fell down, wrenched his arm, and ran away from a Frenchman into the woods. Besides, to tell everything as it really was, would have demanded an effort to tell only that which had happened.

They expected a story of how he was all enveloped in flames, how, forgetting himself, he flew like a storm against a square, how he cut his way through it, slashing to the right and to the left, how his sword glutted on flesh, how he fell down exhausted, and all such things. And he told them so. It is very difficult to tell the truth, and young people are rarely capable of telling it."

Now to take two outstanding men among our more famous American story tellers, Mr. Sinclair Lewis and Mr. Theodore Dreiser, what a difference is immediately noted. As we read, we feel that the one man, no doubt in some secret inner part of himself, has been, at some time in his life, deeply hurt by his contact with life and wants to get even. He seems to want to pay life back, get even with it by showing people up, throwing up in his work constantly the ridiculous, the absurd and pretentious, while in the work of the other man, as we read, we feel constantly a great tenderness for all life.

Now I am not here setting myself up as a judge of the relative value of these two approaches to the story teller's art nor am I attempting here to pass judgment on the value of one of these men's work as against the other, although it is a matter on which I certainly have an opinion. I am only here pointing out a difference of approach. There is truth in both points of view. We are all, if we can take it, perhaps helped by having our absurdities and our weak human pretensions pointed out to us in the figure of another, but it is certainly true also that we all want passionately the sort of understanding of self we sometimes get from the work of the story teller who, out of a kind of love for other humans, identifies himself more closely and with a deeper feeling with us, through the characters of his stories. To see in another only the absurd pretensions that are, often enough, a covering for our own doubts, to go no deeper, may make a man a successful and even a valuable caricaturist but it does not necessarily make him an understanding story teller. In such work there is always the suggestion that you, the story teller, are a bit above the characters of your story. There is very little surrender of self. You stand above and look down. You become the all wise, the seeing one, while, on the other hand, to participate more fully in the lives of the people you put into your stories does, it seems to me, suggest always your being on a level with the people about whom you tell your stories. There is in such participation a kind of real humbleness before life, a knowledge that, no matter how skilfully you present your characters, there is always the realization that you yourself share in their weaknesses, their absurdities, their pretensions.

It was because of this humbleness before life, even in the poor and the downtrodden, that the master story teller Turgenev could write as he did of the Russian serfs, in the time of the Tsars, in his *Annals of a Sportsman*. It was because of this tenderness and humbleness in him that Turgenev, an aristocrat, could identify himself so completely with the poorest and most ignorant of the serfs and that he could tell stories of their lives in a way that so touched the heart of that other aristocrat, the Tsar Alexander, that he was fairly compelled by the feeling aroused in him to free the serfs.

As my own central interest in life is in writing, or rather in story telling, and as I believe profoundly in the importance of good story telling, and as I believe also that any man is at his best when talking of the work that most interests himself, I am trying to put down for you here what is most interesting to me, hoping of course, that what I have to say may also be of interest to you.

A man's work really is his life. For example, when you are dealing with the art of writing you are dealing primarily with the imagaination, and not only your own imagination but the imaginations of others. Now there are two distinct channels in every man's life. We all live on two planes. There is what we call the world of reality and there is the somewhat unreal world of the imagination. These roads do not cross each other but the road of the imagination constantly touches the road of reality. It comes near and it goes away. All of us are sometimes on one road and sometimes on another. I think that we are all living more of our lives on the road of the imagination, or perhaps I had better say in the world of the imagination, than in the real world. You will have to pardon me if I seem to get my figures somewhat mixed. At any rate you will understand what I mean.

Now I have selected here as my subject "Man and His Imagination." I cannot avoid speaking as a professional writer. It seems to me that the obligation of the writer to the imagination is pretty obvious. I am, to be sure, speaking of the writer as a story teller. There is the obligation to himself, to his own imagination, its growth, what he does to it, the obligation to the imaginations of other people, and there is the third and perhaps most important obligation. The writer in his creative mood is creating figures of people, to be true imaginary figures, and there is the writer's tremendous obligation to these imaginary figures. I think this is the most important of all the obligations. It is the obligation least understood. It is, I think the thing to talk about. It is the obligation too often forgotten by our professional writers.

We see it on all sides. Formerly, when I myself began writing, when I found I could not live by my writing, I worked for several years in a Chicago advertising agency. I was employed there as a writer of advertisements. Publishers and editors of some of our more popular magazines used to come to us. They wanted our clients to advertise in their magazines.

Often they outlined for us their plans for the year ahead. "This is the sort of stories we are going to have our writers write," they said. They did not give us actual outlines of stories but often they did speak as a manufacturer of, say automobiles, might have spoken. "We are going to produce this or that model." You get the idea.

Life was not to be touched too closely, to disturb people or make them think. People did not like being made to think, or to be disturbed. The mind might thus be taken from the buying of the goods advertised in the pages of the magazines.

But what is to happen to the imagination of the writer, the story teller? I think you can see that he has got to put it to work in a certain groove, keep it there. He has got to be cautious. Howells, in writing to his friend Mark Twain once said, "We write as we please. Then we throw it away and write what they want." I may be confused here. Twain may have said it to Howells.

At any rate Twain wrote *Innocents Abroad*. He wrote *Roughing It*. Try reading the books now. How dull they are.

Then he wrote *Huckleberry Finn*, leaving his imagination full play over a life he knew. What glorious humor! How living and real the book remains.

I know of course that many of you will never be writers in any professional sense and that you will have no intention of being writers and yet you will all write, you will tell stories, you will spend your lives trying to struggle through the tangle of human relations.

As you will see, I am trying here to bring closer together the writer, the man who in his work must constantly use his imagination, and the man who does not write. I would like, if possible to create a new understanding among us. In America the writer, and in particular the writer whose name is a little up, is put in rather an odd position. Often he is treated too well, often too badly. We are inclined often to set him too much apart. When I was an advertising writer and it was thought desirable to impress some advertiser with my ability they did what they called "staging me." They went and bragged me up, told what a wonder I was. It is a thing too much done to us professional writers. We are called great, geniuses, etc. It sometimes makes it difficult for a man to just go along, feel himself a part of others. They tell us we are torchbearers, preservers of the culture of the people, etc. A man is likely to get that sort of thing up into his own head and it separates him from others. It is like giving a man the Nobel Prize or something of that sort. It should never be done to a man until he is old and feeble—until his usefulness is gone.

And here let me say that it is my belief that we Americans are, in spite of our great achievements, an essentially lonely people, and this may be true because we were, in the beginning, a transplanted people.

And it may also be because of the fact that after our ancestors had come here, to this continent, coming as they did from many lands and from many different cultures . . . I say that it may also be because of the fact that, before we as a people had really got our feet well planted on our American soil, there came the industrial revolution, the so-called machine age.

And in the third place there is something else. Story telling, as we know it here in America has become too much the servant of the dollar. There is a constant corruption of the imagination always going on. The story teller, instead of being absorbed in human life, is made too much to serve, through our magazines, the radio etc., the purpose of selling some toothpaste or some hair invigorator and to do this successfully the story teller must never draw his audience too close to the strangeness of life as we lead it.

And this also I believe, tends to separate us from each other.

It is essentially a restless age. We all move nowadays more rapidly from place to place. It is nowadays more and more difficult for the modern man to center his life, his feelings about one town, one street of a town, one group of friends. It is more difficult for us to begin to know each other.

When I began my own work as a writer and when, after several years of writing in comparative seclusion and when my writing began to be printed and noticed by critics, I was at once called, by most of the critics who noticed my work, a realist, and that was a surprise and something of a shock to me.

I do not know what reality is. I do not think any of us quite know how much our point of view, and, in fact all of our touch with life, is influenced by our imaginations.

In my own experience, for example, and in my work as a writer I have always attempted to use materials that come out of my own experiences of life. I have written a good deal about my father, my mother, a certain grandmother who touched my imagination, and about my brothers and sisters, and it has amused me sometimes, in talking with some of my brothers, to see how poorly my conception of our father and mother fitted into their own conceptions. "Why, I dare say, the woman you have pictured is all right. She is very interesting, but she is not my mother as I knew her," they say.

This whole matter of what we think of as realism is probably pretty tricky. I have often told myself that, having met some persons for the first time, some other human being, man or woman, and having had my first look, I cannot ever even see him or her again.

If this is true, why is it true? It is true because the moment I meet you and if we begin to talk, my imagination begins to play. Perhaps I begin to make up stories about you. This is a trick all writers, and for that matter, all people, do. The writer may merely be more conscious of it. It is our method of work. Very little of the work of the writer is done at his desk or at the typewriter. It is done as he walks about, as he sits in a room with people, and perhaps most of all as he lies in bed at night.

I myself, for example, have had all my life over and over an experience that some of you may also have had. If I have been working intensely, I find myself unable to relax when I go to bed.

Often I fall into a half dream state, and when I do, the faces of people begin to appear before me. They seem to snap into place before my eyes, stay there, sometimes for a short period, sometimes longer. There are smiling faces, leering ugly faces, tired faces, hopeful faces. Almost always they seem to be faces of people I cannot remember ever having met.

However, I am quite sure they are faces of people I have seen.

They may be people I have met quite casually in the street. I have been walking about. At times the faces of people, met thus quite casually, seem full of strange significance. To quote Herman Melville, "Who has ever fathomed the strangeness and wonder of man?" I get sometimes the illusion that every man and woman I meet is crying out to me. Sometimes a single glance at a human face seems to tell a whole life story and there have been times, when I walked thus when I had to go along with bowed head, looking at the sidewalk. I could not bear looking at any more faces.

I have a kind of illusion about this matter. It is, I have no doubt, due to a story teller's point of view. I have the feeling that the faces that appear before me thus at night are those of people who want their stories told and whom I have neglected. Once I wrote a poem on this matter. I think I had better quote it to you. I called my verses,

THE STORY TELLER

Tales are people who sit on the door-
    step of the house of my mind.
It is cold outside and they sit waiting.
I look out at a window.
The tales have cold hands,
Their hands are freezing.
A short thickly-built tale arises and
    thrashes his arms about.
His nose is red and he has two gold teeth.
There is an old female tale that sits
    hunched up in a cloak.
Many tales come to sit for a moment
    on the doorstep and then go away.

It is too cold for them outside.
The street before the door of the house
    of my mind is filled with tales.
They murmur and cry out, they are
    dying of cold and hunger.
I am a helpless man—my hands tremble.
I should be sitting on a bench like a
    tailor.
I should be weaving warm cloth out of
    the threads of thought.
The tales should be clothed.
They are freezing on the doorstep of
    the house of my mind.

Let me try to put this matter as simply as I can. It seems important to me. I am not speaking now of the writing that sets out to put down as closely as possible the realities of life, that is to say, reporting or journalism.

And when it comes to that we all know, or should know, how much the best journalist misses reality. Have you ever had the experience of attending let us say a trial in court, a strike, or even a simple matter like a fight between two men in a street and then later read a description of the experience at the hands of a reporter? The man never sees what you saw.

When it comes to story telling I think that most of us begin our stories on the plane of reality. Something happens that is interesting to us. Among our acquaintances there is some person, a man or woman, having had certain experiences or adventures in life that fascinate us. "What a character that one would make for a story or a novel," we say to ourselves.

And so we go to work. I dare say that most writers are a good deal as I am. They begin their stories out of some such impulse as that suggested above. They use the people around them, often the people they know well, but they do not want to use them too blatantly.

So you begin to hedge. There is a little trick you do. Let us say that you begin with the idea of telling the story of a certain tall, red-haired man, whom you happen to know.

You know this man very well. You know certain circumstances

of his life. In the story you are about to write you will use some of
these circumstances and discard others. You will invent new
situations. Every good story teller is a born inventor.

But in this matter of invention care must also be taken. Your
invention may not at all fit into the theme of your story. You may
be so proud of it that you will be tempted to force it in and thus
destroy your story.

But let us pass that phase of the matter just now. The tall, red-
haired man you are going to write about, let us say, is a personal
friend. You want to protect him so you make certain physical
changes in your man. He is this tall, lean man with red hair and
you make him short and broad-shouldered. Now he has stiff black
hair and rather small, sharp black eyes. Your red-haired friend
was named Turner but you give this new one another name. Let
us say that you call him Bob Wyatt.

But wait. Look! Here is something a bit strange. Your red-
haired friend named Turner has suddenly escaped you. He is
gone. Now there is a new fellow come into your consciousness.
This broad-shouldered, short, black-ahired man named Bob
Wyatt. Do you think he will have the same sort of life, the same
reactions to the experiences of life, that Turner would have? You
will find that he will not.

You have got a new man on your hands. Now I do not mean to
say that this new man, Bob Wyatt, will not have certain
experiences you got from Turner. I do not mean that he will react
in a quite different way. His story will not be Turner's story.

As you go along with Bob Wyatt everything you say begins to
change under your hand. Let me try to explain what I am driving
at by a personal experience. Some two and one-half years ago in
the winter I was in the state of Texas. I was down there on the
Gulf in the town of Brownsville. I am fond of fishing and I like a
warm climate in the winter. I spent the winter down there,
usually working in my hotel room in the morning and fishing in
the afternoon.

One evening I came home from fishing and there was a
telephone call for me. It was from Mr. Henry Morgenthau, our
Secretary of the Treasury. Now it happened that our prohibition
laws are enforced by the Treasury Department. I live in the hills

of Virginia and there is a certain Virginia county, less than fifty miles from my home, that had gone into bootlegging in a rather gigantic way.

There was an odd and startling situation. A mountain county in Virginia that has no large town, that is a rough and rugged mountain country, where the farmers are all poor, had suddenly become an industrial center. Big city gang methods had been introduced into this mountain community. Liquor was being made there in vast quantities. The whole country had been organized under one man and this man was a typical industrial overlord. He was ruling the county largely by terror and there were poor farmers in the country who had got into a situation where they were making liquor and turning it over to this man, themselves constantly facing the chances of a penitentiary sentence, for a wage of less than two dollars a day.

The Treasury Department had sent their secret agents into this county.

Suddenly they had swooped down and had begun making arrests. Practically the whole county was under arrest.

It was this matter that Mr. Morgenthau had called me about. He spoke to me over the telephone from Washington. I think Mr. Morgenthau must be a very human man. He told me that he was sure that among the many people arrested in the Virginia county, all of them facing penitentiary sentences, there were many poor and essentially innocent men. "I want the human story told. Will you go there? Will you attend the trial of these people? Will you attempt to get at the human side of what has happened in this particular community?"

Now I did go into the Virginia county. I spent some weeks there. I got acquainted with people. I attended the trial of these people and among those being tried was a certain young woman rum-runner. I, because I was interested in this woman, rode about with her in a car, dined with her. We had many long talks and afterward I wrote a novel, under the title *Kit Brandon*, with this woman as the central figure.

The point that interests me here and that has I think something to do with what I am trying to say is that since this novel was published I have often been asked a question that writers are always being asked. "Did this woman actually live? Did she actually have the experiences you have set down in this book?"

Now the truth is I do not know. I have forgotten everything the woman told me. I have not seen her for several years and have even forgotten how she looks and I have forgotten everything for the reason I have tried to suggest here.

You see when I began to write I did the thing that practically all writers do. It was another case of Mr. Turner and Bob Wyatt. The particular woman rum-runner with whom I talked had had a hard life. She had definitely decided to make a new try at living in a new way. Naturally I did not want to interfere with her new life. I changed her name. I am quite sure I completely changed her personal appearance. I began to attribute to this woman certain traits no doubt picked up from others. She became—and this is the whole point of what I am trying to say here—completely another person. Other people, perhaps met in other circum-stances in my own life, were introduced into my story and I had to think and feel my way through this new woman's reactions to these people. What I am trying to say is that the new woman, the central figure, in my story no longer lived in the reality of her own life, but that she had a new life in this imaginative world. This is a matter that is a little difficult sometimes to make people understand who are not writers. A book or story that comes alive, that really has form and substance, has its own life and it is right here that violence is so often done to the art of writing.

I would like, if possible, to make myself pretty clear in this matter, and I think that I can perhaps get at it best by simplification. There are no doubt two kinds of story telling. There is the plot short story and if you want to be a successful writer and make a good deal of money by writing, it is perhaps best to become a plot story writer. You see there are plot short stories and plot novels. If you work in this way you begin your story with a plot. To be sure you introduce people into your story, but you make them fit into the plot. This is a thing that is always being done. You see it in plays in our theaters and you see it constantly in the stories by our most successful writers in our popular magazines. There is, let us say, a certain character introduced into a story. He is essentially a very human man but in the plot story I am writing he has to murder his uncle. How easy it is to write the words, "He crept into the dark room. He had a knife in his hand. He crept forward," etc. Murder, you see, is always exciting. You can excite the reader. You can even make him believe temporarily the impossible. In our popular stories the impossible is always being done. People are always being violated. What is not generally understood is that to do violence, to sell out a character in the imaginative world, is as much a crime as to sell people out in the real world. As I have already tried to say, this imaginative world of ours, the imaginative lives we live, are as important to us as are real lives. They may be more important.

Now when it comes to talking about the experiences of a writer I think I should say something that perhaps most of you realize. The work of any writer and for that matter of any artist in any of the seven arts should contain within it the story of his own life. There are certain beliefs I have. One is that every man who writes, writes as well as he can. We are always hearing stories about men writing with their tongues in their cheeks, but the truth is that if, for example a man devotes his life to writing detective stories, he probably believes in the detectives he puts in his stories. If he writes cowboy stories he really believes that cowboys in life are like the cowboys of the stories and movies. They aren't, of course, but he thinks so.

I have myself, I think, been counted among what we call in America the highbrow writers. I am not in the least a highbrow type of man, so I have to ask myself, or did at first, when I first began writing, have to ask myself how it came about that I was called a highbrow. And I concluded finally that it was because I happened to be a man who took writing rather seriously and I took it seriously because I enjoyed it so thoroughly.

I remember reading somewhere a sentence by Joseph Conrad. He said that he only lived fully and richly when he was at work writing.

It seems to me very important, if a man is to get at anything like an intelligent use of his imagination, not to let it get too much out of hand.

A good many years ago I was living in the city of Chicago. I was working at the time in a factory and I remember that in going to

my room from the factory, that was situated near the Loop, in
Chicago, I had to take a train on the elevated railroad. I was young
and strong and my work in the factory did not tire me too much. I
used to come out of the factory and walk down into the Chicago
Loop. I climbed to an elevated station. This would be at a time of
the day when people were pouring out of office buildings. They
came from lofts where men's clothing and women's dresses were
made. They came from offices. They came from factories.

People hurried, a struggling mob, up the stairway to the
elevated platform where I stood. They ran in little droves, like
covies of quail, across the streets, dodging the traffic. A few years
before all this happened to me I had been a soldier. I came out of
the working class and I was a good deal absorbed in the subject of
the injustice of life to the worker. The first thing I ever wrote was
a long book, of some several hundred pages, under the title, *Why I
am a Socialist*. I must have written the book when I was seventeen
or eighteen years old. I had come upon the idea of socialism, the
cooperative commonwealth, and, like most young men, having
got the idea, I had, temporarily, the impression that I was the first
man in the world it had ever come to. I wanted to explain it to all
the world. I wrote and wrote feverishly. I do not know what ever
became of the book. It got lost. Perhaps later I threw it into the
fire.

Anyway, I was standing there, as I have suggested, in the
evening on the platform of the elevated station in the city of
Chicago. I became absorbed, watching the thousands of city
people rushing homeward.

"How wonderful it would be," I thought, "if the workers,
instead of rushing through life like this, a broken disorganized
mob, could be organized, by some leader, into armies." I
remember the sense of power that had come to me, as a young boy
in the army. I remembered a certain occasion. I was in a great
training camp. One day, during maneuvers, I was marching with
some thousands of others along a road. We were in a long file and
for some reason, I dropped out of line. It was a burning hot day
and perhaps I was partially overcome by the sun. At any rate I had
got permission to drop out of line and stood leaning against a tree
beside the road. The long line of men went by me with rhythmic
steps and I stood by the tree trembling. Tears ran from my eyes.

In some way I, for the first time in my life, understood armies, the fascination of the army to the individual man. We all feel so ineffectual in life and suddenly through this physical accord we get with others in physical organization, we begin to feel effectual. Power out of others comes into us. There is a new feeling of strength, of manliness. Fear goes away. I think it is this fact that explains a good deal the power of the fascist state. The individual man does not identify himself with other individual men. He identifies himself instead with the huge vague thing we call the state.

I had been standing as described on the elevated station in the American city and having these thoughts.

"How wonderful if the workers could be organized into armies." I thought of the factory where I myself worked. There were several thousand men employed. I pictured our metting at some appointed place in the early morning and marching as a body to the factory. When the whistle blew in the evening we came out of the factory and fell into ranks. We marched off along the street. I pictured, in fancy, the owner of the factory looking out of his office window. A strange new fear would settle down upon him. He would at last realize the terrible strength of the workers.

I believe that what I pictured to myself thus, as a young man on a summer evening, has since been pretty effectually worked out by the fascists. It seems it doesn't work out exactly as I thought it would but even that is not my point. Some years later, and after I had written several stories and four or five novels, most of which were never published, I took up this theme. I wrote a novel I called *Marching Men*. I imagined a man, in his nature a kind of combination of Abraham Lincoln and John Lewis, organizing the workers as described above and using the methods described above, that is to say I started with such a man. I have not looked at the novel for several years. It was later published but was not a success. I had been thinking too big. My imagination had betrayed me. When later I returned, in my work, to life on a smaller scale, in the individuals about me, I was on solider ground.

This matter of use of the imagination on the grand scale can sometimes lead to very ridiculous results. For example I know two young men who like to go bird hunting in the fall. They are both highly imaginative young men. They have both read a good deal about the American Civil War. They are in a field advancing on a covey of quail. Their bird dogs are pointing the quail.

They begin to speak in tense tones to each other. There is a little game they play. They imagine themselves Lees, Grants or Stonewall Jacksons. They are at Gettysburg or at Fredericksburg. They are no longer merely bird hunters but great men, generals leading armies in the face of enemies.

It is all ridiculous of course and a little amusing.

However, in thinking thus of war and imagining themselves leaders of armies they do not think of war as it really is. They think of it as our historians too often report it. They do not think of the butchery, the terror, the confusion, the stench and horror of actual war.

They are merely pretending, as we all do most of the time, but there is this to be said, that in imagining themselves great generals, engaged in a desperate battle out of which they are to emerge as heroes, they are very likely missing something, the beauty of the trained dogs at work, the fall colors in trees on distant hills, all the living beauty of the country in the fall. They are missing what we all too much miss, the strangeness and wonder of our everyday lives.

All of us who are older can remember with what fervor we read when we were younger. What a rich place our imagined world was. As we grew older it seemed to get less rich. I think it is possible, by the use of the imagination to keep it rather rich.

We all, I dare say, have to face what are called "the facts of life," but I do think we are often inclined to call facts what are not necessarily facts.

And I think also that the actual training of the imagination, the learning to use it has a lot to do with human relations. That has something to do with what I am trying to say here.

There is something you can do. Even if you are not actually practising writers, you can employ something of the writer's technique. When you are puzzled about your own life, as we all are most of the time, you can throw imagined figures of others against a background very like your own, put these imagined figures through situations in which you have been involved. It is a very comforting thing to do, a great relief at times, this occasionally losing sense of self, living in these imagined figures. This thing we call self is often very like a disease. It seems to sap you, take something from you, destroy your relationship with others, while even occasionally losing sense of self seems to give you an understanding that you didn't have before you became absorbed.

May it not be that all the people we know are only what we imagine them to be? If, for example, you are as I was, for a good many years of my own young life, a businessman, on the whole spending my time seeking my own advantage, you lost interest, while, as opposed to this, if you lose yourself in others, life immediately becomes more interesting. A new world seems to open out before you. Your imagination becomes constantly more and more alive.

There is a profound pleasure in all of this. At least I know that when I came to it, I found it the pleasantest experience I had ever had. To be sure I do not want to discount the difficult. It is very hard to understand any other human being. It is difficult to tell truly the story of another, but it is, I think, rather a grand challenge.

But I would like to speak a little more clearly if possible on the subject of what, when we think of writers, we call realists, men who are presumed to deal in realities. I have said that I do not know what reality is. I do not think any man knows. I remember that some years ago I wrote a short essay that has often since been reproduced and has even, I believe, been used in college textbooks. I called it "A Note On Realism."

There is something very confusing to both readers and writers about the notion of realism in fiction. As generally understood it is akin to what is called "representation" in painting. The fact is before you and you put it down, adding a high spot here and there, to be sure. No man can quite make himself a camera. Even the most realistic worker pays some tribute to what is called "art." Where does representation end and art begin? The location of the line is often as confusing to practising artists as it is to the public.

Recently a young writer came to talk with me about our mutual craft. He spoke with enthusiastic admiration of a certain book— very popular a year or two ago. "It is the very life. So closely observed. It is the sort of thing I should like to do. I should like to bring life itself within the pages of a book. If I could do that I would be happy."

I wondered. The book in question had seemed to be good only in spots and the spots had been far apart. There was too much dependence upon the notebook. The writer had seemed to me to have very little to give out of himself. What had happened, I thought, was that the writer of the book had confused the life of reality with the life of the imagination. Easy enough to get a thrill out of people with reality. A man struck by an automobile, a child falling out of a window of a city office building. Such things stir the emotions. No one, however, confuses them with art.

This confusion of the life of the imagination with the life of reality is a trap into which most of our critics seem to me to fall about a dozen times each year. Do the trick over and over, and in they tumble. "It is life," they say. "Another great artist has been discovered."

What never seems to come quite clear is the simple fact that art is art. It is not life.

The life of the imagination will always remain separated from the life of reality. It feeds upon the life of reality, but it is not that life—cannot be. Mr. John Marin painting "Brooklyn Bridge," Henry Fielding writing *Tom Jones*, are not trying in the novel and the painting to give us reality. They are striving for a realization of something out of their own imaginative experience, fed to be sure upon the life immediately about. A quite different matter from making an actual picture of what they see before them.

And here arises a confusion. For some reason—I myself have never exactly understood very clearly—the imagination must constantly feed upon reality or starve. Separate yourself too much from life and you may at moments be a lyrical poet, but you are not an artist. Something within dries up, starves for the want of food. Upon the fact in nature the imagination must constantly feed in order that the imaginative life remain significant. The workman who lets his imagination drift off into some experience altogether disconnected with reality, the attempt of the American to depict life in Europe, the New Englander writing of cowboy life—all that sort of thing—in ninety-nine cases out of a hundred ends in the work of such a man becoming at once full of holes and bad spots. The intelligent reader, tricked often enough by the technical skill displayed in hiding holes, never in the end accepts it as good work. The imagination of the workman has become confused. He has had to depend altogether upon tricks.

The difficulty, I fancy, is that so few workmen in the arts will accept their own limitations. It is only when the limitation is fully accepted that it ceases to be a limitation. Such men scold at life immediately about. "It's too dull and commonplace to make good material," they declare. Off they sail in fancy to the South Seas, to Africa, to China. What they cannot realize is their own dullness. Life is never dull except to the dull.

The writer who sets himself down to write a tale has undertaken something. He has undertaken to conduct his readers on a trip through the world of his fancy. If he is a novelist his imaginative world is filled with people and events. If he has any sense of decency as a workman he can no more tell lies about his imagined people, fake them, than he can sell out real people in real life. The thing is constantly done but no man I have ever met, having done such a trick, has felt very clean about the matter afterward.

On the other hand, when the writer is rather intensely true to the people of his imaginative world, when he has set them down truly, when he does not fake, another confusion arises. Being square with your people in the imaginative world does not mean lifting them over into life, into reality. There is a very subtle distinction to be made, and upon the writer's ability to make this distinction will in the long run depend his standing as a workman.

Having lifted the reader out of the reality of daily life it is entirely possible for the writer to do his job so well that the imaginative life becomes to the reader for the time real life. Little real touches are added. The people of the town that never existed except in the fancy—eat food, live in houses, suffer, have moments of happiness and die. To the writer, as he works, they are very real. The imaginative world in which he is for the time living has become for him more alive than the world of reality ever can become. His very sincerity confuses. Being unversed in the matter of making the delicate distinction that the writer himself sometimes has such a hard time making, they call him a realist. The notion shocks him.

"The deuce, I am nothing of the kind," he says.

"But such a thing could not have happened in a Vermont town."

"Why not? Have you not learned that anything can happen anywhere? If a thing can happen in my imaginative world it can of course happen in the flesh-and-blood world. Upon what do you fancy my imagination feeds?"

My own belief is that the writer with a notebook in his hand is a man who distrusts his own imagination. Such a man describes actual scenes accurately, he puts down actual conversation.

But people do not converse in the book world as they do in life. Scenes of the imaginative world are not real scenes.

The life of reality is confused, disorderly, almost always without apparent purpose, whereas in the artist's imaginative life there is purpose. There is determination to give the tale, the song, the painting, form—to make it true and real to the theme, not to life. Often the better the job is done, the greater the confusion.

I myself remember with what a shock I heard people say that one of my books, *Winesburg, Ohio*, was an exact picture of Ohio village life. The book was written in a crowded tenement district of Chicago. The hint for almost every character was taken from my fellow-lodgers in a large rooming house, many of whom had never lived in a village. The confusion arises out of the fact that others besides practising artists have imaginations. But most people are afraid to trust their imaginations and the artist is not.

Would it not be better to have it understood that realism, in so far as the word means reality to life, is always bad art—although it may possibly be very good journalism?

Which is but another way of saying that all of the so-called great realists were not realists at all and never intended being. *Madame Bovary* did not exist in fact. She existed in the imaginative life of Flaubert and he managed to make her exist in the imaginative life of his readers.

I am about to begin the writing of a story.

If I am to succeed in making the characters of my story real in their world, they, like hundreds of other men and women who live only in my own fanciful world, must live and move within the scope of the story or novel into which I have cast them. If I do tricks with them in the imaginative world, sell them out, I become merely a romancer. If, however, I have the courage to let them really live they will, perhaps, show me the way to a fine story or novel.

But the story or novel will not be an actual picture of life. I will never have had any intentions of making it that.

And so you will see in this matter of the imaginary as opposed to reality what I am trying to say. There is a reality to your book, your story people. They may, in the beginning, be lifted out of life, but once lifted, once become a part of the book, of the story life, realism, in the sense in which the word is commonly used, no longer exists.

There are, you see, these two kinds of realism, the realism of actual life that is the challenge to the journalist and the realism to the book or the story-life. That I should say is the job of your real story teller.

I have spoken here a good deal about the work of the story teller. It was my idea, in attempting to prepare this essay, to center it upon man's imagination. You do not need to be, as I am, a professional story teller to learn to use your imaginations in human contacts.

A young man, an artist, came recently to my house in Virginia. He sat for an evening before the fire in my house. He was a very earnest young man. He was a writer and he began to tell me of the mission he felt he had in life. As a writer he is a man with a great deal of technical skill. He does not like the civilization in which he lives. He is out to do what he can to change that civilization.

However, he is constantly bringing into this work his ideas of what he thinks of as an ideal civilization and as he talked it seemed to me that in the mission he had given himself he has pretty much chucked human beings. In his work he more and more makes them fit into an idea created in his own head.

And human beings are being too much chucked everywhere now. The world is filled with men who are doing what I call, thinking big. Their imaginations have run them off into some vague and terrible world where they think, where they let the imagination play about, not in the little world in which most of us live and in which they must actually live, as I have said, in the people of a house, a street, in the strange, often startling and absorbing, happenings among people about them, acquaintances they see daily on the streets, men and women with whom they associate daily, but in this other huge and I think on the whole rather meaningless world.

You all hear such talk now on all sides. It is shouted at you on the radio, in the newspapers. The imaginations of men are at work not in the little worlds in which they must live but in these other vague huge worlds.

It is this kind of use of the imagination that leads a man to think not of a Spaniard but of what he calls the Spanish people, not of a German he may have sometime known but as the German people. Words like the People, the Capitalists, Proletariat, the Middle-Class, the Americans, phrases like the American Way, are always now on such peoples' lips.

Well we are all Americans here and in our hearts we know that there is no such thing as the American People or the American Way. There are only people, single individuals, each with his own sorrows, often with his tricky envy of others, his moments of love and gladness, his lusts, his secret desire to live the good life and to let others live it, his moments of meanness and crookedness, and perhaps also his sudden upflarings of goodness.

It is all a very dangerous, very tricky matter. It is so easy to slip into this habit of thinking, of using words, in this big vague way. It is a kind of wholesale selling out of people. I was born in the Middle West, lived there until some fifteen years ago when I went to live in the South. I found something I had not known in my boyhood and young manhood in the Middle West. I found more of a tendency to group people in this big loose way. I found people being called Hill Billies, Georgia and Florida Crackers. The word aristocrat was always being used in the South and the way it is used has always irritated me profoundly. I cannot let it pass. I dare say I am also often irritating to my neighbors and friends of the South.

Such and such a man or woman is brought into a conversation. He, or she, is spoken of as belonging to one of the South's aristocratic families.

"And what do you mean by aristocrat?

"Does it mean that he or his father owned slaves?

"Has his family been in the country for several generations?

"Have they money?"

"How did they get it?"

I find myself inclined to point out that there are families who have been in New England for a long time, in the Middle West and Far West for a long time, and that there are others who have made a lot of money, live in big houses, own land and that some of them are served and have been served by their own kind of slaves.

"Does it make a man an aristocrat because his slave is black rather than white?"

Sometimes, aroused by this careless grouping of people, I point out that many of the early large slave-owning families of the Old South, there being big money at that time in the growing of cotton, cotton-cropped all the eastern section of the Old South to death. They wore out the land and then, with their troupes of slaves, moved westward to new lands.

"Does it make a man an aristocrat to destroy the ground under his feet?" I ask.

I speak of this here as a sample of another way in which our imaginations are always being betrayed. The guilt is far from all being in the South. I think that we, of what is called the artist class, are more guilty than any other class in this matter. It is so easy to group people in this way, calling a man, because he is a poor tenant farmer in Georgia, a Georgia Cracker, because he lives on a little mountain farm in the hill country of the Upper South, a Hill Billy, grouping them so, as though there were not all kinds of men and women on Georgia tenant farms, in the hills of the Upper South, many spirited ones, crooked lying ones, honest kind ones, gentle ones.

It is all confusing, all evil. It keeps separating us from one another. There is a not too refined, too subtle cruelty in it in which we, who put our heads up, daring to call ourselves artists, are too much inclined to indulge.

There is a difference, it seems to me, in where and how you put your imaginations to work. It seems to me that the wise thing now is to try at least not to let our imaginations run off too much into this bigness. I know that I have myself tried, from time to time, to be in imagination, a big one. I have tried being a political thinker on the grand scale, looking to the state, to some new form of organization of the state and through the state, through this or that group of political thinkers, trying to give myself to their enthusiasms. I have always, in the end, found myself going cold. So many of these groups have a philosophy I cannot accept. They seem to have some glorious end in view but they also often seem to think that it does not make much difference what methods are used to reach what they think the ideal end. "The ends justify the means we use," they say, but that seems to me a profound untruth. It seems to me that the means always make the ends.

However there is something I think I do know. We live in a country where there has been a tremendous development of all the physical gadgets of life. Man's physical isolation from man has been pretty thoroughly wiped out. The machine age has done that for us and it seems to me a good thing to have done.

There remains however this other kind of isolation. The players who play for us in our theaters do not come among us. They stay in Hollywood in California. In all of our houses now there are voices shouting at us over the radio, but when we go into our houses there is no one there. There is only the voice, far off somewhere. Even in our wars now we shoot at men out of sight, miles away from us. We stay in holes in the ground, even in our killing, and shoot into the air.

We are all going about trying to understand our Hitlers, our Mussolinis, our Chamberlains. We talk big. Our imaginations roam over the world. We are trying to be national thinkers, international thinkers and I presume someone has to do that kind of thinking, that is to say if thinking has anything to do with it.

You see I really believe that, for the most of us, if we are to remain at all sane in what seems too much an insane world, we had better be trying to think small, to stay closer home, to use our imaginations at home.

Sometimes now, as I go about, I hear men saying that we are at a great crisis in what we call civilization. They are saying that we must all choose one or the other of two ways, Communism or Fascism is bound to come. We must be one or the other.

I do not believe it.

As I think you will see I am trying to make here a plea for the right of the story teller, of any imaginative worker, to lead his own life, to build up and maintain his own attitude toward life. I think something of this kind is necessary if the art of the story teller is to go on and grow. I have nothing at all to say against the man or woman whose mind happens to take the economic or political turn. There are no doubt men and women who are able to think clearly and intelligently in terms of masses of people or of people separated definitely into classes. If there were not such people how would any man dare accept office in government.

But I think also there is this other right. I think those of us who choose to work in the imaginative field have a right to demand that we be let alone. I think it is our job to try a little at least to lose ourselves in the lives of others, to try to understand a little what hurts people, what sometimes makes them do strange, sometimes amusing, often apparently unaccountable things. I think we have a right without feeling of guilt or without assertion of superiority to take a certain stand. We ought to really write for ourselves, in the present situation, a kind of new declaration of rights. There is something we ought to say to these others.

"Go on with your own work," we ought to say to them. "I will not try to interfere with what you are doing, or what you think you are doing, and you shall not interfere with me.

"It may be that you know how to correct the social evils of the world but I do not.

"If the power were to be given me to change the whole social structure of life by turning over my hand I would not dare to turn it over."

I think we have a right to say to these people, often I believe quite heroic people, many of them important enough figures in life—

"Let me alone.

"I have my own job to do."

We have, I think, to stay at our own job and find our own kind of morality. I think our morality is outside of all this. As I happen to be one of these men myself I think that our morality, when we can find it, is a true morality.

I think there is a possibility of living by it even in these confused times. I even believe that through the artist's morality there is a chance for all of us to lead something like the good life. I think that we can be priests to the imaginative lives of ourselves and others. I think that is our job. I think that when we lose our own morality and adopt the morality of others we become corrupt, that we are going back on our jobs.

Appendix

A Writer's Conception of Reality

IT must be that I am an uncurable small town man. Either that is true or there is something very special going on here at Olivet and, after some ten days here, I have about concluded that it is not the small town in general that has built up in me a kind of feeling of wonder but Olivet in particular. It has seemed to me a little like something out of the past and at the same time something too which one looks forward to in the future, and, I must say, not always very hopefully. Just now and in most of the places in which I have been—I should say ever since the World War, I have felt a certain tenseness. It has been rather hard to work in. Everyone seems to be trying to think nationally and internationally. The old human interest of one man in another seems to have got lost somewhere. People seem more and more to be separating themselves into groups and classes. A man like myself, never anything but a somewhat liberal democrat, finds his name put into a book called "The Red Network" labeled there as a communist writer; in many places the anti-Jewish feeling apparently growing stronger—often, I have noticed, in places where there are no Jews and among men who know personally no Jews; prejudice against the negro, often stronger in the North now than in the South; and all of these impulses leading to a new suspicion by man of man and making more prevalent and more marked our human loneliness.

Here in Olivet I have seemed to find these impulses that do so much to destroy human relationships strangely absent. I came here, as a man goes into most new places, now-a-days, a little afraid. The fear is gone. I may be a bit nervous about trying to speak to you here tonight but I am not afraid of you. Since I have been here I do not believe I have heard the words capitalist or proletariat used once. What a relief. Here I have heard talk of music, of painting, of the art of living and even, strangely enough, of education. It is a little like coming, after a long and stormy sea voyage onto some quiet bay, and I feel rather like congratulating the young men and women who are here seeking an education that they can live here, for a time, in this atmosphere, before going out to tackle what they will find they must tackle.

I am here tonight to make a public lecture, the first one I have tried to make for two or three years. I am a professional writer with, I admit, a good many marks of the eternal amateur on me, and so I have written out what I want to say. When a man has sat at a desk for as many hours through as many years as I have, he finds that his thoughts, when he has any, run more naturally down through his arms and fingers than up to his mouth and lips.

Just the same, as you have probably been told that I was going to try to tell you something of a writer's conception of realistic fiction, I think I ought to try to keep the talk as much as possible, on the subject of realism. I do not know what reality is. I do not think any of us quite know how much our point of view, and, in fact all of our touch with life, is influenced by our imaginations.

In my own experience, for example, and in my work as a writer I have always attempted to use materials that came out of my own experiences of life. I have written a good deal about my father, my mother, a certain grandmother who touched my imagination, and about my brothers and sisters, and it has amused me sometimes, in talking with some of my brothers, to see how poorly my conception of our father and mother fitted into their own conceptions. "Why, I dare say, the woman you have pictured is all right. She is very interesting, but she is not my mother as I knew her," they say.

This whole matter of what we think of as realism is probably pretty tricky. I have often told myself that, having met some person for the first time, some other human being, man or woman, and having had my first look, I cannot ever even see him or her again.

If this is true, why is it true? It is true because the moment I meet you and if we begin to talk, my imagination begins to play. Perhaps I begin to make up stories about you. This is a trick all writers, and for that matter, all people, do. The writer may merely be more conscious of it. It is our method of work. Very little of the work of the writer is done at his desk or at the typewriter. It is done as he walks about, as he sits in a room with people, and perhaps most of all as he lies in bed at night.

I myself, for example, have all my life had over and over an experience that some of you may also have had. If I have been working intensely, I find myself unable to relax when I go to bed. Often I fall into a half dream state, and when I do, the faces of people begin to appear before me. They seem to snap into place before my eyes, stay there, sometimes for a short period, sometimes longer. There are smiling faces, leering ugly faces, tired faces, hopeful faces. Almost always they seem to be faces of people I cannot remember ever having met.

However, I am quite sure they are faces of people I have seen.

They may be people I have met quite casually in the street. I have been walking about. At times the faces of people, met thus, quite casually seem full of a strange significance. To quote Herman Melville, "Who has ever fathomed the strangeness and wonder of man?" I get sometimes the illusion that every man and woman I meet is crying out to me. Sometimes a single glance at a human face seems to tell a whole life story and there have been times, when I walked thus when I had to go along with bowed head, looking at the sidewalk. I could not bear looking at any more faces.

I have a kind of illusion about this matter. It is, I have no doubt, due to a story teller's point of view. I have the feeling that the faces that appear before me thus at night are those of people who want their stories told and whom I have neglected. Once I remember that I wrote a poem on this matter. I think I had better recite it to you. I called my verses,

THE STORY TELLER*

Tales are people who sit on the doorstep of the house of my mind.
It is cold outside and they sit waiting.
I look out at a window.
The tales have cold hands,
Their hands are freezing.
A short thickly-built tale arises and threshes his arms about.
His nose is red and he has two gold teeth.
There is an old female tale that sits hunched up in a cloak.
Many tales come to sit for a moment on the doorstep and then go
     away
It is too cold for them outside.
The street before the door of the house of my mind is filled with
     tales.
They murmur and cry out, they are dying of cold and hunger.
I am a helpless man—my hands tremble.
I should be sitting on a bench like a tailor.
I should be weaving warm cloth out of the threads of thought.
The tales should be clothed.
They are freezing on the doorstep of the house of my mind.
I am a helpless man—my hands tremble.
I feel in the darkness but cannot find the doorknob.
I look out at a window.
Many tales are dying in the street before the house of mind.

Now when it comes to talking about the experiences of a
writer I think I should say something that perhaps most of you
realize. The work of any writer and for that matter of any artist in
any of the seven arts should contain within it the story of his own
life. There are certain beliefs I have. One is that every man who
writes, writes as well as he can. We are always hearing stories
about men writing with their tongues in their cheeks, but the
truth is that if, for example, a man devotes his life to writing
detective stories, he probably believes in the detectives he puts in
his stories. If he writes cowboy stories he really believes that

---

* Reprinted from "A New Testament" by Sherwood Anderson.

cowboys in life are like the cowboys of the stories and the movies. They aren't, of course, but he thinks so.

I have myself, I think, been counted among what we call in America the high-brow writers. I am not in the least a high-brow type of man, so I have to ask myself, or did at first, when I first began writing, have to ask myself how it came about that I was called a high-brow. And I concluded finally that it was because I happened to be a man who took writing rather seriously and I took it seriously because I enjoyed it so thoroughly.

I remember reading somewhere a sentence by Joseph Conrad. He said that he only lived fully and richly when he was at work writing.

I have always thought of myself as a man who came into writing, let us say, by the back door. I had a rather adventurous youth. I was a laborer, a farm hand and factory hand until I was twenty-two or twenty-three years old. I was as a youth always a passionate reader.

And I did not read in order to learn to write. I had no notion of being a writer, although it is probable that I always instinctively wanted to be a story teller. My father was a rather famous story teller in the little town in which we lived, and I very much admired that quality in him.

And there were other good story tellers about. I sought them out. I think I perhaps instinctively watched their technique. I became more or less a wanderer and have been one all of my life. For a time, for two or three years, I led the life of a wandering vagabond, a tramp, working just enough to live. I speak of this because I think it was for me a time of learning, or at least trying to learn.

And here I would like to speak of something. When I was a lad there was a good deal of something going on that may be rather on the wane now. There was this talk heard on all sides, of America being the great land of opportunity. At that time, such talk pretty much meant getting on, if possible, growing rich, getting to be something big in the world. A lad heard it on all sides and it was not unkindly meant. The idea of accumulation of possessions got all mixed up with the idea of happiness and it was rather confusing. I know it got me confused and I suffered for it. I think I should say to some of the students here who have heard me talk to smaller groups that, if I have kept emphasising this idea, there is a reason. I have spoken here a good deal, perhaps too much, of my own particular experiences in life. It may be I am rather a nut on the subject, that I too much resent the years I myself spent trying to be what I did not want to be. Some years ago I was asked to deliver what is called the William Vaughn Moody series of lectures in the University of Chicago, and through all the lectures I tried to emphasize the idea of smallness as opposed to bigness, that is to say the desirability of being just a man going along rather than something outstanding and special.

The truth probably is that I wanted to get out of the scramble as much as I could for a particular reason. I had a hunch. It may be that I gradually realized as I grew out of childhood into young manhood, that I was losing something. All of us who are older can remember with what fervor we read when we were younger. What a rich place our imagined world was. As we grew older it seemed to get less rich. I suppose I wanted to keep it rich.

We all, I dare say, have to face what are called "the facts of life", but I do think we are often inclined to call facts what are not necessarily facts.

And I think also that the actual training of the imagination, the learning to use it has a lot to do with human relations. That has something to do with what I want to try to say here.

There is something you can do. Even if you are not actually practising writers, you can employ something of the writer's technique. When you are puzzled about your own life, as we all are most of the time, you can throw imagined figures of others against a background very like your own, put these imagined figures through situations in which you have been involved. It is a very comforting thing to do, a great relief at times, this occasionally losing sense of self, living in these imagined figures. This thing we call self, as I said here in a talk the other evening, is often very like a disease. It seems to sap you, take something from you, destroy your relationship with others, while even occasionally losing sense of self seems to give you an understanding that you didn't have before you became absorbed.

May it not be that all the people we know are only what we imagine them to be? If, for example, you are as I was at the time of which I am now speaking, a business man, on the whole spending my time seeking my own advantage, you lose interest, while, as opposed to this, as you lose yourself in others, life immediately becomes more interesting. A new world seems to open out before you. Your imagination becomes constantly more and more alive.

And there is a profound pleasure in all of this. At least I know that when I came to it, I found it the pleasantest experience I had ever had. To be sure I do not want to discount the difficult. It is very hard to understand any other human being. It is difficult to tell truly the story of another, but it is, I think, rather a grand challenge. I hope you will pardon me for speaking thus seriously about that which interests me so profoundly. You see I am interested in writing. I am a man in love with his craft.

But I would like to speak a little more clearly if possible on the subject of what, when we think of writers, we call realists. I have said that I do not know what reality is. I do not think any man knows. I remember that some years ago I wrote a short essay that has often since been reproduced and has even, I believe, been used in college text books. I called it "A Note on Realism." I think I will read some extracts from it.

"There is something very confusing to both readers and writers about the notion of realism in fiction. As generally understood it is akin to what is called 'representation' in painting. The fact is before you and you put it down, adding a high spot here and there, to be sure. No man can quite make himself a camera. Even the most realistic worker pays some tribute to what is called 'art'. Where does representation end and art begin? The location of the line is often as confusing to practicing artists as it is to the public."

Recently a young writer came to talk with me about our mutual craft. He spoke with enthusiastic admiration of a certain book— very popular a year or two ago. "It is the very life. So closely observed. It is the sort of thing I should like to do. I should like to bring life itself within the pages of a book. If I could do that I would be happy."

I wondered. The book in question had only seemed to me good in spots and the spots had been far apart. There was too much dependence upon the notebook. The writer had seemed to me to have very little to give out of himself. What had happened, I thought, was that the writer of the book had confused the life of reality with the life of the imagination. Easy enough to get a thrill out of people with reality. A man struck by an automobile, a child falling out at the window of a city office building. Such things stir the emotions. No one, however, confuses them with art.

This confusion of the life of the imagination with the life of reality is a trap into which most of our critics seem to me to fall about a dozen times each year. Do the trick over and over, and in they tumble. "It is life," they say. "Another great artist has been discovered."

What never seems to come quite clear is the simple fact that art is art. It is not life.

The life of the imagination will always remain separated from the life of reality. It feeds upon the life of reality, but it is not that life—cannot be. Mr. John Marin painting Brooklyn Bridge, Henry Fielding writing "Tom Jones", are not trying in the novel and the painting to give us reality. They are striving for a realization in art of something out of their own imaginative experiences, fed to be sure upon the life immediately about. A quite different matter from making an actual picture of what they see before them.

And here arises a confusion. For some reason—I myself have never exactly understood very clearly—the imagination must constantly feed upon reality or starve. Separate yourself too much from life and you may at moments be a lyrical poet, but you are not an artist. Something within dries up, starves for the want of food. Upon the fact in nature the imagination must constantly feed in order that the imaginative life remain significant. The workman who lets his imagination drift off into some experience altogether disconnected with reality, the attempt of the American to depict life in Europe, or New England, or writing of cowboy life—all that sort of thing—in ninety-nine cases out of a hundred ends in the work of such a man becoming at once full of holes and bad spots. The intelligent reader, tricked often enough by the technical skill displayed in hiding holes, never in the end accepts it as good work. The imagination of the workman has become confused. He has had to depend altogether upon tricks. The whole job is a fake.

The difficulty, I fancy, is that so few workmen in the arts will accept their own limitations. It is only when the limitation is fully accepted that it ceases to be a limitation. Such men scold at the life immediately about. "It's too dull and commonplace to make good material," they declare. Off they sail in fancy to the South Seas, to Africa, to China. What they cannot realize is their own dullness. Life is never dull except to the dull.

The writer who sets himself down to write a tale has undertaken something. He has undertaken to conduct his readers on a trip through the world of his fancy. If he is a novelist his imaginative world is filled with people and events. If he has any sense of decency as a workman he can no more tell lies about his imagined people, fake them, than he can sell out real people in real life. The thing is constantly done but no man I have ever met, having done such a trick, has felt very clean about the matter afterward.

On the other hand, when the writer is rather intensely true to the people of his imaginative world, when he has set them down truly, when he does not fake, another confusion arises. Being square with your people in the imaginative world does not mean lifting them over into life, into reality. There is a very subtle distinction to be made, and upon the writer's ability to make this distinction will in the long run depend his standing as a workman.

Having lifted the reader out of the reality of daily life it is entirely possible for the writer to do his job so well that the imaginative life become to the reader for the time real life. Little real touches are added. The people of the town—that never existed except in the fancy—eat food, live in houses, suffer, have moments of happiness and die. To the writer, as he works, they are very real. The imaginative world in which he is for the time living has become for him more alive than the world of reality ever can become. His very sincerity confuses. Being unversed in the matter of making the delicate distinction that the writer himself sometimes has such a hard time making, they call him a realist. The notion shocks him. "The deuce, I am nothing of the kind," he says. "But such a thing could not have happened in a Vermont town." Why not? Have you not learned that anything can happen anywhere? If a thing can happen in my imaginative world it can of course happen in the flesh and blood world. Upon what do you fancy my imagination feeds?"

My own belief is that the writer with a notebook in his hand is always a bad workman, a man who distrusts his own imagination. Such a man describes actual scenes accurately, he puts down actual conversation.

But people do not converse in the book world as they do in life. Scenes of the imaginative world are not real scenes.

The life of reality is confused, disorderly, almost always without apparent purpose, whereas in the artist's imaginative life there is purpose. There is determination to give the tale, the song, the painting, form—to make it true and real to the theme, not to life. Often the better the job is done, the greater the confusion.

I myself remember with what a shock I heard people say that one of my own books, "Winesburg, Ohio", was an exact picture of Ohio village life. The book was written in a crowded tenement district of Chicago. The hint for almost every character was taken from my fellow-lodgers in a large rooming house, many of whom had never lived in a village. The confusion arises out of the fact that others besides practicing artists have imaginations. But most people are afraid to trust their imaginations and the artist is not.

Would it not be better to have it understood that realism, in so far as the word means reality to life, is always bad art—although it may possibly be very good journalism?

Which is but another way of saying that all of the so-called great realists were not realists at all and never intended being. Madame Bovary did not exist in fact. She existed in the imaginative life of Flaubert and he managed to make her exist in the imaginative life of his readers.

I have been writing a story. A man is walking in a street and suddenly turns out of the street into an alley-way. There he meets another man and a hurried whispered conversation takes place. In real life they may be but a pair of rather small bootleggers, but they are not that to me.

When I began writing, the physical aspect of one of the men, the one who walked in the street, was taken rather literally from life. He looked strikingly like a man I once knew, so much like him in fact that there was a confusion. A matter easy enough to correct.

A stroke of my pen saves me from realism. The man I knew in life had red hair he was tall and thin.

With a few words I have changed him completely. Now he has black hair and a black mustache. He is short and has broad shoulders. And now he no longer lives in the world of reality. He is a denizen of my own imaginative world. He can now begin a life having nothing at all to do with the life of the red-haired man.

If I am to succeed in making him real in this new world he, like hundreds of other men and women who live only in my own fanciful world, must live and move within the scope of the story or novel into which I have cast him. If I do tricks with him in the imaginative world, sell him out, I become merely a romancer. If, however, I have the courage to let him really live he will, perhaps, show me the way to a fine story or novel.

But the story or novel will not be a picture of life. I will never have had any intentions of making it that.

And so you will see in this matter of realism what I am trying to say. There is a reality to your book, your story people. They may, in the beginning, be lifted out of life, but once lifted, once become a part of the book, of the story life,—realism, in the sense in which the word is commonly used, no longer exists.

There are, you see, these two kinds of realism, the realism to actual life that is the challenge to the journalist and the realism to the book or the story-life. That I should say is the job of your real story teller.

Textiles: A Radio Play

STATION announcements. *We have here a short play that sings the song of the weavers, the clothmakers. Weaving is one of man's oldest crafts. It may have started even before man began stirring the ground and scattering seeds. Man came naked into a cold and a hot world. In spite of the richness of our age there are still millions of men, women, and children miserably clad, but man's cunning brain has made the machines that can now clothe all mankind. Here come the weavers, the clothmakers.*

[*There is heard the sound of men's and women's footsteps approaching.*]

Voice (*a woman*). What's this? Where are we?

Voice (*a man*). Why have you brought us into this room?

Voice (*a woman*). What are these little disks?

Voice (*a man*). These little disks are microphones. Speak; sing into them; tell your story. The air is free. Your voices will carry far. Out over the states men, women, and children will be sitting in their houses and listening.

Voice (*another man*). The microphone is also a part of the new world. It is a new wonder like the loom, when man first invented it. It is brother to the great cloth mills, with the millions of singing spindles, the thousands of dancing looms.

Voice (*a woman*). The radio is still strange, a wonder to us; but

413

think how strange and ever terrible must have seemed the first power loom.

Chorus (men's and women's voices).

The great woolen mills.
The spinners of yarn,
Of silk,
Of linen,
Of rayon.

[*The above is a chant. It breaks off.*]

Voice (a man). But wait. But wait. You must begin far back. You must tell the story of cloth. Tell them who you are. Yours is a workers' story. If you sing, sing first of beginnings.

Chorus. Oho! Oho!
We are the men and women of cloth.
We are the weavers.
We are the makers of cloth.
We are of one of the oldest crafts in
   the world.
The pride of the old workers is ours.

Voice (a man). Ours is the old, old story of the workers. It began with heavy, brutal labor. Our fathers were brothers to the low-browed man with the hoe.

Voice (another man). But a few began to think. They used their brains. Inventions began. Man was naked and cold. From the time of Adam, or whoever it was who first walked the earth, conscious of manhood, man has felt the bitterness of cold winds and the burning heat of the sun.

Chorus.
We, the weavers, began when first man
   began to dig in the earth.
When seeds were first scattered over
   the earth, we began.
We began with the wool of sheep.
We followed on the heels of those who
   clothed themselves with hides and
   furs.
We were among the first to grasp new
   tools with our hands.

We kept on getting new knowledge.

Voice (a man). When the cotton plant was found, we made the fiber of the cotton boll into cloth.

Voice (another man). We took the wild flax from the field. We broke it. We ripped out the fiber. We made linen. A long time later with the help of the scientist we made cloth of wood. We made cloth of rayon.

Voice (a man). We made the first machines. We made the distaff. We carded the wool. We made the spinning wheel. We built the first looms. We ran the looms with our hands and our feet.

Voice (a woman). But some were afraid, some protested. They were afraid man would be robbed of his work.

Voice (another woman). They are still afraid. It is fear that makes men ugly. They are afraid of the great modern machines. Look now far back—to the sixteenth century.

[*There is heard the low murmur of angry voices of men and women in the distance.*]

Voice (a woman). Kill the inventor.
Voice (a man). Destroy the loom.

[*Sound of a struggle—low, in the distance. It dies down.*]

Voice (another man). Listen. It is the mayor of the old city of Danzig speaking. It is the year fifteen hundred and twenty-nine. A man has invented a loom that will weave fifty ribbons at once. The people are furious with fear. "We will lose our work," they cry.

[*Again the sound of struggle in the distance, machinery being broken, angry voices.*]

Voice (louder—a man). Stop! Stop. (*Sound of struggle stops.*) Inventor, I sentence you to be beheaded. We will destroy your loom. We will go back to the old way.

Chorus (laughter).
Ha! Ha!
The old way.

The old way.
Back! Back!
Man can never go back!

Voice (a woman). There was sweetness in the old way. The women made cloth for their families. There were no power looms. They did it all by hand. Listen, you will hear the song of the wheel.

[*There is heard a soft whirling sound, and women's voices are heard chattering softly. This is simply a murmuring sound. The words are not distinct. The voices are soft, as of women contentedly working together. There is an occasional soft laughter.*]

Voice (a woman). I shall make my daughter a dress. It is for her marriage day.
Voice (another woman). But Mary, it takes so long. If it were me, I wouldn't wait.

[*Sound of soft women's laughter*]

Voice (a woman—louder). Compared with our age, the age of the wheel and the hand loom was a simple age.

Voice (a woman—louder). Compared with our age, the age of the wheel and the hand loom was a simple age.
Chorus.
    When we weavers began, how could
        we look into the future?
    We wove cloth for our neighbors.
    There were no fast ships, no railroads,
        no steamboats.
    The great machines had not come.
    It was the day of the ox and the cart.
Voice (a man). Look. Who is this coming?
Voice (a woman). It is the prophet of fear.
Voice (another woman). It is the prophet of defeat.
Voice (another woman). It is he who says nothing can be done.
Voice (another woman). He is always saying human nature cannot be changed.

Voice (another woman). It is he who says all man's efforts must end in defeat.

Voice (another woman). He thinks life isn't worth living.

Voice (another woman). How old he looks.

Voice (another woman). How sour he looks.

Voice (a man). He croaks like the croak of a frog.

Voice (another man—this is to be a croaking, complaining voice). So, here you are—children of hope, eh? Fools, you would do better to listen to me.

Voice (a man—answering). Hello, croaker—prophet of defeat. What's eating you now?

Croaker. So you have begun to sing of an age of plenty, eh? You had better listen to me. It would have been better for man to let all tools alone. The tools led to the machines. The machines will destroy you.

Voice (a man). Yes, croaker—man of fear, we are here to sing of a new day. The machine will clothe man as he was never clothed before.

Voice (a woman). There will come the age of plenty.

Voice (a man). All will be clothed.

Voice (a woman). My mother, a worker, had one new dress in three years.

Voice (another woman). It took my grandmother nearly a year to make the cloth for a dress.

Chorus.

    The age of plenty may already be here.

    We can already do it.

    All can be beautifully clothed.

    Already a river of beautiful cloth can flow out of our milles.

Voice (a man). The mills should never stop.

Voice (another man). Men and women should walk in pride— filled with the pride of man's accomplishments.

Chorus.

    Let the millions of spindles sing.

    Let the looms dance with joy.

    Let the river of cloth flow.

    The day of plenty is here.

[*Again the croaking, complaining voice is heard.*]

Croaking Voice. The machine will destroy you all. Man has invented the loom. From the first the loom has thrown man out of his work. When you rob a man of his work, you destroy him. Listen.

[*The* voice *quits talking, and there is a sound of the clatter of hand looms. Complaining voices are heard above the clatter.*]

Voice (a woman). But we cannot get the cloth we help to make. We are of the old workers. We are poor and miserably clad.

Voice (another woman). The mills close. They are dark and silent, and we walk the streets in fear.

Voice (a man). They say we do not want to work.

Chorus. It is a lie, a lie.

Croaker (His voice now high and sharp—a sneer in it). I told you. I told you. There is but one hope. Destroy it all. Go back. Go back. Go back to the day of the handwork.

Voice (a woman). No. No. Never the old days. They put me at work when I was a child of eight. I worked from daylight till dark, summer and winter. Before I was a woman grown, I was already worn out.

Voice (a man). How could such women, the weavers of the old days, be good wives? How could they be good mothers?

Voice (a woman). I was ragged. I was almost naked. I made cloth, but I went always in rags. The new day is already a thousand times better than that.

Croaker. I tell you again that it will be better to destroy the looms.

Chorus. We'll never do it. We'll solve it. We'll solve it.

Croaker. The machine is taking man from his work.

Chorus. We will find a way. We will find a way.

Croaker. Those who cannot work will starve.

Chorus. With the new machines there is also food for all.

Croaker. It would have been better for man to let all tools and machines alone.

Chorus. It is the machine that will make the new age—the age of plenty.

Croaker. I tell you the machine will destroy you all.

[*The* croaking voice *is interrupted.*]

Voice (a man). Listen, men and women, you workers, will you accept the voice of defeat?

Voice (a woman). But sometimes we are afraid.

Voice (a man). Come on, let us keep to the story. Let us tell them that we workers are builders.

Chorus. We want the new world. We have the machines. We want all men and women beautifully clothed.

Voice (a man). But wait. Go on with the story.

Chorus.

Now the day of the hand loom has passed.

Life is speeding up.

Men are working.

Men are thinking.

Man has discovered the power in steam.

The motor is coming.

Man has applied power to the looms.

How the looms dance.

Faster, faster, faster.

Voice (a man). Ha! Now we have freed ourselves from the heavy, brutal labor. We have come out of the dark little rooms. The great light, singing factories are building. The work is lighter.

Chorus. Faster, faster, faster.

Voice (a woman). See the river of cloth flow.

Voice (a man). It is a river, a Mississippi of cloth.

Voice (a woman). Look—it is my daughter going to church.

Voice (another woman). My daughter is going to her wedding.

Voice (a man). Now at night, when I return from work, my bed is covered with warm blankets.

Voice (a woman). How white and soft the sheets.

Chorus.

Now we have many new and beautiful kinds of cloth.

We have soft and beautiful cloth of cotton,

Of silk,

Of wool,

Of linen,
Of rayon.

We make
Damasks,
Chiffons,
Jerseys,
Crepe.

We make
Lace and tapestries,
Zephyrs and brocades,
Tweeds and muslins,
Velvets and satins.

We will make hundreds, thousands of new kinds of cloth.

Croaker. Ha! I tell you the machines will destroy you. Look. Now the looms grow in number. Man has found the secret of power. Listen and you will hear the clatter of the new looms. They will rob more and more men of their work. I tell you when you rob man of his work you destroy him. Listen. Fools. Fools. You will be kicked into the streets. You will be turned out of your houses. The machines will fix you.

Voice (a woman). It is true, true.

Croaker. Ha, you thought you were smart. You racked your brains, making always more and more machines. You discovered the power of steam, of electricity. You harnessed rivers. You made the great mills. You thought you were smart.

Voice (a man). But we wanted to make an end of poverty, of fear.

Croaker. And you only threw yourselves out of work. I told you. Ha! Fools. Fools. You had better destroy the machines. Destroy the factories.

Voice (a man). He may be right. More and more of us are being thrown out of work.

Voice (a woman). He is right. I worked and saved to educate my son. I sent him to college. Now he can find no work.

Voice (a man). All they talk of is relief. We do not want relief. We are men. We want our work.

Croaker. I told you. I told you. Come on. Do as I say. Break up the machines. Destroy. Destroy.

Voices. No. No.

Other Voices. Yes. Yes. Come on. Come on.

[*There is a loud, intense sound of struggle—cries of pain—the sound of hammers against metal, of glass being broken. It becomes a strong metallic laugh. It is broken by the loud, sharp sound of a factory whistle—and then silence.*]

Voice (a woman). It was a mistake. It can't be done that way.

Voice (a man). Man cannot destroy the work of his own hands.

Voice (a woman). It is cowardly, cowardly.

Voice (another woman). We have come out of darkness and poverty. We cannot go back.

Voice (a man—angry). You croaker—you are a fool. You are a false leader.

Voice (a woman). There are too many false leaders.

Voice (a man). Let us kill the croaker. Let us kill fear.

[*There is heard the low rumbling sound, as though of a mob forming.*]

Voice (a woman—pleading). No. Please. There has been too much killing. It is too brutal. It solves nothing. It has gone on too long.

Croaker. Ha. Fools. Fools. You cannot kill me. You cannot kill fear. Fear will win. Better destroy. There is joy in destruction.

Voice (a man). It is true that we are being thrown out of work.

Voice (a woman). But we can bring such richness into the world.

Voice (another woman). There are so many millions of us—of us, the workers.

Voice (a man). Where are the thinkers? We want thinkers now. We want the best brains in the world.

Voice (a woman). Let them quit thinking of new machines for a time. Let them think of us.

Voice (another woman). Men are always talking of the new world, the better life for all, the good life.

Chorus.

It is coming.
It is coming.
The machines are a part of it.
The machines are making it.
Do not lose courage.
Croaker. Pipedreams. Pipedreams. You are fools, fools.
Destroy. Go back. Go back. Go back. Go back. Destroy. Destroy.
Go back. Go back.

[*The voice of the* croaker *has become a chant. It merges into a
new sound—the sound of men marching. The marching
rhythm drowns out the voice of the* croaker. *The march stops.*]

Voice (a woman). Look. Who are these? Look. The whole
earth, as far as the eyes can see, is covered with men and women.
They are marching.
Voice (another woman). Who are they? Where are they
going?

[*Again is heard the sharp, loud sound of a factory whistle and the
heavy, rhythmic sound of marching. It stops again.*]

Voice (a woman). Who are you? Tell us. Who are you?
Voice (a man). We are the textile workers of the new day. We
are going to the factories. We are going to make more and more
cloth. We are the men and women of the age of plenty.
*Chorus (loud and clear as though a great army of men and
women were shouting).*

We are the makers of textiles.

We make cloth of cotton,
    Of silk,
    Of wool,
    Of linen,
    Of rayon.

We make
    Damasks,
    Chiffons,

        Jerseys,
        Crepe.

    We make
        Lace and tapestries,
        Zephyrs and brocades,
        Tweeds and muslins,
        Velvets and satins.

    We will make hundreds, thousands of new kinds of cloth.

    Croaker. You are fools. You are the new slaves of the machines.
    Chorus.
        We are the ones who will free men.
        We will clothe all men, all women, all children.
        We will clothe them with rick, many-colored cloth.
    Croaker. You are marchers, marching to your own destruction.
    Chorus.
        We have been leaderless, but will find leaders.
        We want only to work.
        We are the clothmakers.

    We make cloth of cotton,
        Of silk,
        Of wool,
        Of linen,
        Of rayon.

    We make
        Damasks,
        Chiffons,
        Jerseys,
        Crepe.

    We make
        Lace and tapestries,
        Zephyrs and brocades,
        Tweeds and muslins,
        Velvets and satins.

We will make hundreds, thousands of new kinds of cloth.

Croaker. You are a mob of fools. Be yourselves. Quit pipedreaming. Turn back. Destroy the machines before they destroy you. Turn back. Turn back. Turn back. Turn back.

[*The* croaker's *voice becomes a chant. It is drowned in a loud outbreak of laughter.*]

Laugh. Laugh. I will laugh last. You'll see. You'll see. The machines will throw you all out of work. Confess it. You all hate the factories. Go now and destroy them.
Voice (a man). Let the marchers speak. Do you hate your work? Do you hate the factories?
Voices (this is a great shout). No.
Chorus.
    Why should we be afraid?
    Look what we have already done.
    The day of the heavy, brutal, degrading labor has passed.
    Listen to the singing of the motors.

[*The singing, purring song of motors is heard.*]

    Listen to the factories and mills calling us.

[*There is an outburst of factory whistles.*]

    We are the children of the factories.
    The factories are our children.
    We have come out of the dark little rooms.
    We have come out of rags and nakedness.
    The march of men is long, long.
Croaker. Man is marching to defeat. He is marching to destruction.
Voice (a woman). Our story is a long one. It is true we have come up slowly out of the darkness.
Voice (a man). The whole story of man could be told in the story of our work, in the story of textiles.
Voice (a woman). When first we began to make cloth, the traders took it.

Voice (a man). The traders floated in boats down rivers to trade with strange tribes.

Voice (a woman). It was thus we first began to hear of other peoples.

Voice (a man). Treaties were made. Nations began to form.

Voice (a woman). Ships began to sail the seven seas carrying our textiles.

Voice (a man). Columbus, when he sailed into the West, took bales of brightly colored cloth.

Voice (a woman). Venice became great. The ships of Venice sailed over the known world, taking the work of our hands, bringing home treasure.

Croaker. Yeah! Yeah! And the rich got richer. The poor got poorer. Misery grew. It will always grow. The machines will destroy you. Power will destroy you.

Chorus.

> Knowledge was growing, slowly, slowly.
> England became the mistress of the seas.
> What did it?
> It was the work of our hands.
> England became the workshop of the world.
> The power loom had come.
> There were always more and more mills.
> They loaded the ships with the work of our hands.

Croaker. Yeah! They would not let their looms be sent out to America. They had to be brought out by stealth. What did it lead to? It led to war, war, war. The machines lead to nothing but wars.

Chorus.

> We fought.
> We got our freedom.
> We made a new nation.
> We made America.
> We built our own ships.
> We filled them with the works of our own hands.

Voice (a woman). We clothed those who went into the West to open the land.

Voice (a man). The mills of New England went down into the South.

Voice (a woman). Life changed in the North, in the South. The cities grew.

Voice (a man). There were new cities, new towns of workers.
Croaker. And all the time you were destroying yourselves.
Chorus.

All the time we were bringing the age of plenty.
Faster and faster our fingers flew.
Faster and faster and the million spindles.
Faster and faster the looms were dancing.
More and more mills.
More and more mills.
Hear the singing of the mills.

[*All this to be accompanied by a soft purring sound of machines humming smoothly.*]

We were making more and more cloth of cotton,
Of silk,
Of wool,
Of linen,
Of rayon.

We have
Damasks,
Chiffons,
Jerseys,
Crepe.

We have
Lace and tapestries,
Zephyrs and brocades,
Tweeds and muslins,
Velvets and satins.

We will make hundreds, thousands of new kinds of cloth.

[*All this still accompanied by the singing sound of the machines.*]

Croaker. Fools. Fools. Stop it. Stop it. Will you never learn what fools you are? You have got more and more mills, but you have got also strikes and lockouts. The new machines throw more and more of you out of work. As I told you long ago, you are marching to your own destruction. There will be no work. No work. No work.

[*Again the above becomes a chant that is presently drowned out by the singing of the machines that become louder. Then again silence.*]

Chorus. When the crops of the farmer fail, he does not quit plowing the ground.

Voice (a man). He is a farmer. He plows again when the spring showers soften the ground.

Voice (a man). We are clothmakers. We will make cloth.

Chorus. We will find a way. We will find a way.

Voice (a woman). Already we have mills to clothe the world.

Voice (a woman). We will make more and more beautiful cloth for men and women.

Chorus.

   Let the mills hum.
   Let the cloth pour out.
   Let there be a great river of cloth.
   Let us have a Mississippi of cloth.

Voice (a man). Now let the thinkers think.

Voice (a woman). Let the planners plan.

Chorus.

   Give attention to us.
   We are the makers of cloth.
      Plant the fields.
      Grow the cotton.
      Grow the flax.
      Make the rayon.
   Turn the sheep loose on the hills.
   Our land is rich.
   Let us march into the age of plenty.
      Think.
      Work.
      Plan.
      Think.
      Work.
      Plan.

Croaker. Ha! Pipedreams. Pipedreams. Pipedreams.

[*The* croaker's *voice is drowned in a great outburst of laughter.*]

Chorus. From a few, working in dark little rooms we workers in cloth, in textiles, have become millions.

Voice (a man). Listen.

Voice (a woman). Listen. You will hear the voice of the new day. You will hear the voice of the age of plenty.

Chorus. We will in some way make it. We will make it. We will make it.

Voice. We will make the good life for our children, our sons, our daughters.

Voice (a man). The day of plenty can already be made.

Voice. Listen to the song of the day of plenty. Listen to the song of the factories.

Chorus (singing a verse from a hymn).

> Mine eyes have seen the glory of the coming of the Day;
> We are trampling out the vintage where the grapes of wrath
>   are stored,
> We have loosed the mighty power of the factories grim and
>   gray;
> Our truth is marching on.

[*The factory whistles begin to sound off. The effect is that of one of the circus calliopes that used to go in circus parades through the streets of American towns. The whistles break into the tune of the song "The Battle Hymn of the Republic." The sound is accompanied by cheers, and a loud voice rises above the din.*]

Voice. March, men. March, women.

Voice (a woman—loud and shrill above the din). March to the mills. March toward the age of plenty.

[*The play ends with the heavy sound of marching feet, accompanied by the shrill sound of factory whistles and the cheering of the marchers. At the last these sounds should grow a little dim, as though the marchers were pouring into the factories. Then a solitary voice.*]

Voice (that of a woman singing).

> We are the makers of cloth, of textiles.

We want to help make the age of plenty.
We are not afraid of work.
We are not afraid of the factories, of the machines,
Help us, thinkers.
Planners, plan for us.

We are the makers of cloth of cotton,
    Of silk,
    Of wool,
    Of linen,
    Of rayon.

We make
    Damasks,
    Chiffons,
    Jerseys,
    Crepe.

We make
    Lace and tapestries,
    Zephyrs and brocades,
    Tweeds and muslins,
    Velvets and satins.
We will make hundreds, thousands of new kinds of cloth.

[*The song dies, and in the distance is heard the sound of tramping
feet, and cheers, growing more and more faint. At the last—in
the distance, faintly a song comes from the workers.*]

He has sounded forth the trumpet that shall never call
    retreat;
He is sifting out the hearts of men before His judgment seat;
O be swift, my soul, to answer Him! be jubilant my feet;
Our day is marching on.

Sources

Theordore Dreiser's *Free and Other Stories* from Introduction to *Free and Other Stories*. New York; The Modern Library, 1925.

Stephen Crane's *Midnight Sketches and Other Impressions* from Introduction to "Midnight Sketches and Other Impressions." Volume XI of *The Work of Stephen Crane*, ed. Wilson Follett. New York: Knopf, 1926.

Eugene Jolas' *Cinema* from Introduction to *Cinema*. New York: Adelphia, 1926.

Philip McKee's *Big Town* from Foreword to *Big Town*. New York: John Day, 1931.

Walt Whitman's *Leaves of Grass* from Introduction to *Leaves of Grass*. New York: Crowell, 1933.

George Sklar and Albert Maltz's *Peace on Earth* from Foreword to *Peace on Earth*. New York: Samuel French, 1934.

Carl Sandburg from *The Bookman*, 54(December 1921), 360-361.

Albert Maurer from "An Exhibition of Paintings by Alfred H. Maurer" (1924).

431

Betrayed from *The Golden Book*, 1(May 1925), 743-744.

Jerome Blum from "Communications," *American Spectator*, 1(September 1933).

City Plowman from *America and Alfred Stieglitz*, ed. Waldo Frank, et. al. New York: Doubleday, 1934.

Paying for Old Sins from *The Nation*, 139(July 11, 1934), 49-50.

Burt Emmett from *The Colophon*, 1, New Series(Summer 1935).

Lindsay and Masters from *The New Republic*, 85(December 25, 1935), 194-195.

A Good One from *The New Republic*, 85 (January 8, 1936), 259.

V. F. Calverton from *The Modern Quarterly*, 11(Fall 1940), 41.

Maury Maverick in San Antonio from *The New Republic*, 102(March 25, 1940), 398-400.

Living in America from *The Nation*, 120 (June 10, 1925), 657-658.

A Great Factory from *Vanity Fair*, 27(November 1926), 51-52.

Prohibition from *Vanity Fair*, 27(February 1927), 68, 96.

In a Box Car from *Vanity Fair*, 31(October 1928), 76, 114.

Domestic and Juvenile from *Vanity Fair*, 34(March 1930), 35-37.

Look Out, Brown Man! from *The Nation*, 131(November 26, 1930), 579-580.

The Cry in the Night from *Vanity Fair*, 37(September 1931), 49-50, 80.

I Want to Be Counted from *New Masses*, 7 (February 1932), 3-6.

To Remember from *American Spectator*, 1(May 1933), 172-174.

Delegation from *The New Yorker*, 9(December 9, 1933), 36, 38.

The Lineup from *American Spectator*, 2 (June 1934), 1.

Give a Child Room to Grow, from *Parents Magazine*, 11(April 1936), 17.

Here They Come from *Esquire*, 13(March 1940), 80-81.

Little People and Big Words from *Reader's Digest*, 39(September 1941), 118-120.

New Orleans from *Vanity Fair*, 26(August 1926), 36, 97.

Chicago—A Feeling from *Vanity Fair*, 27(October 1926), 53, 118.

The Far West from *Vanity Fair*, 27(January 1927), 39-40, 104.

Small Town Notes from *Vanity Fair*, 30 (June 1928), 58, 120.

The Man at the Filling Station from *Vanity Fair*, 30(August 1928), 53, 88, 90.

Let's Go Somewhere from *Outlook*, 151(February 13, 1929), 247, 278, 280.

Country Town Notes from *Vanity Fair*, 32(May 1929), 63, 112, 126.

Small Town Notes from *Vanity Fair*, 32(July 1929), 48, 110.

Country Squires from *Vanity Fair*, 33(October 1929), 63, 128.

At Amsterdam from *New Masses*, 8(November 1932), 11.

Delegation from *The New Yorker*, 9(December 9, 1933), 36, 38.

Winter Day's Walk in New York from *The American Spectator*, 2 (January 1934), 15.

City Scapes from *The American Spectator*, 2 (February 1934), 2.

Stewart's on the Square from *The New Yorker*, 10 (June 9, 1934), 77-80.

Factory Town from *The New Republic*, 62 (March 26, 1930), 143-144.

Cotton Mill from *Scribner's Magazine*, 88 (July 1930), 1-11.

City Gangs Enslave Moonshine Mountaineers from *Liberty*, 12(November 2, 1935), 12-13.

The Time and the Towns from *America as Americans See It*, ed. Fred J. Ringel. New York: Harcourt, Brace, 1932.

The New Note from *Little Review*, 1(March 1914), 23.

New Orleans, the Double Dealer and the Modern Movement in America from *Double Dealer*, 3(March 1922), 119-126.

Educating an Author from *Vanity Fair*, 28(May 1927), 47-48.

America on a Cultural Jag from *Saturday Review of Literature*, 4(December 3, 1927), 364-365.

The Future of Japanese and American Writing from *The Jiji Shimpo* [*Current News*], Japan, January 1928.

Nearer the Grass Roots from *Nearer the Grass Roots*. San Francisco: The Westgate Press, 1929.

On Being Published from *The Colophon*, Pt. 1(February 1930).

How I Came to Communism from *The New Masses*, 8(September 1932), 8-9.

They Come Bearing Gifts from *The American Mercury*, 21(October 1930), 129-137.

When Are Authors Insulted from *The Bookman*, 75(October 1932), 564-565.

Why Men Write from *Story*, 8 (January 1936), 2, 4, 103, 105.

The Story Teller's Job from *The Bookbuyer*, 2(December 1936), 8.

Why I Write from *Writer*, 49(December 1936), 363-364.

Belief in Man from *New Masses*, 21(December 15, 1936), 30.

Personal Protest from *The Canadian Forum*, 17(August 1937), 168-169.

The Situation in American Writing from *Partisan Review*, 6(Fall 1939), 103-105.

So You Want to Be a Writer from *Saturday Review of Literature*, 21(December 9, 1939), 13-14.

Man and His Imagination from *The Intent of the Artist*, ed. Augusto Centeno. Princeton, N.J.: Princeton Univ. Press, 1941.

A Writer's Conception of Reality from *A Writer's Conception of Reality* [An address delivered on January 20, 1939 at Olivet College]. Olivet, Michigan: Olivet College, 1939.

BOWLING GREEN STATE UNIVERSITY

DISCARDED

LIBRARY